# AQA Mathematics

## Book 2

## Higher (Linear)

GCSE

Series Editor
**Paul Metcalf**

Series Advisor
**Andy Darbourne**

Lead Authors
**Sandra Burns**
**Shaun Procter-Green**
**Margaret Thornton**

Authors
**Tony Fisher**
**June Haighton**
**Anne Haworth**
**Gill Hewlett**
**Steve Lomax**
**Jan Lucas**
**Andrew Manning**
**Ginette McManus**
**Howard Prior**
**David Pritchard**
**Dave Ridgway**
**Kathryn Scott**
**Paul Winters**

Nelson Thornes

This edition published in 2013 by:
Nelson Thornes Ltd
Delta Place
27 Bath Road
CHELTENHAM
GL53 7TH
United Kingdom

13 14 15 16 / 10 9 8 7 6 5 4 3 2

A catalogue record for this book is available from the British Library

ISBN 978 1 4085 2151 9

Cover photograph: Purestock/Getty Images

Illustrations by Rupert Besley, Roger Penwill, Angela Knowles and Tech-Set Limited

Page make-up by Tech-Set Limited, Gateshead

Printed in China by 1010 Printing International Ltd

**Photo acknowledgements**
**Alamy:** p12, p17, p114, p132, p188
**Fotolia:** p57, p71, p94, p97, p111, p134, p168, p209, p250, p261
**iStockphoto:** p34, p49, p62, p66, p85, p126, p217
**Wikipedia/Plimpton322:** p143

# Contents

Introduction                                                         5

## Chapter 1 Representing data                                       7

1.1 Stem-and-leaf diagrams                        8    1.4 Box plots                                  19
1.2 Line graphs and frequency polygons            11   1.5 Histograms                                 24
1.3 Cumulative frequency diagrams                 14       Chapter 1 Assess                           28

## Chapter 2 Properties of circles                                   32

2.1 Angle properties of circles                   33       Chapter 2 Assess                           42
2.2 Tangents and chords                           38

## Chapter 3 Fractions and decimals                                  46

3.1 One quantity as a fraction of another         47   3.4 Upper and lower bounds                     56
3.2 Calculating with fractions                    49   3.5 Calculating with bounds                    57
3.3 Rounding                                      51       Chapter 3 Assess                           59

## Chapter 4 Probability                                             62

4.1 Mutually exclusive events                     63   4.4 Dependent events and conditional
4.2 Relative frequency                            65       probability                                72
4.3 Independent events and tree diagrams          69       Chapter 4 Assess                           75

## Chapter 5 Formulae                                                77

5.1 Substitution and writing formulae             78       Chapter 5 Assess                           85
5.2 Changing the subject of a formula             81

## Chapter 6 Enlargements                                            88

6.1 Enlargement and scale factor                  89   6.4 Similar shapes and scale factors           99
6.2 Centres of enlargement                        92       Chapter 6 Assess                           105
6.3 Negative scale factors                        97

## Chapter 7 Trigonometry 1                                          108

7.1 Calculating the side of a right-angled             7.3 Trigonometry in three dimensions           116
    triangle using trigonometry                   109       Chapter 7 Assess                           118
7.2 Calculating angles using trigonometry         113

## Chapter 8 Percentages and ratios                                  120

8.1 Increasing or decreasing by a percentage      121  8.3 Using ratios and proportion                126
8.2 Writing one quantity as a percentage               8.4 Direct and indirect proportion             130
    of another                                    124       Chapter 8 Assess                           134

## Chapter 9 Quadratics                                              136

9.1 Factorising quadratic expressions             137  9.7 Solving quadratic equations by using the
9.2 Factorising harder quadratic expressions      139      quadratic formula                          147
9.3 Simplifying algebraic fractions               141  9.8 Solving quadratic equations graphically    150
9.4 Solving quadratic equations by factorising    141  9.9 Algebraic proof                            155
9.5 Solving equations with fractions              144      Chapter 9 Assess                           157
9.6 Solving quadratic equations by completing
    the square                                    145

## Chapter 10  Simultaneous equations                                                  160

| 10.1 | Solving simultaneous equations by elimination | 161 |
| 10.2 | Solving simultaneous equations by substitution | 163 |
| 10.3 | Solving simultaneous linear equations graphically | 167 |
| 10.4 | Solving simultaneous equations algebraically, where one is linear and one is quadratic | 171 |
| 10.5 | Solving simultaneous equations graphically, where one is linear and one is quadratic | 172 |
| | Chapter 10 Assess | 176 |

## Chapter 11  Construction                                                            179

| 11.1 | Drawing triangles accurately | 180 |
| 11.2 | Constructions | 183 |
| 11.3 | Similar shapes | 188 |
| 11.4 | Congruent shapes | 193 |
| | Chapter 11 Assess | 198 |

## Chapter 12  Loci                                                                    200

| 12.1 | Constructing loci | 201 |
| | Chapter 12 Assess | 205 |

## Chapter 13  Cubic, circular and exponential functions                               207

| 13.1 | Cubic functions | 208 |
| 13.2 | Reciprocal functions | 212 |
| 13.3 | Circular functions | 214 |
| 13.4 | Exponential functions | 217 |
| 13.5 | Graph recognition and graphs of loci | 219 |
| | Chapter 13 Assess | 223 |

## Chapter 14  Trigonometry 2                                                          228

| 14.1 | The sine rule | 229 |
| 14.2 | The cosine rule | 232 |
| 14.3 | Finding the area of a triangle using trigonometry | 235 |
| | Chapter 14 Assess | 236 |

## Chapter 15  Vectors                                                                 239

| 15.1 | Vectors | 240 |
| 15.2 | Vector geometry | 244 |
| | Chapter 15 Assess | 246 |

## Chapter 16  Area and volume 2                                                       249

| 16.1 | Arcs and sectors | 250 |
| 16.2 | Volumes and surface areas of pyramids, cones and spheres | 253 |
| | Chapter 16 Assess | 257 |

## Chapter 17  Transforming functions                                                  259

| 17.1 | Transforming functions | 260 |
| | Chapter 17 Assess | 267 |

| Glossary | 269 |
| Index | 272 |

# Introduction

Nelson Thornes has developed these resources to ensure that the book and the accompanying online resources offer you the best support for your GCSE course.

All resources have been reviewed by subject experts so you can feel assured that they closely match the specification for this subject.

The print and online resources together unlock blended learning; this means that the links between the activities in the book and the activities online blend together to maximise your understanding of a topic and help you achieve your potential.

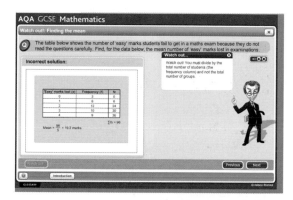

These online resources are available on  which can be accessed via the internet at www.kerboodle.com/live, anytime, anywhere.

If your school or college subscribes to kerboodle you will be provided with your own personal login details. Once logged in, access your course and locate the required activity.

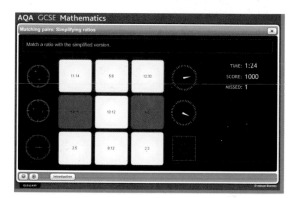

For more information and help on how to use kerboodle visit www.kerboodle.com.

## How to use this book

To help you unlock blended learning, we have referenced the activities in this book that have additional online coverage in Kerboodle by using this icon:

The icons in this book show you the online resources available from the start of the new specification and will always be relevant.

In addition, to keep the blend up-to-date and engaging, we review customer feedback and may add new content onto Kerboodle after publication!

# Welcome to GCSE Mathematics

This book has been written by teachers who not only want you to get the best grade you can in your GCSE exam, but also to enjoy maths. Together with Book 1 it covers all the material you will need to know for AQA GCSE Mathematics Higher (Linear). Look out for calculator or non-calculator symbols (shown below) which tell you whether to use a calculator or not.

In the exam, you will be tested on the Assessment Objectives (AOs) below. Ask your teacher if you need help to understand what these mean.

**AO1**  recall and use your knowledge of the prescribed content

**AO2**  select and apply mathematical methods in a range of contexts

**AO3**  interpret and analyse problems and generate strategies to solve them.

Each chapter is made up of the following features:

### Objectives

The objectives at the start of the chapter give you an idea of what you need to do to get each grade. Remember that the examiners expect you to do well at the lower grade questions on the exam paper in order to get the higher grades. So, even if you are aiming for a Grade C you will still need to do well on the Grade G questions on the exam paper.

On the first page of every chapter, there are also words that you will need to know or understand, called Key Terms. The box called 'You should already know' describes the maths that you will have learned before studying this chapter. There is also an interesting fact at the beginning of each chapter which tells you about maths in real life.

###  Learn...

The Learn sections give you the key information and examples to show how to do each topic. There are several Learn sections in each chapter.

### Practise...

Questions that allow you to practise what you have just learned.

**E** The bars that run alongside questions in the exercises show you what grade the question is aimed at. This will give you an idea of what grade you're working at. Don't forget, even if you are aiming at a Grade C, you will still need to do well on the Grades G–D questions.

These questions are Functional Maths type questions, which show how maths can be used in real life.

These questions are problem solving questions, which will require you to think carefully about how best to answer.

These questions are harder questions.

These questions should be attempted **with** a calculator.

These questions should be attempted **without** using a calculator.

### Assess

End of chapter questions test your skills. Some chapters feature additional questions taken from real past papers to further your understanding.

### Hint

These are tips for you to remember whilst learning the maths or answering questions.

### Study tip

Hints to help you with your study and exam preparation.

# 1 Representing data

## Objectives

Examiners would normally expect students who get these grades to be able to:

**D**

construct a histogram (frequency diagram) with equal class intervals

construct and interpret an ordered stem-and-leaf diagram

construct and interpret line graphs

**C**

construct a frequency polygon

**B**

construct and interpret a cumulative frequency diagram for continuous or grouped data

use a cumulative frequency diagram to estimate median and inter-quartile range

construct and interpret a box plot

compare two sets of data using a box plot referencing average and spread

**A**

construct a histogram with unequal class intervals

**A***

interpret a histogram with unequal class intervals.

## Key terms

stem-and-leaf diagram

back-to-back stem-and-leaf diagram

line graph

frequency polygon

frequency diagram

histogram

cumulative frequency diagram

cumulative frequency

lower quartile

upper quartile

inter-quartile range

## Selling more phones than ever

May 2010
48 sold

June 2010
96 sold

*Did you know?*

## Misleading diagrams

Charts and diagrams can sometimes be misleading.

Look at the diagram showing mobile phone sales in May and June. The sales in June are twice that in May and the dimensions of the phone in June are twice that in May – but does the advert look correct?

You need to be very careful to make sure your work is not misleading.

## You should already know:

✔ the measures of average: mean, mode and median

✔ how to find and work with the range

✔ types of data, e.g. discrete and continuous, qualitative and quantitative

✔ the meaning of inequality signs

✔ how to work with percentages and fractions.

# Learn... 1.1 Stem-and-leaf diagrams

**Stem-and-leaf diagrams** are a useful way of representing data.

They are used to show discrete data, or continuous data that has been rounded.

Stem-and-leaf diagrams need a key to show the 'stem' and 'leaf'.

For two-digit numbers the first digit is the stem and the second digit is the leaf.

It is often useful to provide an ordered stem and leaf diagram where the items are placed in order.

```
1 | 1  6  7  8  9
2 | 2  2  7  7  7  8  9
3 | 1  4  6
```

Key: 3 | 1 represents 31

> **Study tip**
>
> You will lose marks if you do not have a key for the 'stem' and 'leaf'.
>
> You will also lose marks if the diagram is not ordered.

If the numbers are decimals such as 5.4, the stem would be the 5 and the leaves would represent the decimal parts.

---

**Example:** A sample of 25 children in a primary school record how many portions of fruit and vegetables they eat in a week.

23  37  14  32  42  38  15  33  27  20  31  19  18

26  25  38  31  32  28  34  25  22  17  12  22

**a** Draw an ordered stem-and-leaf diagram for the data.

**b** Work out the range of the results.

**c** Work out the median number of portions eaten.

**Solution:** **a** The data runs from 12 to 42 and the values are all tens and units.

The stem will represent the tens and the leaf will represent the units.

The unordered stem-and-leaf diagram looks like this.

**Unordered stem-and-leaf diagram showing portions of fruit and vegetables eaten**

```
1 | 4  5  9  8  7  2
2 | 3  7  0  6  5  8  5  2  2
3 | 7  2  8  3  1  8  1  2  4
4 | 2
```

Key: 4 | 2 represents 42 portions of fruit and vegetables

The ordered stem-and-leaf diagram looks like this:

**Ordered stem-and-leaf diagram showing portions of fruit and vegetables eaten**

```
1 | 2  4  5  7  8  9
2 | 0  2  2  3  5  5  6  7  8
3 | 1  1  2  2  3  4  7  8  8
4 | 2
```

Key: 4 | 2 represents 42 portions of fruit and vegetables

**b** Range = highest value − lowest value

= 42 − 12

= 30

**c** The median is the middle value when values are put in order.

In an ordered stem-and-leaf diagram the data are already ordered.

There are 25 values so the median is the $\left(\frac{25+1}{2}\right)$th value or the 13th value.

Counting along this gives 26 portions. (Note that if the total was much above 25 you can simply halve the frequency to find the median, as when the sample size is large the difference is negligible.)

**Study tip**

Don't forget to include the stem number in your answer.

For example, here you must say that the median is 26, not 6.

---

*Example:* Two data sets can be shown at the same time on a **back-to-back stem-and-leaf diagram**.

This example of a back-to-back stem-and-leaf diagram compares the portions of fruit eaten by boys and girls. (Each side of the diagram then needs a label.)

| Boys | | Girls |
|---:|:---:|:---|
| 9 4 2 | 1 | 5 7 8 |
| 5 3 2 0 | 2 | 2 5 6 7 8 |
| 8 4 2 2 1 | 3 | 1 3 7 8 |
| | 4 | 2 |

Key: 9 | 1 represents 19          Key: 1 | 7 represents 17

Notice the leaves run backwards in order of size on the left.

This also means you need a key for **each side** of the diagram.

---

## Practise... 1.1 Stem-and-leaf diagrams

**1** The prices paid for a selection of items from a supermarket are as follows.

45p   32p   38p   21p   66p   54p   60p   44p   35p   42p   44p

**a** Show the data in an ordered stem-and-leaf diagram.

**b** What was the range of the prices paid?

**c** What was the median price paid?

**d** What was the modal price paid?

**e** What percentage of the prices were under 50p?

**2** The marks obtained by some students in a test were recorded as follows.

8   20   9   21   18   22   19   13   22   24

14   9   25   10   19   20   17   14   12

**a** Show this information in an ordered stem-and-leaf diagram.

**b** What was the highest mark in the test?

**c** Write down the median of the marks in the test.

**d** Write down the range of the marks in the test.

**e** The pass mark for the test was 15 marks.
What fraction of the students passed the test?

**D**

**3** The times taken to complete an exam paper were recorded as follows.

2 h 12 min    1 h 53 min    1 h 26 min    2 h 26 min    1 h 50 min
1 h 46 min    2 h 05 min    1 h 43 min    1 h 49 min    2 h 10 min
1 h 49 min    1 h 55 min    2 h 06 min    1 h 57 min

**a** Convert all the times to numbers.

**b** Show the converted data in an ordered stem-and-leaf diagram.

**C**

**4** Look again at the data in Question 3.

Convert all the times to minutes.

Draw a new ordered stem-and-leaf diagram for this new data.

Comment on the similarities or otherwise of the new diagram with the one from Question 3.

**5** The number of visitors to a small museum each day in July was counted.

The set of data has the following.

Minimum value of 23          Maximum value of 65
Median of 44                 Modes of 42 and 55

Draw a possible stem-and-leaf diagram, making up data values which satisfy these conditions.

**6** A village football team played 32 games during one season.

The numbers of spectators for the first 31 games are shown in the stem-and-leaf diagram.

```
18 | 4  6
19 | 0  2  3  5
20 | 3  3  7  9  9  9  9
21 | 0  1  5  5  6  7  8  8  9
22 | 3  4  4  6  9
23 | 2  5
24 | 7  8
```

Key: 18 | 4 represents 184 spectators

**a** The number of spectators at the 32nd game increases the range by 14.
Work out two possible values for the number of spectators at the 32nd game.

**b** Do either of these possible values affect the median of the number of spectators after 31 games? Explain your answer.

**c** Do either of the possible values found in part **a** affect the modal number of spectators after 31 games? Explain your answer.

**7** Emma is investigating this hypothesis:

'Girls take longer to complete an exercise than boys'.

She collects the data shown in this back-to-back stem-and-leaf diagram.

| Girls | | Boys |
|---|---|---|
| 7 7 6 5 4 2 2 | 1 | 1 6 7 8 9 |
| 7 6 4 3 2 1 | 2 | 2 2 7 7 7 8 9 |
| 7 0 | 3 | 1 4 6 |

Key: 3 | 2 represents 23 minutes          Key: 3 | 4 represents 34 minutes

Compare the time taken by girls and boys to complete the exercise.

Write some conclusions that Emma might make about her hypothesis.

8    Declan is investigating reaction times for Year 7 and Year 11 students.

In an experiment he obtains these results.

| Year | Times (tenths of a second) | | | | | | | | | | | | | | |
|---|---|---|---|---|---|---|---|---|---|---|---|---|---|---|---|
| 7 | 18 | 19 | 09 | 28 | 10 | 04 | 11 | 14 | 15 | 18 | 09 | 27 | 28 | 06 | 05 |
| 11 | 07 | 20 | 09 | 12 | 21 | 17 | 11 | 12 | 15 | 08 | 09 | 12 | 08 | 16 | 19 |

**a**    Show this information in a back-to-back stem-and-leaf diagram.

**b**    Declan thinks Year 7 have quicker reaction times than Year 11.
Use your diagram to show whether he is correct.

**c**    Explain how Declan might improve his experiment.

 **Learn...    1.2  Line graphs and frequency polygons**

### Line graphs

A **line graph** is a series of points joined with straight lines.

Line graphs show how data change over a period of time.

Here is an example of a line graph showing shop sales over a period of time.

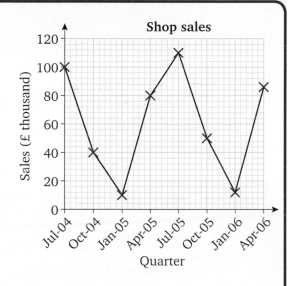

### Frequency polygons

A **frequency polygon** is a way of showing continuous grouped data in a diagram.

Points are plotted at the midpoint of each class interval.

For a frequency polygon, the groups may have equal or unequal widths.

The frequency polygon is an example of a **frequency diagram**.

Another type of frequency diagram is a **histogram**.

Histograms are discussed in Learn 7.5

*Example:*    50 people were asked how long they had to wait for a train.

The table below shows the results.

| Time, $t$ (minutes) | Frequency |
|---|---|
| $5 \leqslant t < 10$ | 16 |
| $10 \leqslant t < 15$ | 22 |
| $15 \leqslant t < 20$ | 11 |
| $20 \leqslant t < 25$ | 1 |

Draw a frequency polygon to represent the data.

**Solution:**   For a frequency polygon, the points are plotted at the midpoint of each class interval.

E.g. the midpoint for $5 \leqslant t < 10$ is $\dfrac{5 + 10}{2} = 7.5$

> **Study tip**
>
> Make sure that the axes are labelled with a continuous scale and not the class intervals.

**Frequency polygon to show waiting times**

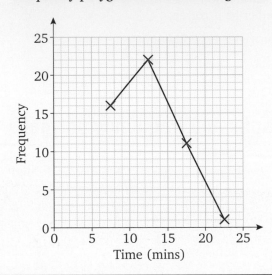

> **Study tip**
>
> There is no need to draw lines beyond the first and last plots.

## 1.2 Line graphs and frequency polygons

**Practise...**

D   C   B   A   A*

**1**   A new freezer is switched on for the first time at 9 o'clock one morning.

The temperature is noted every 10 minutes.

The readings (°C) for the next three hours are:

| 17.4 | 15.1 | 12.3 | 9.2 | 6.6 | 3.0 | 0.2 | −2.3 | −4.4 |
| −7.1 | −9.9 | −12.0 | −14.5 | −16.6 | −18.3 | −19.1 | −19.5 | −19.6 |

**a**   Draw a fully labelled line graph to show these data.

**b**   What do you think the temperature of the freezer will be 24 hours later? Give a reason for your answer.

**2**   The table shows the times of runners in a fun run.

| Time, $t$ (minutes) | Frequency |
| --- | --- |
| 5 up to 10 | 40 |
| 10 up to 15 | 125 |
| 15 up to 20 | 100 |
| 20 up to 25 | 55 |
| 25 up to 30 | 15 |

**a**   How many runners took part in the fun run?

**b**   Draw a frequency polygon to represent the data.

**3**  **a**  The table shows the time taken for 100 students to solve a simple puzzle.

| Times for 100 students | |
|---|---|
| Time, $x$ (seconds) | Frequency |
| $10 \leqslant x < 20$ | 30 |
| $20 \leqslant x < 30$ | 35 |
| $30 \leqslant x < 40$ | 20 |
| $40 \leqslant x < 50$ | 10 |
| $50 \leqslant x < 60$ | 5 |

Draw and label the frequency polygon for these students.

**b**  This table shows the time taken for 100 adults to solve the same puzzle.

| Times for 100 adults | |
|---|---|
| Time, $x$ (seconds) | Frequency |
| $10 \leqslant x < 20$ | 40 |
| $20 \leqslant x < 30$ | 22 |
| $30 \leqslant x < 40$ | 15 |
| $40 \leqslant x < 50$ | 13 |
| $50 \leqslant x < 60$ | 10 |

On the same axes draw and label the frequency polygon for these adults.

**c**  Write down two comparisons shown by the frequency polygons between the students and the adults.

**4**  The frequency polygons show the times taken by sprinters in a series of 200 m races at a school.

The data is shown for boys and girls separately.

Compare the times of the boys and girls.

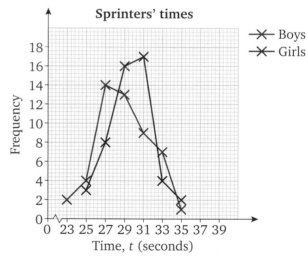

**5**  The principal of a college thinks that attendance becomes worse as the week progresses.

The table shows the number of students present during morning and afternoon registration.

| Day | Mon | Mon | Tue | Tue | Wed | Wed | Thu | Thu | Fri | Fri |
|---|---|---|---|---|---|---|---|---|---|---|
| Session | am | pm | am | pm | am | pm | am | pm | am | pm |
| Number | 220 | 210 | 243 | 215 | 254 | 218 | 251 | 201 | 185 | 152 |

**a**  Show this information on a graph.

**b**  There are 260 students in the college.
Work out the percentage attending each registration session.
Give your answers to the nearest whole number.

**c**  Do your answers to parts **a** and **b** support the principal?
Explain your answer.

**6** The duration of the 25 most popular films of 2008 are as follows.

| | | | |
|---|---|---|---|
| 1 hour 54 minutes | 2 hours 3 minutes | 1 hour 34 minutes | 2 hours 23 minutes |
| 2 hours 22 minutes | 2 hours 12 minutes | 1 hour 23 minutes | 1 hour 49 minutes |
| 1 hour 44 minutes | 2 hours 43 minutes | 2 hours 1 minute | 2 hours 10 minutes |
| 1 hour 30 minutes | 1 hour 39 minutes | 1 hour 28 minutes | 2 hours 54 minutes |
| 1 hour 39 minutes | 1 hour 57 minutes | 2 hour 2 minutes | 1 hour 21 minutes |
| 1 hour 40 minutes | 3 hours 6 minutes | 2 hours 29 minutes | 1 hour 52 minutes |
| 2 hours 9 minutes | | | |

Use suitable class groupings to draw a frequency diagram for these data.

# Learn... 1.3 Cumulative frequency diagrams

A **cumulative frequency diagram** (or cumulative frequency curve) is used to estimate the median and quartiles of a set of data.

To find the **cumulative frequency**, you add the frequencies in turn to give you a 'running total'.

Cumulative frequencies are plotted at the upper class bound. The upper class bound is the highest possible value for each class interval.

The cumulative frequency diagram is formed by joining the points with a series of straight lines or a smooth curve.

The total cumulative frequency can be divided by four to find the quartiles and the median. This is shown in the example that follows.

*Example:* The frequency distribution shows the length of 80 phone calls to an internet help line.

**a** Construct a column of cumulative frequencies.

**b** Draw a cumulative frequency diagram for the data.

**c** Use your diagram to estimate:

  **i** the median length of phone call

  **ii** the **lower quartile**

  **iii** the **upper quartile**

  **iv** the **inter-quartile range**.

**d** Estimate the percentage of calls over 25 minutes.

| Time, $t$ (minutes) | Frequency |
|---|---|
| $0 < t \leqslant 10$ | 9 |
| $10 < t \leqslant 20$ | 23 |
| $20 < t \leqslant 30$ | 31 |
| $30 < t \leqslant 40$ | 12 |
| $40 < t \leqslant 50$ | 5 |

*Solution:* **a** It is useful to add an extra column to the table. This can be used to show the cumulative frequencies.

| Time, $t$ (minutes) | Frequency | Cumulative frequency |
|---|---|---|
| $0 < t \leqslant 10$ | 9 | 9 |
| $10 < t \leqslant 20$ | 23 | 9 + 23 = 32 |
| $20 < t \leqslant 30$ | 31 | 32 + 31 = 63 |
| $30 < t \leqslant 40$ | 12 | 63 + 12 = 75 |
| $40 < t \leqslant 50$ | 5 | 75 + 5 = 80 |

**Study tip**

Check your final total by adding up all the frequencies.

9 + 23 + 31 + 12 + 5 = 80 so the total cumulative frequency is correct.

(Notice the value 80 was given in the question.)

**b**  The upper class bounds for each interval are shown below.

| Time, $t$ (minutes) | Upper class bound |
|---|---|
| $0 < t \leqslant 10$ | 10 |
| $10 < t \leqslant 20$ | 20 |
| $20 < t \leqslant 30$ | 30 |
| $30 < t \leqslant 40$ | 40 |
| $40 < t \leqslant 50$ | 50 |

**Study tip**

To draw a cumulative frequency diagram, cumulative frequencies are plotted at the upper class bound for each class interval.

The points to be plotted are (10, 9), (20, 32), (30, 63), (40, 75) and (50, 80).

(0, 0) can also be plotted as no calls are below zero minutes long.

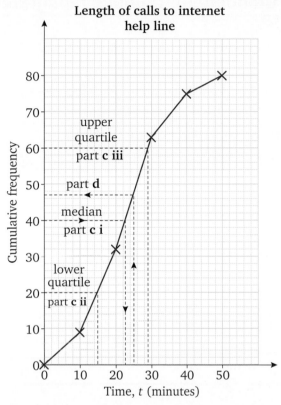

Length of calls to internet help line

**c  i**  The median is read off at the halfway point in the whole of the data set.

There are 80 values, so the median is the $\frac{1}{2} \times$ 80th value = 40th value

From the graph, median = 22.5 minutes

(Note the median is the $\frac{(n+1)}{2}$th value which is $\frac{81}{2} = 40.5$ but when $n$ is large it is simpler to just halve the cumulative frequency. The difference in outcome is negligible. This idea is also used in the position of the quartiles.)

**ii**  The lower quartile is read off at the point one quarter along the data.

There are 80 values, so the lower quartile is the $\frac{1}{4} \times$ 80th value = 20th value

From the graph, lower quartile = 15 minutes

**iii**  The upper quartile is read off at the point three quarters along the data set.

There are 80 values, so the upper quartile is the $\frac{3}{4} \times$ 80th = 60th value

From the graph, upper quartile = 29 minutes

**iv**  The inter-quartile range is the difference between the upper and lower quartiles. It gives you the spread of the middle 50% of the data and is important for comparing the spread of different data sets.

The inter-quartile range = upper quartile − lower quartile

$$= 29 - 15$$
$$= 14 \text{ minutes}$$

(This means there is a 14 minute range across the middle 50% of the data.)

**d**    To find an estimate of the percentage of calls over 25 minutes:

Draw a line from 25 minutes on the horizontal axis to the cumulative frequency graph.

From the graph, reading across = 47 calls.

There are 47 calls **below** 25 minutes.

There are $80 - 47 = 33$ calls **above** 25 minutes.

This represents $\frac{33}{80}$ calls $= \frac{33}{80} \times 100\% = 41.25\%$

## Practise... 1.3 Cumulative frequency diagrams 𝒌 D C B A A*

**B**

**1**    Complete the cumulative frequency columns for these frequency tables.

**a**

| Height, $h$ (cm) | Frequency | Cumulative frequency |
|---|---|---|
| $100 < h \leqslant 120$ | 5 | 5 |
| $120 < h \leqslant 140$ | 12 | $5 + 12 = 17$ |
| $140 < h \leqslant 160$ | 10 | $17 + 10 =$ |
| $160 < h \leqslant 180$ | 7 | |
| $180 < h \leqslant 200$ | 4 | |

**b**

| Weight, $w$ (kg) | Frequency | Cumulative frequency |
|---|---|---|
| $10 < w \leqslant 11$ | 300 | 300 |
| $11 < w \leqslant 12$ | 254 | 554 |
| $12 < w \leqslant 13$ | 401 | |
| $13 < w \leqslant 14$ | 308 | |
| $14 < w \leqslant 15$ | 126 | |

**c**

| Time, $t$ (seconds) | Frequency | Cumulative frequency |
|---|---|---|
| $10 \leqslant t < 30$ | 43 | 43 |
| $30 \leqslant t < 50$ | 65 | |
| $50 \leqslant t < 70$ | 72 | |
| $70 \leqslant t < 90$ | 55 | |

**d**

| Height, $h$ (feet) | Frequency | Cumulative frequency |
|---|---|---|
| $100 \leqslant h < 150$ | 1 | |
| $150 \leqslant h < 200$ | 15 | |
| $200 \leqslant h < 250$ | 34 | |
| $250 \leqslant h < 300$ | 46 | |
| $300 \leqslant h < 350$ | 16 | |
| $350 \leqslant h < 400$ | 9 | |

**2**    For each of the tables in Question 1, draw a cumulative frequency diagram.

**B**

**3**  The cumulative frequency diagram shows the mass of 100 gerbils in a pet shop.

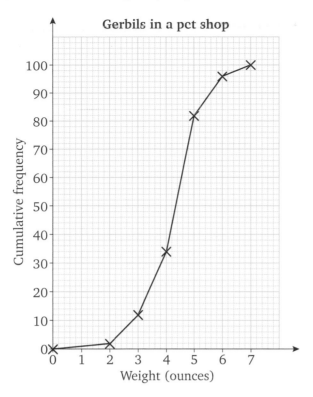

Use the diagram to estimate:

**a**    the median

**b**    the lower quartile

**c**    the upper quartile

**d**    the inter-quartile range

**e**    the percentage of gerbils under 2 ounces

**f**    the percentage of gerbils over 5.5 ounces.

**4**  The frequency distribution shows the lifetimes of 1000 light bulbs in hours.

| Lifetime, $l$ (hours) | Frequency | Cumulative frequency |
|---|---|---|
| $50 < l \leqslant 100$ | 80 | |
| $100 < l \leqslant 150$ | 240 | |
| $150 < l \leqslant 200$ | 390 | |
| $200 < l \leqslant 250$ | 200 | |
| $250 < l \leqslant 300$ | 90 | |

**a**    Copy and complete the table.

**b**    Draw the cumulative frequency diagram.

**c**    Use your diagram to estimate:

    **i**    the median

    **ii**    the lower quartile

    **iii**    the upper quartile

    **iv**    the inter-quartile range

    **v**    Estimate the percentage of light bulbs lasting beyond one week of continuous use.

**d**    Explain why your answers to the parts in **c** are estimates.

**5** The data represent the weights of 100 newborn babies.

| Weight, $w$ (kg) | Frequency | Cumulative frequency |
|---|---|---|
| $0 < w \leqslant 1$ | 1 | 1 |
| $1 < w \leqslant 2$ | $a$ | 18 |
| $2 < w \leqslant 3$ | 72 | $b$ |
| $3 < w \leqslant 4$ | $c$ | 98 |
| $4 < w \leqslant 5$ | $d$ | $e$ |

**a** Find the values indicated with letters in the table.

**b** Draw a cumulative frequency diagram for the data.

**c** Estimate the inter-quartile range of the babies' weights.

**6** Speeds on some roads are constantly monitored. If the upper quartile of actual car speeds is above the speed limit, speed cameras are considered to enforce the speed limit.

**a** For these data, speed cameras were not considered. What was the speed limit?

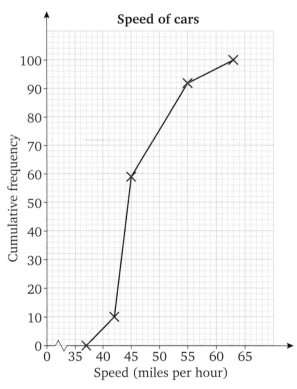

Speed of cars

| Speed, $s$ (mph) | Frequency |
|---|---|
| $55 < s \leqslant 60$ | 27 |
| $60 < s \leqslant 65$ | 36 |
| $65 < s \leqslant 72$ | 40 |
| $72 < s \leqslant 80$ | 11 |
| $80 < s \leqslant 95$ | 6 |

**b** A different road has a speed limit of 70 miles per hour.

Comment on the need for consideration of speed cameras in light of the data in the table.

Give a reason for your answer.

**7** The hourly pay of employees at a certain company is shown in the table.

The company is situated in a country outside of the UK.

The minimum wage is $\frac{2}{3}$ of the median pay.

**a** Estimate the minimum wage of this country.

**b** Are there any employees working for the minimum wage? Justify your answer and if so, estimate the percentage doing so.

| Hourly pay, $p$ (euro) | Frequency |
|---|---|
| $4 < p \leqslant 5$ | 17 |
| $5 < p \leqslant 6$ | 56 |
| $6 < p \leqslant 7$ | 55 |
| $7 < p \leqslant 8$ | 101 |
| $8 < p \leqslant 9$ | 39 |

**8** The cumulative frequency diagram represents the length of service of workers at a company.

Use the diagram to complete the missing information in this company report.

The company has _____ employees and all but six have been with the company for at least _____ years.

The median length of service is _____ years. This is an increase of 2.6 years on the figure of two years ago which was _____ years.

The inter-quartile range is 10% less than two years ago when the figure was _____ years.

I am pleased to be able to recommend _____ workers for long service awards as they have worked for more than 35 years.

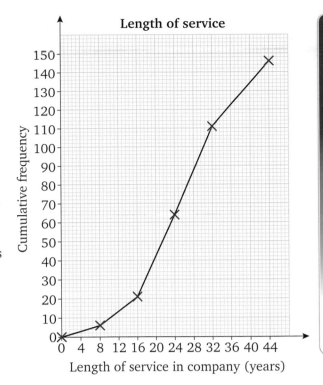

Length of service

Length of service in company (years)

---

## Learn... 1.4 Box plots

A box plot (sometimes called a box-and-whisker diagram) is another way to show information about a frequency distribution.

The box plot provides a visual summary of information.

It can be used to compare two or more distributions.

The box plot shows the following information.
- the minimum and maximum values
- the lower and upper quartiles
- the median

*Example:* The box plot shows the length of songs in a record collection (recorded in minutes).

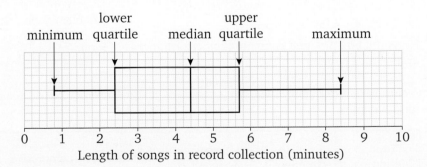

Length of songs in record collection (minutes)

Write down:

**a** the minimum song length

**b** the maximum song length

**c** the median song length

**d** the lower quartile song length

**e** the upper quartile song length.

*Solution:* From the diagram, you can see that:

    **a**    the minimum song length was 0.8 minutes long

    **b**    the maximum song length was 8.4 minutes long

    **c**    the median song length was 4.4 minutes long

    **d**    the lower quartile song length was 2.4 minutes long

    **e**    the upper quartile song length was 5.7 minutes long.

Box plots are sometimes drawn at the base of a cumulative frequency diagram.

This is because the measures are often estimated from the diagram.

Box plots can be put together to compare two or more data sets.

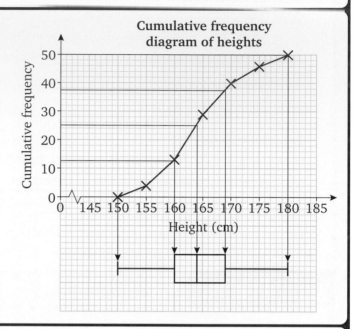

**Cumulative frequency diagram of heights**

*Example:* A group of men competed against a group of women in a series of puzzles.

The times to finish obtained by each person are summarised in the table.

| Time, $t$ (minutes) | Male frequency | Female frequency |
|---|---|---|
| $0 < t \leqslant 10$ | 3 | 5 |
| $10 < t \leqslant 20$ | 11 | 16 |
| $20 < t \leqslant 30$ | 35 | 21 |
| $30 < t \leqslant 40$ | 27 | 29 |
| $40 < t \leqslant 50$ | 4 | 9 |

    **a**    Use a suitable diagram to obtain estimates of measures for a box plot.

    **b**    Draw the box plot and compare the performances of men and women.

**Study tip**

You will see the words 'use a suitable diagram' in examination questions. Here a cumulative frequency diagram is the suitable diagram but you will have to choose.

*Solution:*    **a**    A cumulative frequency diagram is a suitable diagram to obtain estimates of measures for a box plot.

| Time, $t$ (minutes) | Male frequency | Female frequency | Male cumulative frequency | Female cumulative frequency |
|---|---|---|---|---|
| $0 < t \leqslant 10$ | 3 | 5 | 3 | 5 |
| $10 < t \leqslant 20$ | 11 | 16 | 14 | 21 |
| $20 < t \leqslant 30$ | 35 | 21 | 49 | 42 |
| $30 < t \leqslant 40$ | 27 | 29 | 76 | 71 |
| $40 < t \leqslant 50$ | 4 | 9 | 80 | 80 |

The upper class values will be 10, 20, 30, …, and so on.

Drawing both graphs on the same axes:

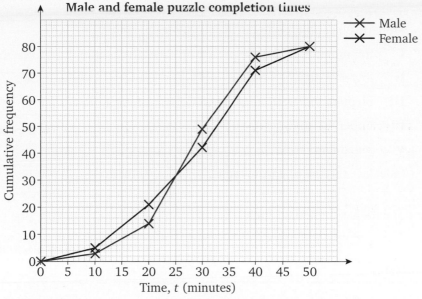

**Male and female puzzle completion times**

b   To obtain the box plots, use the cumulative frequency diagrams.

The median is read off at the halfway point in the whole of the data set.

There are 80 values, so the median is the $\frac{1}{2} \times$ 80th value = 40th value

The lower quartile is read off at the halfway point in the bottom half of the data.

There are 80 values, so the lower quartile is the $\frac{1}{4} \times$ 80th value = 20th value

The upper quartile is read off at the halfway point in the top half of the data set.

There are 80 values, so the upper quartile is the $\frac{3}{4} \times$ 80th = 60th value

The minimum for both groups has to be taken as 0.

The maximum for both groups has to be taken as 50

Putting all the results into a table you get estimates as follows:

|  | Minimum | Lower quartile | Median | Upper quartile | Maximum |
|---|---|---|---|---|---|
| Data for women | 0 | 19.5 | 29 | 36 | 50 |
| Data for men | 0 | 22 | 27.5 | 34 | 50 |

Showing this information as a pair of box plots:

**Box plot showing average times to complete puzzles**

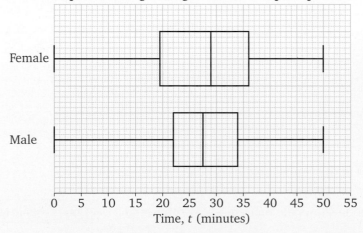

> **Study tip**
>
> When making comparisons between two sets of data try to make one comment about average and one comment about the spread.

The box plots show that on average men do better.

The median shows that women took a higher average time.

The box plots also show that men are more consistent than women, as the inter-quartile range (the width of the box part) is narrower.

Also women have more really quick times and more really slow times.

# Practise... 1.4 Box plots

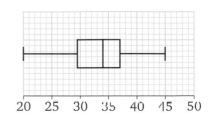

**B**

**1**   **a**   From this box plot, write down the following values.

    **i**   minimum

    **ii**   lower quartile

    **iii**   median

    **iv**   upper quartile

    **v**   maximum

  **b**   Calculate the inter-quartile range.

**2**   A set of data has these measures.

| | Minimum | Lower quartile | Median | Upper quartile | Maximum |
|---|---|---|---|---|---|
| Data value | 10 | 29 | 37 | 50 | 66 |

  **a**   Draw a box plot for these data.

  **b**   Explain why the inter-quartile range is 21.

**3**   The box plots below show the ages of all of the people in two villages.

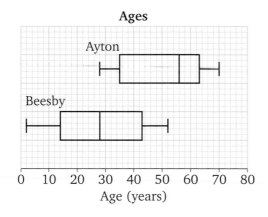

Ages

  **a**   Complete the table for the two villages.

| | Ayton | Beesby |
|---|---|---|
| Minimum age | | |
| Maximum age | | |
| Lower quartile age | | |
| Upper quartile age | | |
| Median | | |

  **b**   Compare the ages in the two villages.

**4**   The frequency distribution shows the times taken by runners in the 'Race for Life'.

  **a**   Draw a cumulative frequency diagram for these data.

  **b**   Draw a box plot for these data.

  **c**   The previous year, the median race time had been 37.1 minutes with an inter-quartile range of 9.9 minutes. Compare the results for this year and the previous year.

| Time, $t$ (minutes) | Frequency |
|---|---|
| 25 up to 30 | 27 |
| 30 up to 35 | 215 |
| 35 up to 40 | 307 |
| 40 up to 45 | 147 |
| 45 up to 50 | 104 |

**5** The cumulative frequency diagram opposite shows the waiting times at a main post office.

The box plot below shows the waiting times at a village post office.

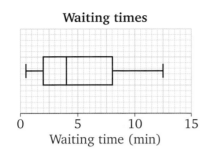

**Waiting times**

Waiting time (min)

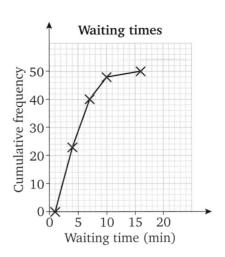

Compare the waiting time at the two post offices.

**6** Match the cumulative frequency distribution with the box plot.

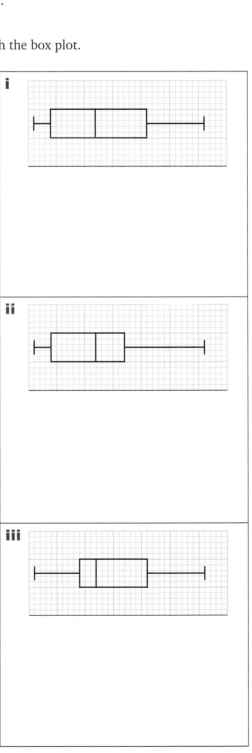

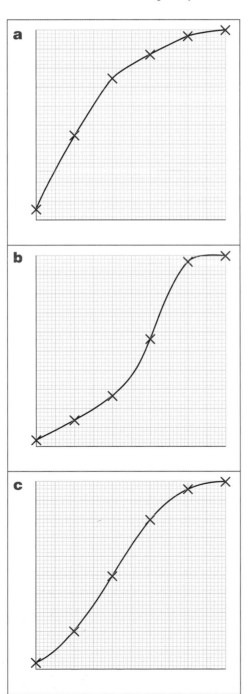

**7**   The box plot shows information about hourly sales in a small corner shop over a period of time.

**Hourly sales**

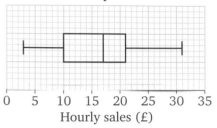

Hourly sales (£)

The shop is taken over by a new manager.

One month later, the following data are collected.

| Hourly sales (£) | Frequency |
|---|---|
| £5 up to £10 | 11 |
| £10 up to £15 | 23 |
| £15 up to £20 | 63 |
| £20 up to £25 | 2 |
| £30 up to £35 | 1 |

Write a report on the sales figures before and after the shop is taken over by the new manager. Include measures obtained from suitable diagrams.

## Learn...   1.5  Histograms  (k)

### Histograms

A histogram is a way of showing continuous grouped data in a diagram.

The area of the bar represents the frequency.

For a histogram, the groups may have equal or unequal widths.

The histogram is an example of a frequency diagram.

Another type of frequency diagram is a frequency polygon.

Frequency polygons were discussed earlier in Learn 7.2 Line graphs and frequency polygons.

### Histograms with equal group widths

In a histogram, the area of the bars represents the frequency.

If the group widths are equal, bars are drawn to the height of the frequency.

**Example:**   50 people were asked how long they had to wait for a train.

The table below shows the results.

| Time, $t$ (minutes) | Frequency |
|---|---|
| $5 \leqslant t < 10$ | 16 |
| $10 \leqslant t < 15$ | 22 |
| $15 \leqslant t < 20$ | 11 |
| $20 \leqslant t < 25$ | 1 |

Draw a histogram to represent the data.

*Solution:*    Use a continuous scale for the *x*-axis.

As the groups are all equal width, bars are drawn to the height of the frequency.

The areas will then be proportional to the frequency.

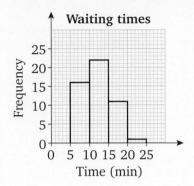

**Study tip**

You may be asked to draw a frequency diagram. You have a choice of drawing a histogram or a frequency polygon.

If the classes are of equal width it is usually easier to draw a histogram. If you draw a frequency polygon you will have to get the midpoints correct.

## Histograms with unequal group widths

For a histogram, the groups may have equal or unequal widths.

In a histogram, the area of the bars represents the frequency.

If the group widths are unequal, bars are drawn to the height of the frequency density.

$$\text{Frequency density} = \frac{\text{frequency}}{\text{class width}}$$

*Example:*    The table shows the waiting times in seconds for a phone to be answered in a call centre.

**a**    Draw a fully labelled histogram for these data.

**b**    Estimate the proportion of calls for which the waiting time is more than 4 seconds.

| Time, $t$ (seconds) | Frequency |
|---|---|
| $0 < t \leqslant 2$ | 38 |
| $2 < t \leqslant 3$ | 32 |
| $3 < t \leqslant 3.5$ | 30 |
| $3.5 < t \leqslant 5$ | 45 |
| $5 < t \leqslant 10$ | 55 |

*Solution:*    **a**    Use a continuous scale for the *x*-axis.

As the groups are unequal width, bars are drawn to the height of the frequency density.

$$\text{Frequency density} = \frac{\text{frequency}}{\text{class width}}$$

It is useful to add extra columns to the table.

A column can be used to show the class width. This is the upper class bound take away the lower class bound.

The other column can be used to show the frequency density.

| Time, $t$ (seconds) | Frequency | Class width | Frequency density $= \dfrac{\text{frequency}}{\text{class width}}$ |
|---|---|---|---|
| $0 < t \leqslant 2$ | 38 | 2 | $38 \div 2 = 19$ |
| $2 < t \leqslant 3$ | 32 | 1 | $32 \div 1 = 32$ |
| $3 < t \leqslant 3.5$ | 30 | 0.5 | $30 \div 0.5 = 60$ |
| $3.5 < t \leqslant 5$ | 45 | 1.5 | $45 \div 1.5 = 30$ |
| $5 < t \leqslant 10$ | 55 | 5 | $55 \div 5 = 11$ |

Now the first bar is drawn from 0 to 2 to a height of 19 and so on.

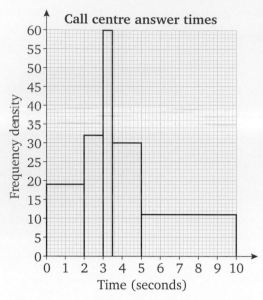

**b** Above 4 seconds is all of the calls for the $5 < t \leqslant 10$ class and two thirds of the calls for the $3.5 < t \leqslant 5$ class (as 4 is one third along the length of the class).

This estimate is therefore $55 + \frac{2}{3} \times 45 = 55 + 30 = 85$ calls

## Practise... 1.5 Histograms  🄺

**D A**

**1** The heights of people auditioning for a play are given in the table.

| Height, $h$ (cm) | Frequency |
|---|---|
| $100 < h \leqslant 120$ | 24 |
| $120 < h \leqslant 140$ | 20 |
| $140 < h \leqslant 160$ | 13 |
| $160 < h \leqslant 180$ | 6 |
| $180 < h \leqslant 200$ | 7 |

**a** Draw a fully labelled histogram for these data.

**b** What would be different about the histogram if the final class was $180 < h \leqslant 220$ instead of $180 < h \leqslant 200$?

**A**

**2** The table shows the wages of workers in a factory.

| Wages, $x$ (£) | Frequency |
|---|---|
| $100 < x \leqslant 200$ | 120 |
| $200 < x \leqslant 250$ | 165 |
| $250 < x \leqslant 300$ | 182 |
| $300 < x \leqslant 350$ | 197 |
| $350 < x \leqslant 400$ | 40 |
| $400 < x \leqslant 600$ | 6 |

**a** Draw a suitable diagram for these data.

**b** Estimate the number of workers earning more than £387.50.

**3**  Draw fully labelled histograms for these sets of data.

**a**

| Time, $t$ (hours) | Frequency |
|---|---|
| $0 < t \leqslant 20$ | 3 |
| $20 < t \leqslant 30$ | 11 |
| $30 < t \leqslant 35$ | 35 |
| $35 < t \leqslant 45$ | 27 |
| $45 < t \leqslant 95$ | 4 |

**b**

| Speed, $s$ (mph) | Frequency |
|---|---|
| $55 < s \leqslant 60$ | 25 |
| $60 < s \leqslant 65$ | 35 |
| $65 < s \leqslant 72$ | 42 |
| $72 < s \leqslant 80$ | 12 |
| $80 < s \leqslant 95$ | 6 |

**c**  From each histogram estimate the median of the distribution.

> **Hint**
>
> The median is halfway along the data and so will divide the total area under the bars into two equal parts.

**4**  The distribution of ages of people at a hotel is shown in the histogram below.

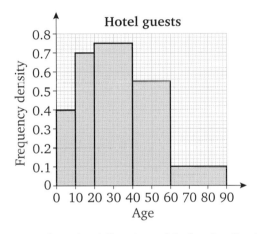

Complete the following table for the distribution.

| Age, $a$ (years) | $0 < a \leqslant 10$ | $10 < a \leqslant 20$ | $20 < a \leqslant 40$ | $40 < a \leqslant 60$ | $60 < a \leqslant 90$ |
|---|---|---|---|---|---|
| Number | 4 | | | | |

**⚠ 5**  A ski resort regularly measures the depth of snow.

The frequency table shows the depth of snow throughout the season.

**a**  Criticise the labelling of the table.

**b**  Construct a fully labelled histogram for the data.

| Depth, $d$ (cm) | Frequency |
|---|---|
| 10–50 | 12 |
| 50–80 | 27 |
| 80–100 | 28 |
| 100–120 | 19 |
| 120–200 | 64 |

**⚠ 6**  The table shows some of the percentages of a sample of tins of beans within various groups of weights.

**a**  Copy and complete the table.

**b**  Draw a fully labelled histogram to show all the data appropriately.

| Weight, $w$ (g) | Percentage |
|---|---|
| $390 < w \leqslant 400$ | 10 |
| $400 < w \leqslant 401$ | 26 |
| $401 < w \leqslant 402$ | 17 |
| $402 < w \leqslant 405$ | 33 |
| $405 < w \leqslant 412$ | |

**7** A restaurant group advertise that they sell a particular drink in 500 ml servings.

Over a period of time trading standards officers sample these drinks.

The table shows the volumes of the sample of drinks.

| Volume, v (ml) | Frequency |
|---|---|
| $490 < v \leqslant 495$ | 8 |
| $495 < v \leqslant 498$ | 18 |
| $498 < v \leqslant 501$ | 21 |
| $501 < v \leqslant 505$ | 44 |
| $505 < v \leqslant 510$ | 13 |

**a** Draw a fully labelled histogram for these data.

**b** Estimate the proportion of drinks which were under the advertised volume.

**c** Comment on your answer to part **b** in the context of the question.

**8** Virgil likes to read his morning paper for half an hour before going to work.

He has to leave for work at 8.15am.

The table shows the arrival times for the newspaper over the last few months.

| Arrival time (am) | Frequency |
|---|---|
| 7.00–7.20 | 12 |
| 7.20–7.40 | 42 |
| 7.40–7.55 | 45 |
| 7.55–8.05 | 23 |
| 8.05–8.30 | 15 |

**a** Draw a fully labelled histogram to show the data.

**b** Estimate the proportion of times:

  **i** Virgil has time to read the newspaper for half an hour in the morning.

  **ii** Virgil has to leave for work before the newspaper arrives.

**9** The histogram shows the distribution of weights of apples.

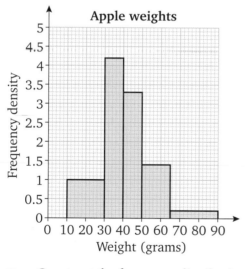

**a** Construct the frequency distribution for these weights.

**b** Calculate an estimate of the mean weight of apples.

# Assess

**D** **1** Rod and Annette went fishing every month for six years.

They kept the following record of the number of fish caught each month.

One number needs to be filled in before you can draw a graph.

Construct a fully labelled histogram for the data.

| Number caught | Frequency |
|---|---|
| $0 \leqslant n \leqslant 10$ | 3 |
| $10 < n \leqslant 20$ | 17 |
| $20 < n \leqslant 30$ | 31 |
| $30 < n \leqslant 40$ | 19 |
| $40 < n \leqslant 50$ | ? |

**2**   The heights of 40 workers in a factory are given in the diagram below.

|       Females       |     |      Males      |
|--------------------:|:---:|:----------------|
| 9 | 14 |  |
| 9 8 2 | 15 |  |
| 9 9 8 7 6 6 6 4 4 3 1 | 16 | 2 4 7 9 9 |
| 8 7 5 3 3 2 2 1 | 17 | 2 2 4 5 5 8 |
| 2 | 18 | 3 3 6 9 |
|  | 19 | 1 |

Key: 7 | 16 represents 167 cm              Key: 18 | 3 represents 183 cm

**a**   Explain why the median male height is 174.5 cm.

**b**   Show that only about 19% of males are shorter than the median female height.

**c**   Compare the ranges of the male and female heights.

**d**   Produce a similar diagram for data from your class.

**3**   The number of workers in the canteen in a hospital is shown in the line graph.

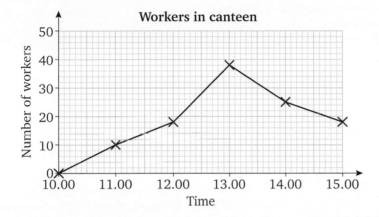

**a**   At what time is the canteen busiest?

**b**   What time do you think the canteen opens?
Give a reason for your answer.

**c**   Complete this table:

| Time | 10.00 | 11.00 | 12.00 | 13.00 | 14.00 | 15.00 |
|------|-------|-------|-------|-------|-------|-------|
| Number of workers in canteen |  |  |  |  |  |  |

**d**   Is a line graph a suitable diagram for these data?
Give a reason for your answer.

**e**   Display the data in a suitable diagram of your choice.

**4**   The ages of passengers on a train are shown in the frequency table.

**a**   Calculate the cumulative frequencies for these data.

**b**   Hence draw a cumulative frequency diagram.

**c**   Use your diagram to estimate the following:

   **i**   median

   **ii**   lower quartile

   **iii**   upper quartile

   **iv**   inter-quartile range.

| Age, $a$ (years) | Frequency |
|------------------|-----------|
| $0 \leqslant a < 5$ | 11 |
| $5 \leqslant a < 10$ | 32 |
| $10 \leqslant a < 15$ | 28 |
| $15 \leqslant a < 20$ | 35 |
| $20 \leqslant a < 30$ | 45 |
| $30 \leqslant a < 50$ | 58 |
| $50 \leqslant a < 65$ | 115 |
| $65 \leqslant a < 90$ | 76 |

**B**

**5**   The cumulative frequency diagram shows the ages of passengers on an aircraft.

Use this diagram and your results from Question 4 to draw two box plots on the same axis.

Compare the ages of travellers on the train and the aircraft.

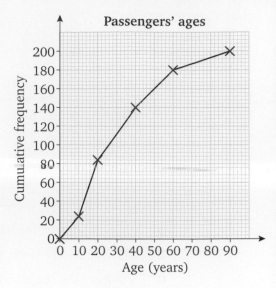

**A**

**6**   **a**   Draw a fully labelled histogram using the train data from Question 4.

**b**   Use the histogram to obtain an estimate of the median age. How does this compare to your answer in Question 4 part **c i**?

**7**   **a**   The frequency distribution shows the heights of 150 trees in a country park.

Draw **two** different frequency diagrams for these data.

| Country park | |
|---|---|
| Height, $h$ (metres) | Frequency |
| $5 < h \leqslant 10$ | 48 |
| $10 < h \leqslant 15$ | 55 |
| $15 < h \leqslant 20$ | 27 |
| $20 < h \leqslant 25$ | 16 |
| $25 < h \leqslant 30$ | 4 |

**b**   The frequency distribution shows the heights of 90 trees in a local park.

Donna wants to draw a diagram to compare the heights of the two sets of trees.

She draws the frequency polygon for the local park.

| Local park | |
|---|---|
| Height, $h$ (metres) | Frequency |
| $0 < h \leqslant 5$ | 7 |
| $5 < h \leqslant 10$ | 51 |
| $10 < h \leqslant 15$ | 23 |
| $15 < h \leqslant 20$ | 3 |
| $20 < h \leqslant 30$ | 6 |

**Tree heights**

What mistake has she made?

**c**   Draw suitable diagrams to compare the heights of the two sets of trees.

**d**   Nick wants to compare the medians and quartiles for the two sets of trees. Draw suitable diagrams to make estimates of the medians and quartiles.

**e**   Use your information to compare the heights of the two sets of trees.

# Practice questions

**1**  **a**  This histogram shows the test scores of 100 female students.

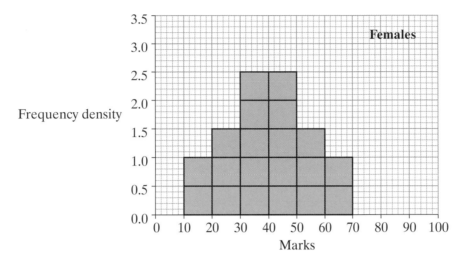

   **i**   What is the median score? *(1 mark)*

   **ii**  What is the inter-quartile range? *(1 mark)*

**b**  This histogram is incomplete.
   It shows some of the test scores for 100 male students.
   The median test score for males is the same as for females.
   The upper quartile for the males is 50.

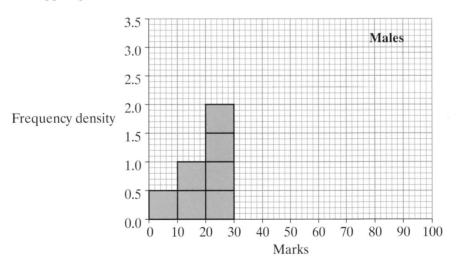

   **i**   What is the lower quartile for the male students? *(1 mark)*

   **ii**  Complete a possible histogram. *(3 marks)*

AQA 2004

## Objectives

Examiners would normally expect students who get these grades to be able to:

### B

know the angle and tangent properties of a circle

### A

understand the angle and tangent properties of a circle

understand the alternate segment theorem.

*Did you know?*

## Crop circles

Crop circles are patterns made in fields of wheat, barley or corn. When crop circles were first spotted, they were normally quite simple patterns of different-sized circles. More recent crop circles are much more detailed and involve complex geometric patterns. There have been many theories about the origins of crop circles ranging from works of art to paranormal activity involving messages from extraterrestrial beings. Whatever the answer, there is no doubt that crop circles involve a lot of mathematics.

## You should already know:

✔ the definition of a circle and the meaning of terms including centre, radius, chord, diameter, circumference, tangent, arc, sector and segment

✔ basic proofs such as the angle sum of a triangle is 180°, the exterior angle of a triangle is equal to the sum of the interior opposite angles

✔ and understand angle properties of parallel lines including corresponding angles and alternate angles on a transversal.

### Key terms

angle subtended
arc
chord
cyclic quadrilateral
supplementary angles
tangent
alternate segment

## Learn...    2.1 Angle properties of circles ⓚ

There are four angle properties of circles you need to know.

- The **angle subtended** by an **arc** (or **chord**) at the centre of a circle is twice the angle subtended at any point on the circumference.
- The angle subtended at the circumference by a semicircle is a right angle.
- Angles subtended by the same arc (or chord) are equal.
- The opposite angles of a **cyclic quadrilateral** add up to 180°.

### The angle subtended by an arc (or chord) at the centre of a circle is twice the angle subtended at any point on the circumference

The angle subtended by the arc $PQ$ at $O$ (the centre) is twice the angle at $R$ (the circumference).

angle $POQ = 2 \times$ angle $PRQ$

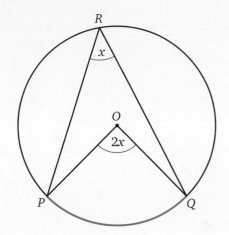

### The angle subtended at the circumference by a semicircle is a right angle

The angle subtended by the arc $PQ$ at $O$ (the centre) is twice the angle at $R$ (the circumference).

The angle at $O$ is 180° so the angle at $R$ (the circumference) is 90°.

Angle $PRQ = 90°$

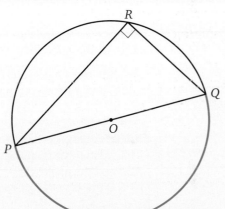

### Angles subtended by the same arc (or chord) are equal

The angle at $D$ and the angle at $C$ and the angle at $E$ are subtended by the same arc $AB$. Therefore, these angles are the same.

angle $ADB$ = angle $ACB$ = angle $AEB$

The angle at $A$ and the angle at $B$ are subtended by the same arc $EC$. Therefore these angles are the same.

angle $EAC$ = angle $EBC$

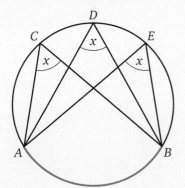

### The opposite angles of a cyclic quadrilateral add up to 180°

A cyclic quadrilateral is any quadrilateral where the four vertices lie on the circumference of a circle.

The opposite angles of a cyclic quadrilateral add up to 180° (i.e. they are **supplementary angles**).

For the cyclic quadrilateral $EFGH$

$e + g = 180°$

$f + h = 180°$

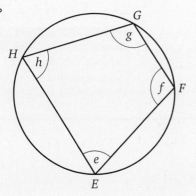

**Example:** *P*, *Q*, *R* and *S* are points on the circumference of a circle.

*PR* is a diameter and angle *SQR* = 58°

**a** Write down the value of *x*.

**b** Calculate the value of *y*.

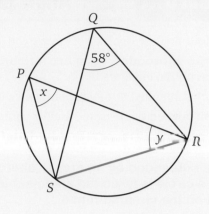

Not drawn accurately

**Study tip**

The words 'Not drawn accurately' mean that you must not use the diagram to measure angles.

**Solution:**

**a** $x = 58°$     Angles subtended by the same chord *RS* are equal.

**b** $\angle PSR = 90°$     Angle subtended at the circumference by a semicircle is a right angle.

$y = 180° - (\angle SPR + \angle PSR)$     Angles of a triangle add up to 180°.

$y = 180° - (58° + 90°)$

$y = 32°$

---

**Example:** The arc *AC* subtends an angle of 110° at the centre of the circle.

Calculate the angle *ADC* and the angle *ABC* giving reasons for your answers.

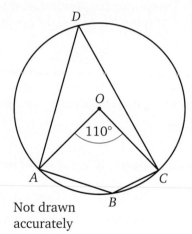

Not drawn accurately

**Study tips**

The order of the questions (i.e. calculate the angle *ADB* and the angle *ABC*) usually suggests that angle *ADB* is the easier angle to find first.

The word 'calculate' in this type of question means that you must work out the angles and **not** measure them.

**Solution:** Angle *ADC* is the angle at the circumference.

So angle *ADC* = 55°     angle at centre = 2 × angle at circumference

Angle *ABC* = 180° − ∠*ADC*     Opposite angles of a cyclic quadrilateral add up to 180°.

      = 180° − 55°

      = 125°

**Hint**

Alternatively, you could use the fact that the angle at centre = 2 × angle at the circumference.

The reflex angle *AOC* = 250° so angle *ABC* = 125°

**Study tip**

Always remember to check that your answers are sensible.

# Practise... 2.1 Angle properties of circles

The shapes in these exercises are not drawn accurately.

**1** Calculate the marked angle on the following diagrams giving a reason for your answer.

The centre of the circle is marked O.

**a**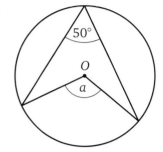

**b**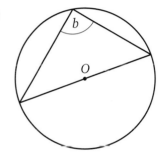

**c**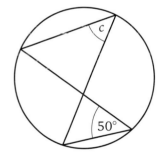

**d**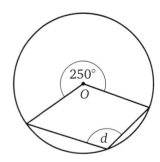

**e**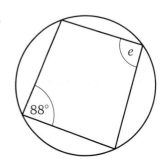

**f**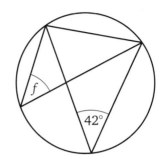

**g**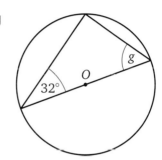

**h**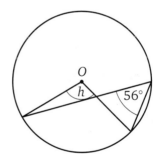

**i**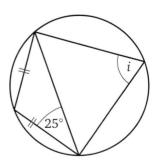

**j**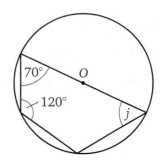

**k**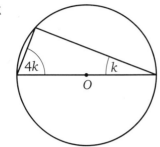

**l**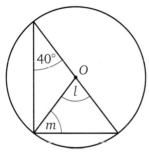

**m**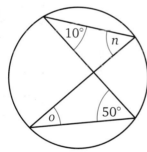

**n**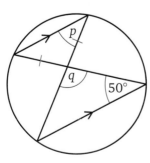

**o**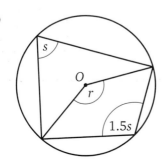

**B**

**2**  Write down whether the following are True or False.

   **a**   Angles subtended by the same arc of a circle at points on the circumference are equal.

   **b**   The angle subtended by a chord at the centre of a circle is twice the angle subtended at the circumference.

   **c**   The opposite pairs of angles of a quadrilateral both add up to 180° (they are supplementary).

   **d**   The angle subtended at the circumference by the diameter of a circle is a right angle.

   **e**   Adjacent angles in a cyclic quadrilateral are both complementary (i.e. they both add up to 90°).

   **f**   The angle subtended by a chord at the centre of a circle is half the angle subtended by the same chord at the circumference.

**3**  Sarah says that a trapezium cannot be a cyclic quadrilateral.

   Is Sarah correct?
   Give a reason for your answer.

**4**  $D$ is the centre of the circle shown.

   Assad thinks angle $ADC$ is 65° because the angle at the centre is twice that subtended at the circumference.

   Show Assad is incorrect by working out angle $ADC$.

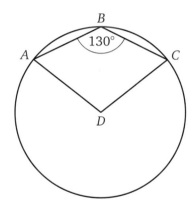

**A**

**5**  The lines $PR$ and $QS$ pass through the centre of the circle at $O$.

   Angle $QRP = 52°$

   Write down the angle $QSP$ and angle $QOR$.
   Give reasons for your answers.

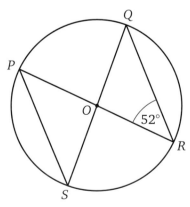

**6**  $LN$ is the diameter of the circle.

   Angle $NLM = x°$ and angle $MNL = 2x°$

   Work out the value of $x$.

   What is the size of angle $MNL$?

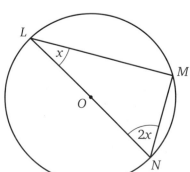

**7**   **a**   Write down the value of *x*.

   **b**   Calculate the value of *y*.

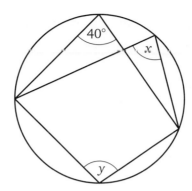

**8**   *PQ = PS*

Angle *QPS* = 100°

Show that angle *SRP* = 40°

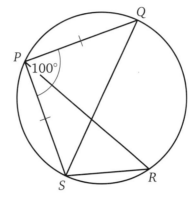

**9**   A quadrilateral *PQRO* is drawn inside a circle centre *O*.

Angle *OPQ* = 65° and angle *POR* = 150°

Calculate the other two angles of the quadrilateral.
Show all your working.

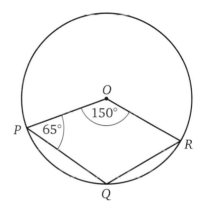

**10**   Prove the following circle properties.

   **a**   The angle subtended by an arc at the centre of a circle is
        twice the angle subtended at any point on the circumference.

   **b**   The angles subtended by the same arc (or chord) are equal.

   **c**   The angle subtended at the circumference by a semicircle
        is a right angle.

   **d**   Opposite angles of a cyclic quadrilateral add up to 180 degrees.

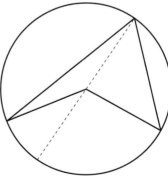

**11**   Work out angles *a* and *b*.

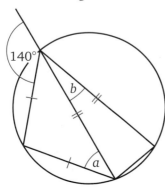

**12**   Work out angle *x*.

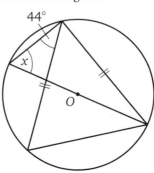

## Learn... 2.2 Tangents and chords

**Tangent**

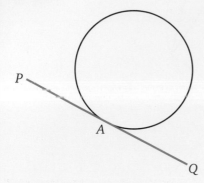

**Chord**

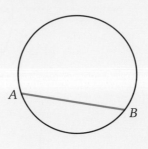

A **tangent** is a straight line that touches a circle at one point only.
*PQ* is a tangent to the circle.
It touches the circle at *A*.

A chord is a straight line joining two points on the circumference of a circle. *AB* is a chord of the circle.
A diameter is a chord that passes through the centre of the circle.

### Tangent properties

You need to know the following tangent properties.

- The tangent at any point on a circle is perpendicular to the radius at that point.
- Tangents from an external point are equal in length.

**The tangent at any point on a circle is perpendicular to the radius at that point.**

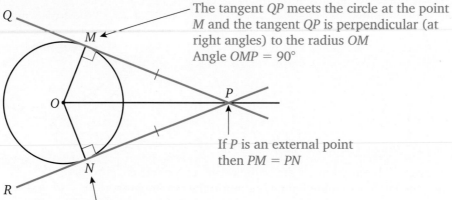

The tangent *QP* meets the circle at the point *M* and the tangent *QP* is perpendicular (at right angles) to the radius *OM*
Angle *OMP* = 90°

If *P* is an external point then *PM* = *PN*

Also, the tangent *RP* meets the circle at the point *N* and the tangent *RP* is at right angles to the radius *ON*
Angle *ONP* = 90°

**Tangents from an external point are equal in length.**

So *PM* = *PN* where *P* is the external point.

### Chord properties

You need to know the following chord properties.

- The perpendicular line from the centre of the circle to a chord bisects the chord.
- The perpendicular bisector of any chord passes through the centre.

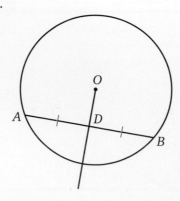

The perpendicular line from the centre to a chord *OD* bisects the chord *AB*.

The perpendicular bisector of the chord *AB* will pass through the centre.

## Alternate segment theorem

The **alternate segment** theorem says that the angle between the tangent and the chord is the same as the angle in the alternate segment.

The tangent *PQ* touches the circle at *A*. The angle between the tangent and the chord *AC* is the same as the angle subtended by the chord *AC*.

angle *PAC* = angle *CBA*

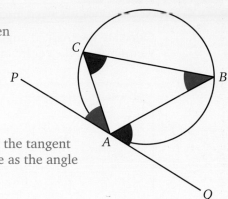

Similarly, the angle between the tangent and the chord *AB* is the same as the angle subtended by the chord *AB*.

angle *QAB* = angle *ACB*

*Example:*   A chord of length 16 cm is 6 cm from the centre of a circle.

Calculate the radius of the circle.

*Solution:*   Drawing a diagram will help to answer the question.

The chord *AB* is 6 cm from the centre of a circle.

The line from the centre to the chord *OP* is perpendicular to the chord.

The perpendicular from the centre to a chord bisects the chord.

So *AP* = *PB* = 8 cm

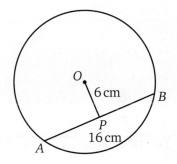

The radius of the circle *OA* can be found using Pythagoras' theorem.

Not drawn accurately

$OA^2 = OP^2 + AP^2$

$OA^2 = 6^2 + 8^2$

$OA^2 = 36 + 64$

$OA = \sqrt{100}$

$OA = 10$ cm

The radius of the circle is 10 cm.

*Example:*   *PQ* is a tangent to the circle centre *O*.

∠*CAP* = 60°

Calculate the angle *ABC*, angle *AOC* and the angle *OAC*.

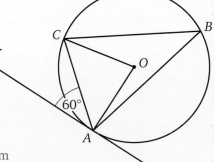

*Solution:*   angle *ABC* = 60°   using the alternate segment theorem

angle *AOC* = 120°   angle at centre = 2 × angle at circumference

angle *OAC* = 90° − angle *CAP*   Tangent is perpendicular to the radius.

angle *OAC* = 90° − 60°

angle *OAC* = 30°

Note that there are many other ways to find the value of angle *OAC*. For example, by using the fact that angle *OAC* is a base angle of the isosceles triangle *OAC*.

**Study tip**

Always remember to check that your answers are sensible.

## Practise... 2.2 Tangents and chords  (k)      D C B A A*

**B**

**1** Calculate the marked angle on the following diagrams, giving a reason for your answer. The centre of the circle is marked O. The diagrams are not drawn accurately.

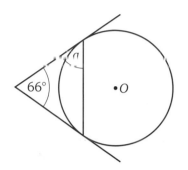

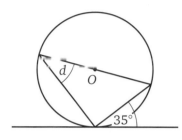

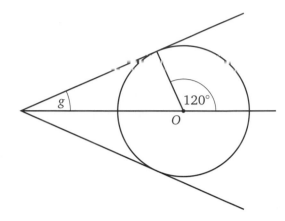

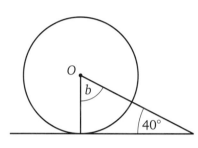

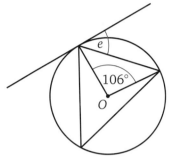

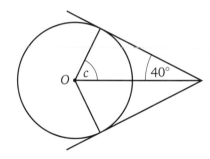

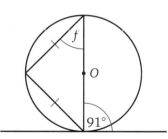

**2** Write down whether the following are True or False.

**a** The perpendicular bisector of a chord in a circle passes through the centre of the circle.

**b** The angle between the tangent and the chord is the same as the angle in the alternate segment.

**c** A tangent is a straight line that touches a circle at one or more points on the circumference.

**d** The tangent at any point on a circle is perpendicular to the radius at that point.

**e** Tangents from an external point to the circumference of a circle are equal in length.

**3** Tangents PS and RS meet the circle at P and S respectively.
SOQ is a straight line passing through the centre of the circle O.
Angle PSO = 22°

Calculate:

**a** angle RSO

**b** angle POR

**c** angle PQR.

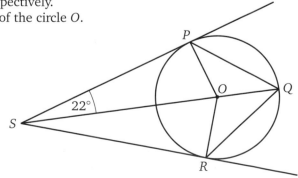

**4**   In the diagram below points $Q$ and $R$ lie on a circle centre $O$.
PQ is a tangent to the circle at $Q$. Angle $QPR = 40°$ and angle $QOR = 80°$

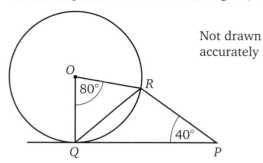

Not drawn
accurately

Prove that triangle $QPR$ is isosceles.

**Hint**

You may find it easier to
draw a diagram.

**5**   A chord of length 24 cm is located 5 cm from the centre of a circle.

Calculate the radius of the circle.

**6**   A chord $PQ$ is 12 cm from the centre of a circle of radius 15 cm.

What is the length of the chord?

**7**   XY is a tangent to the circle, touching at the point $A$.

$AB = BC$ and $CD = DA$

Angle $XAB = 48°$

Calculate:

**a**   angle $BCA$

**b**   angle $ABC$

**c**   angle $DAC$.

Give reasons for your answers.

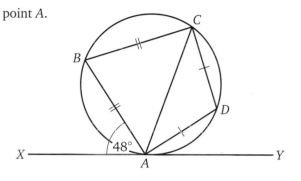

**8**   PQ and QC are tangents.

The tangent $PQ$ meets the circle at $B$.

The centre of the circle is $O$

Angle $PBA = 82°$ and angle $PQC = 40°$

Calculate the values of $x$ and $y$.

Remember to show your working.

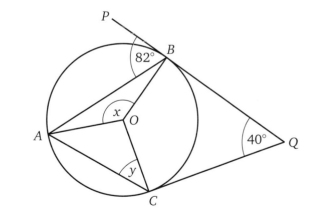

**9**   Tangents $PR$ and $PT$ meet the circle at
$Q$ and $S$ respectively.

$WQ = WS$

Show that angle $RQW$ = angle $TSW$

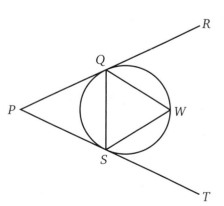

**10**   Prove that the angle between the tangent and the chord is the same as the angle
in the alternate segment.

**11** The perpendicular bisector of a chord passes through the centre of a circle.

Write down how you might use this fact to find the centre of any circle.

 **12** Work out the angle *x*, giving reasons for your answer.

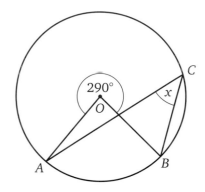

# 2 **Assess** ⓚ

**B** **1** For each question part, calculate the marked angles.
The centre of the circle is labelled *O*.

**a**
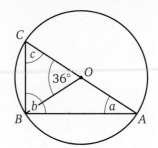

**e**
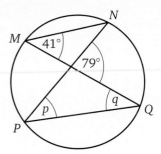

**b**
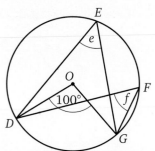

**f**
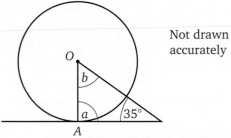

Not drawn accurately

**c**
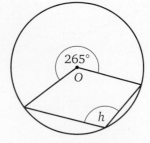

**g**
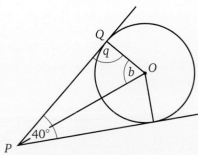

**d**
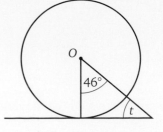

**h**

**2**   *AD* is a diameter of the circle centre *O*.
Angle *ADC* = 60° and angle *ACB* = 35°

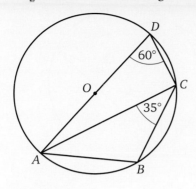

Not drawn
accurately

Calculate:

**a**   angle *DCA*

**b**   angle *DAC*

**c**   angle *ABC*

**d**   angle *DAB*.

**3**   A chord *AB* is drawn on a circle centre *O*.
The length of the chord is 16 cm.
The radius of the circle is 10 cm.

Calculate the area of the triangle *AOB*.
State the units of your answer.

**4**   A quadrilateral is drawn inside a circle centre *O*.

Angle *OPQ* = 55° and angle *POR* = 150°.

Calculate the other angles of the quadrilateral.
Remember to show all your working.

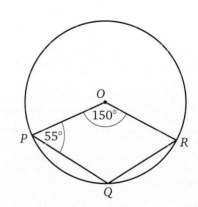

Not drawn
accurately

**5**   For each question part, calculate the marked angles.

**a**

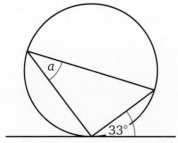

**c**

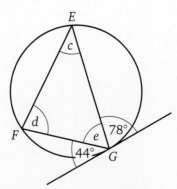

**b**

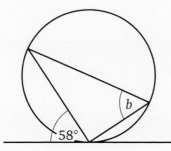

**d**

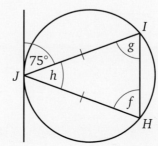

**A**

**A**

**6** A, B and C are three points on a circle.

PQ is a tangent to the circle, which touches the circle at A.

The angle AOB = 102°

Calculate the angle QAB.

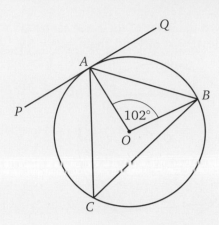

**7** PA is a tangent to the circle centre O.
PB is a straight line passing through O.
Angle PAC = 35°

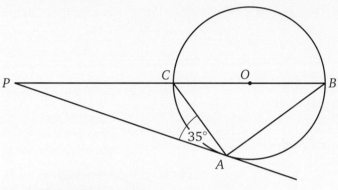

Not drawn accurately

Calculate the angle CBA and the angle CPA.
Give reasons for your answers.

**A\***

**8** XY is the tangent to the circle touching at the point A.

AB = BC and CD = DA    Angle XAB = x

Calculate, leaving your answer in terms of x:

**a**    angle BCA

**b**    angle ABC

**c**    The angle ADC = 102°

Find the value of x.

Give a reason for your answer.

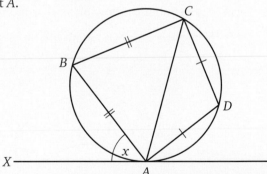

# Practice questions &#9426;

**1**    **a**    $P$, $Q$ and $R$ are points on the circumference of a circle, centre $O$.
$PR$ is a diameter of the circle.

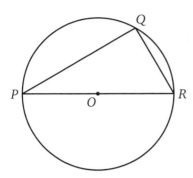

Not drawn
accurately

Write down the size of angle $PQR$.      *(1 mark)*

   **b**    $T$ is also a point on the circumference of the circle in part **a**.
Angle $QTR = 27°$

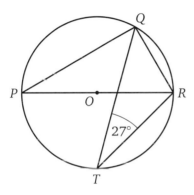

Not drawn
accurately

     **i**    Write down the size of angle $RPQ$.      *(1 mark)*

     **ii**    Work out the size of angle $PRQ$.      *(1 mark)*

   **c**    $S$ is another point on the circumference of the circle in part **a**.
$QS$ is a diameter of the circle.
Angle $PRS = 38°$

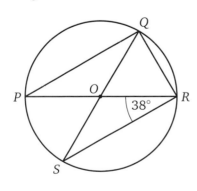

Not drawn
accurately

Work out the size of angle $SQR$.      *(1 mark)*

AQA 2008

# 3 Fractions and decimals

## Objectives

Examiners would normally expect students who get these grades to be able to:

### D
find one quantity as a fraction of another

solve problems involving fractions

### C
add and subtract mixed numbers

multiply and divide fractions

round numbers to significant figures

round numbers to decimal places

find the reciprocal of a number

### B
find upper and lower bounds

### A/A*
use upper and lower bounds in calculations.

## Key terms

numerator
denominator
equivalent fraction
mixed number
rounding
significant figures
lower bound
upper bound
decimal places
reciprocals

## Did you know?

### Fractions and decimals in music

Why do musical instruments sound different from each other? A lot of it has to do with fractions. Pluck a guitar string and you hear a certain note, but mixed in with the main note there are quieter, higher notes. You can bring out one of these notes, called 'harmonics', by lightly touching the string halfway along when you pluck it. In fact a vibrating string naturally produces harmonics that correspond to $\frac{1}{2}, \frac{1}{3}, \frac{1}{4}, \frac{1}{5}$ ... of its length all at the same time. The tubes of air in wind instruments, like trumpets and saxophones, do the same. The construction of an instrument, and the way it's played, affect how loud the different harmonics are, compared with one another. That's why a violin sounds different from a clarinet.

Decimals come into music too. The pitch of a note (how high or low it is) depends on the number of times per second it makes the air (and therefore your eardrums) vibrate. The faster the vibrations, the higher the note. Play a note on a keyboard, and then the nearest note above it: the higher note causes vibrations approximately 1.05946... times faster than the lower note.

## You should already know:

✔ what equivalent fractions are

✔ how to add and subtract simple fractions

✔ how to calculate fractions of quantities

✔ how to express simple decimals and percentages as fractions

✔ how to order decimals.

**Reminder:** You will be allowed to use a calculator in this unit. Make sure you know how to use the fraction (  or  ) button on your calculator.

Calculators will simplify your fractions as well. Just put in the fraction using the fraction button then press = to get the simplest form.

## Learn...   3.1  One quantity as a fraction of another

To work out one quantity as a fraction of another, write the first quantity as the **numerator** and the second as the **denominator** then simplify the fraction.

To work out 35 as a fraction of 50, write 35 out of 50 as a fraction, $\frac{35}{50}$, then simplify to $\frac{7}{10}$     $\frac{35}{100}$ and $\frac{7}{10}$ are **equivalent fractions**.

So 35 is seven-tenths of 50.

*Example:*     What is 25 cm as a fraction of 2 m?

*Solution:*     2 m is 200 cm.

So the fraction is $\frac{25}{200}$,

which simplifies to $\frac{1}{8}$.

## Practise...   3.1 One quantity as a fraction of another   (k)     D  C  B  A  A*

**D**

**1**     What is:

    **a**   15p as a fraction of 30p       **d**   20 minutes as a fraction of two hours

    **b**   15p as a fraction of £3         **e**   100 g as a fraction of 1.3 kg

    **c**   20 minutes as a fraction of an hour    **f**   200 g as a fraction of 1.3 kg?

**2**     Kevin says '50p as a fraction of £500 is $\frac{1}{10}$.' Is Kevin right? Explain your answer.

**3**     Here is a list of the heights of 12 students, measured to the nearest centimetre and arranged in order.

    155 cm    159 cm    161 cm    162 cm    162 cm    165 cm
    167 cm    169 cm    172 cm    174 cm    175 cm    177 cm

    **a**   What fraction of students have heights:

        **i**   less than 166 cm         **iii**  between 161.5 cm and 173 cm?

        **ii**  more than 166 cm

    **b**   What fraction of students have heights below 161.5 cm?

**4**     **a**   The students in a class of 28 take a test.
        What fraction of them passed the test if the number passing was as follows:

        **i**   14     **ii**   12     **iii**   13     **iv**   18     **v**   20?

    **b**   If the fraction passing the test was $\frac{3}{4}$, how many students passed?

    **c**   Explain why you should never get an improper (top-heavy) fraction in a question like this.

**5**     In a dance class there are 25 women and 15 men.

    **a**   What is the fraction of men in the class?

    **b**   What is the fraction of women in the class?

**D**

**6** Here is a list of test marks of a class of 30 students, arranged in order.

a What fraction of the students got under 40 marks?

b What fraction of the students got a mark between 60 and 70?

c The pass mark was 50 marks. What fraction of the students passed the test?

d What should the pass mark be for two-thirds of the students to pass the test?

e What mark separates the top tenth of the class from the rest?

```
22   25
30   33   37
42   43   46   46
53   54   55   55   56
61   61   63   64   64   67   68   68   69
73   75   78   79
81   87
95
```

**7** What is:

a $x$ as a fraction of $10x$

b $5b$ as a fraction of $25b$

c $x$ as a fraction of $x^2$?

**8**

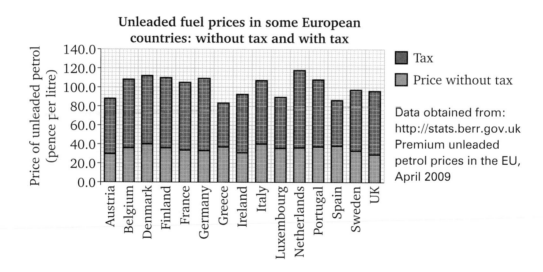

**Unleaded fuel prices in some European countries: without tax and with tax**

Legend:
- Tax
- Price without tax

Data obtained from: http://stats.berr.gov.uk Premium unleaded petrol prices in the EU, April 2009

The graph shows how the total price paid for unleaded petrol is made up.

a Estimate the fraction of the total price paid in tax in the UK.

b Which country pays the highest fraction in tax?

c Which country pays the lowest?

d Would it affect your answers if the prices were in euros instead of in pence? Explain your answer.

**9** Here are 32 students' test marks. Three-quarters of the students passed the test. What could the pass mark have been?

```
14
23   29
33   34   36
46   47
54   53   56   56   56   59   59
60   60   61   64   65   67   68   68
70   71   71   73   75   76   77
80   82
```

## Learn... 3.2 Calculating with fractions

In this unit you will be using a calculator to work with fractions.

With a calculator, you can use the fraction button

 or $\boxed{a\frac{b}{c}}$

to do all fraction calculations.

For example, to do the calculation $\frac{3}{4} + \frac{2}{5}$, do this:

 3 ▶ 4 ▶ ⊞  2 ▶ 5 ⊟

or   3 $\boxed{a\frac{b}{c}}$ 4 ⊞ 2 $\boxed{a\frac{b}{c}}$ 5 ⊟

which gives the answer $\frac{23}{20}$ or $1\frac{3}{20}$

> **Study tip**
>
> Make sure you know how to put **mixed numbers** into your calculator using the fraction button and how to convert between mixed numbers and top-heavy fractions.

**Example:**    Dave makes fleece hats to sell on his market stall. Each hat needs $\frac{3}{8}$ of a yard of fabric. How many hats can he make from $2\frac{1}{2}$ yards of fabric?

**Solution:**    To find how many hats can be made, divide $2\frac{1}{2}$ by $\frac{3}{8}$

 5 ▶ 2 ▶ ÷  3 ▶ 8 ⊟ $\frac{20}{3}$ ⊟ $6\frac{2}{3}$

So Dave can make 6 hats with enough fabric for $\frac{2}{3}$ of a hat left over.

## Practise... 3.2 Calculating with fractions    D C B A A*

**1**    Zeb spends $\frac{2}{5}$ of his pocket money on clothes, $\frac{1}{3}$ on CDs and $\frac{1}{4}$ on going to the cinema. What fraction of his pocket money has he spent altogether?

**2**    A group of students and teachers are on a trip.

$\frac{1}{4}$ of the group are Year 9. Of the remainder, $\frac{2}{5}$ are Year 10.
There are also 19 students from Year 11 and 8 teachers.
How many people are in the group altogether?

**3**    There are red, blue and green discs in a bag.

$\frac{1}{3}$ of the discs are red.

$\frac{2}{5}$ of the discs are blue.

There are 12 green discs.

How many red discs are there?

**4**    Here is a fraction pattern.

$$\frac{1}{2} \qquad\qquad\qquad = \frac{1}{2}$$
$$\frac{1}{2} + \frac{1}{4} \qquad\qquad = \frac{3}{4}$$
$$\frac{1}{2} + \frac{1}{4} + \frac{1}{8} \qquad = \frac{7}{8}$$
$$\frac{1}{2} + \frac{1}{4} + \frac{1}{8} + \frac{1}{16} \qquad =$$
$$\frac{1}{2} + \frac{1}{4} + \frac{1}{8} + \frac{1}{16} + \frac{1}{32} =$$

**a**    Find the sums for the last two rows of the pattern.

**b**    What is the sum of the tenth row of the pattern?

**c**    What do you think will happen to the sum of the rows as you keep adding more and more terms?

D

**5** The same T-shirt is available in two different shops.

Which shop gives the better price? Show how you worked out the answer.

**Tees 'R' Us**

Normally £7.50
Now With
One Third Off!!!

**Getting Shirty**

USUAL
PRICE £9 BUT
$\frac{£}{5}$ OFF TODAY!!!

Super T

**6** In a sale, everything is offered with 'one quarter off'. Work out the sale prices of these items, rounding to the nearest penny if necessary.

**a** A sweater costing £24

**b** A dress costing £69.99

**c** A pair of trousers costing £24.99

**d** A pen costing 89p

**7** In America, dress material is sold in yards and fractions of yards. A jacket needs $2\frac{1}{2}$ yards of material and a skirt needs $1\frac{3}{4}$ yards.

**a** How much material is needed altogether?

**b** The material costs $15 a yard. How much will the material for the jacket and skirt cost?

**8** A video game runs at a frame rate of 35 frames a second. The movement of a car takes 15 frames ($\frac{15}{35}$ of a second). Going round a corner and stopping takes a further 30 frames. How much time is taken by these two scenes?

**9** A recipe for biscuits needs two-thirds of a cup of sugar.
A pudding needs $1\frac{3}{8}$ cups of sugar.

Lucy has two cups of sugar.

Does she have enough to make the biscuits and the pudding?

**10** Thirty years ago in the UK, lengths used to be measured in yards and fractions of a yard. Here is a problem from that time.

A room measures $4\frac{1}{4}$ yards by $3\frac{3}{8}$ yards. The door is $\frac{7}{8}$ of a yard wide.
What length of skirting board is needed for this room?

**11** *A* and *B* are two whole numbers.

**a** One-fifth of *A* is equal to one-quarter of *B*.

**i** Which number is bigger, *A* or *B*? Explain how you know.

**ii** Find possible values for *A* and *B*. How many pairs are there?

**iii** For each pair, work out the fraction $\frac{A}{B}$. What do you notice?

**b** Three-quarters of *A* is equal to two-thirds of *B*. Work out the fraction $\frac{A}{B}$

**12**   Here are two strips of card.

The top one is divided into quarters. The bottom one is divided into sixths.

Work out the total width of the diagram.

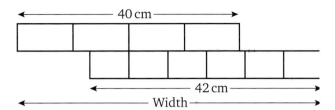

---

## Learn... 3.3 Rounding

### Rounding

Numbers can be **rounded** to make them easy to work with and to understand. For example, if parents want to know how many students there are in a school, they probably want to know the approximate number, 900 for example, rather than the exact answer 936.

Rounded to the nearest 100, 936 is 900. It is between 900 and 1000 and nearer to 900.

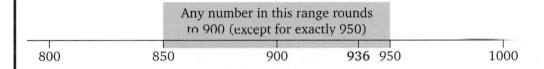

Rounded to the nearest 10, 936 is 940. It is between 930 and 940 and nearer to 940.

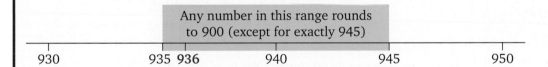

The diagrams also show that 936 to the nearest 50 is 950 and to the nearest 5 is 935. You need to be able to round numbers to different degrees of accuracy like this.

What is 950 to the nearest 100? It is exactly halfway between 900 and 1000 so it is not nearer to either. The usual rule is that numbers halfway between round up. So 950 is 1000 to the nearest 100.

You also need to be able to round decimal numbers to the nearest **integer** (whole number), to one **decimal place** (d.p.), two decimal places and so on.

---

*Example:*   What is 7.846 to one decimal place?

*Solution:*   7.846 is between 7.8 and 7.9 and nearer to 7.8. So 7.846 to one decimal place is 7.8

Any number in this range rounds
to 7.8 (except for exactly 7.85)

| 7.7 | 7.75 | 7.8 | 7.846 7.85 | 7.9 |

To two decimal places, 7.846 is 7.85; it is between 7.84 and 7.85 and nearer to 7.85

## Significant figures

936 students in the school rounded to one **significant figure** (s.f) is 900.

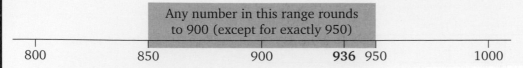

0.0936 rounds to 0.09

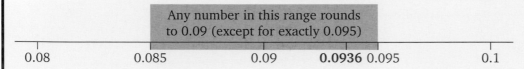

936 is 900 (one significant figure).

0.0936 is 0.09 (one significant figure).

The figure 9 in each number gives the approximate size. Both numbers also need zeros to show the place value of the 9. These zeros are not significant figures.

Note the difference between significant figures and decimal places: 936 is 940 (two significant figures) 0.0936 is 0.094 (two significant figures, three decimal places).

(Zeros **can** be significant; for example, the number 1020 has three significant figures, 1, 0 and 2. The zero in the units position is not significant. It is just there for place value.)

---

*Example:*  Round these numbers to:

    **a** the nearest integer     **b** one decimal place     **c** one significant figure.

        **i** 44.79      **iii** 204.45

        **ii** 0.5678    **iv** 0.0235

> **Hint**
>
> To round to the nearest integer, think which integers lie on either side of the number.

*Solution:*  **a** 44.79 is between 44 and 45.

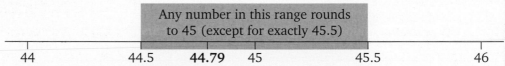

44.79 is more than 44.5 so is nearer to 45 than to 44. To the nearest integer, 44.79 is 45. The other numbers are rounded in a similar way.

    **a** **i**     45       **iii**   204

        **ii**    1        **iv**   0

To round to one decimal place, identify the numbers with one decimal place on either side: 44.79 is between 44.7 and 44.8

44.79 is greater than 44.75 so it is nearer to 44.8 than to 44.7. It rounds to 44.8

    **b** **i**     44.8    **iii**   204.5

        **ii**    0.6     **iv**   0.0

To round to one significant figure, look at the first two non-zero digits, which are 44. This is nearer to 40 than to 50, so to one significant figure 44.79 is 40.

    **c** **i**     40       **iii**   200

        **ii**    0.6     **iv**   0.02

## Expressing fractions as decimals

Any fraction can be expressed as a decimal.
Some simple examples are $\frac{1}{2} = 0.5$, $\frac{3}{4} = 0.75$, $\frac{3}{10} = 0.3$

Make sure that you are familiar with simple examples like these.

To express a fraction as a decimal, use your calculator to divide the numerator by the denominator.

$\frac{3}{4} = 3 \div 4 = 0.75$ (Make sure that your calculator is set to give a decimal answer, not a fraction answer.)

0.75 is a **terminating decimal**. $3 \div 4$ works out exactly; the calculation comes to an end after two decimal places. Some fractions become **recurring decimals**; the calculation does not come to an end but one digit, or a group of digits, repeats forever.

$\frac{5}{11} = 5 \div 11 = 0.454545...$ 　　　This can also be written as $0.\dot{4}\dot{5}$

$\frac{2}{3} = 2 \div 3 = 0.666...$ 　　　　　This can also be written as $0.\dot{6}$

The calculator display shows that $\frac{2}{3}$ is 0.6666666667. The calculator can show only a limited number of digits and it rounds the final one in the display.

When decimals are used in calculations, you have to round them appropriately.

$\frac{2}{3}$ rounded to:

one decimal place is　　0.7

two decimal places is　　0.67

three decimal places is　0.667

four decimal places is　0.6667

and so on.

### Expressing fractions as percentages

To express a fraction as a percentage, change the fraction to a decimal and then multiply the decimal by 100%.

$\frac{3}{4} = 0.75$

$0.75 \times 100\% = 75\%$

> **Study tip**
>
> In calculations, use all the figures already in your calculator whenever possible. Do not re-enter the number unless you really have to.

*Example:*　　**a**　What is $\frac{5}{12}$ as a decimal? Write your answer correct to three significant figures.

　　　　　　**b**　Write $\frac{5}{12}$ as a percentage.

*Solution:*　　**a**　$\frac{5}{12} = 5 \div 12 = 0.41666... = 0.417$ to three significant figures.

　　　　　　**b**　$\frac{5}{12} = 5 \div 12 = 0.41666...$

　　　　　　　　$= 0.41666... \times 100\%$

　　　　　　　　$= 42\%$, correct to the nearest whole percent.

> **Study tip**
>
> Make sure you always divide the numerator by the denominator when changing a fraction to a decimal.

### Arranging fractions in order

When fractions are expressed as decimals or percentages, you can put them in order.

It is not easy to see which fraction, $\frac{3}{4}$ or $\frac{7}{9}$, is bigger when they are in fraction form, but in decimals $\frac{3}{4} = 0.75$ and $\frac{7}{9} = 0.77777...$ so you can see that $\frac{7}{9}$ is a bit bigger than $\frac{3}{4}$

*Example:*　　Arrange these in order of size, starting with the smallest.

　　　　　　$\frac{2}{3},$ 　　$\frac{3}{5},$ 　　62%, 　　$\frac{11}{18},$ 　　0.65, 　　$\frac{7}{11}$

*Solution:*　　$\frac{2}{3} = 0.666...,$ $\frac{3}{5} = 0.6,$ 62% $= 0.62,$ $\frac{11}{18} = 0.6111...,$ 0.65 $= 0.65,$ $\frac{7}{11} = 0.636363...$

　　　　　　So the order of size is $\frac{3}{5}, \frac{11}{18}, 62\%, \frac{7}{11}, 0.65, \frac{2}{3}$

## Reciprocals

When two numbers multiply together to make 1, the numbers are the **reciprocals** of each another.
So 2 and $\frac{1}{2}$ are the reciprocals of each other because $2 \times \frac{1}{2} = 1$

The reciprocal of any fraction $\frac{a}{b}$ is $\frac{b}{a}$ because $\frac{a}{b} \times \frac{b}{a} = 1$

The reciprocal of any number $x$ (integer, decimal or fraction) is $\frac{1}{x}$ because $x \times \frac{1}{x} = 1$

Your calculator can work out reciprocals both as fractions and as decimals; look for the button labelled
or $\boxed{x^{-1}}$ and find out how to use it.

*Example:*     Find the reciprocals of $\frac{1}{3}$, 0.2, $\frac{9}{20}$, 0.89

*Solution:*     Reciprocal of $\frac{1}{3} = \frac{3}{1} = 3$

To find the reciprocal of 0.2, enter 0.2 into your calculator, press the $\boxed{x^{-1}}$ key then $\boxed{=}$
The answer is 5

Reciprocal of $\frac{9}{20} = \frac{20}{9} = 2\frac{2}{9}$

Reciprocal of $0.89 = \frac{1}{0.89} = 1.12$ to three significant figures. (Enter 0.89 into your

calculator, press the $\boxed{x^{-1}}$ key, then $\boxed{=}$)

---

## Practise...    3.3 Rounding Ⓚ      

**D**

**1**    Round these numbers:

    **a**   to one significant figure    **b**   to two significant figures    **c**   to three significant figures.

      **i**   12.89     **ii**   54.5     **iii**   109.87     **iv**   4.756     **v**   0.836

**2**    The number of wild tigers in India is 1500 to
the nearest 500.
What is the biggest number of wild tigers
there could be in India?
What is the least number?

**3**    Express these fractions as percentages.

    **a**   $\frac{4}{5}$      **b**   $\frac{9}{10}$      **c**   $\frac{11}{20}$      **d**   $\frac{23}{50}$      **e**   $\frac{67}{100}$

**4**    Arrange these in order of size, starting with the smallest.

    $\frac{5}{12}$,    0.4,    $\frac{4}{9}$,    45%,    $\frac{3}{7}$,    $\frac{7}{16}$

**5**    There are three girls and seven boys in the chess club. One more boy and one more girl join the club.

    Is the fraction of girls in the club now more, less or the same?
Show how you found your answer.

**C**

**6**    **a**   Which of these fractions are equivalent to recurring decimals?

       **i**   $\frac{3}{5}$      **ii**   $\frac{9}{11}$      **iii**   $\frac{5}{6}$      **iv**   $\frac{7}{20}$      **v**   $\frac{4}{15}$

    **b**   Can you say which fractions become recurring decimals without working them out?
Explain what you have found out, using examples.

**7** **a** Match up each number with its reciprocal. The first has been done for you.

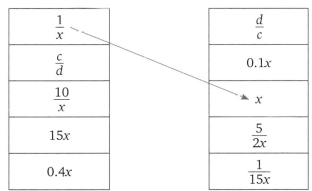

| $\frac{5}{9}$ |
|---|
| 1 |
| 0.4 |
| 15 |
| 7 |

| 1 |
|---|
| $\frac{1}{7}$ |
| 2.5 |
| $1\frac{4}{5}$ |
| 0.066… |

**b** What happens when you multiply a number by its reciprocal?

**8** **a** Which number is the reciprocal of itself?

**b** Use your calculator to try to find the reciprocal of zero. What happens?

**9** **a** Multiply 150 by $\frac{1}{4}$. What do you have to multiply the answer by to get back to 150?

**b** Choose another number. Multiply it by 2.5. What do you have to multiply the answer by to get back to the original number?

**c** What do your answers to parts **a** and **b** tell you about reciprocals?

**⚠ 10** Express the decimal 0.1296 as a fraction in its lowest terms.

**⚠ 11** Match up each number with its reciprocal. The first has been done for you.

| $\frac{1}{x}$ |
|---|
| $\frac{c}{d}$ |
| $\frac{10}{x}$ |
| $15x$ |
| $0.4x$ |

| $\frac{d}{c}$ |
|---|
| $0.1x$ |
| $x$ |
| $\frac{5}{2x}$ |
| $\frac{1}{15x}$ |

**⚙ 12** Jake got 12 marks out of 25 in his first maths test and 14 out of 30 in his second.

In which test did he do better?
Show how you found your answer.

**⚙ 13** Pigs have an average weight of 150 pounds and a stomach weighing 6 pounds.
Sheep have a different digestive system. They have an average weight of 120 pounds and a stomach system weighing 30 pounds.

**a** What percentage of a pig's total weight is the weight of its stomach?

**b** What percentage of a sheep's total weight is the weight of its stomach system?

C

# Learn... 3.4 Upper and lower bounds

Continuous measurements can never be completely accurate and it is helpful to know how accurate they are.

Suppose that the weight of a person is measured as 62 kg to the nearest kilogram on bathroom scales.

This means that the weight is nearer to 62 kg than it is to either 61 kg or 63 kg. It can be half a kilogram either side of 62 kg.

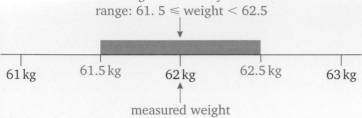

The real weight can be anywhere in the
range: $61.5 \leqslant$ weight $< 62.5$

61 kg    61.5 kg    62 kg    62.5 kg    63 kg

measured weight

If $W$ kg is the weight, $61.5 \leqslant W < 62.5$

61.5 kg is the **lower bound** of the weight and 62.5 kg is the **upper bound**.

A weight less than 61.5 kg would be rounded to 61 kg.

A weight greater than 62.5 kg would be rounded to 63 kg.

---

**Example:**   The weight of a package, $P$ kg, is 4 kg to the nearest kilogram.

  **a**   What are the upper and lower bounds of the weight?

  **b**   Copy and complete this statement:   ___ $\leqslant P <$ ___

**Solution:**   **a**   4 kg to the nearest kilogram means it can be half a kilogram either way.
      So the upper bound is 4.5 kg and the lower bound is 3.5 kg.

    **b**   $3.5 \leqslant P < 4.5$

---

# Practise... 3.4 Upper and lower bounds

**C**

**1**   These numbers have been rounded to the nearest integer.
Write down their upper and lower bounds.

  **a**   15    **b**   157    **c**   100    **d**   4    **e**   0

**2**   Write down the upper and lower bound of these volumes measured to the nearest cubic centimetre ($cm^3$).

  **a**   100 $cm^3$    **b**   15 $cm^3$    **c**   245 $cm^3$    **d**   1000 $cm^3$    **e**   500 $cm^3$

**3**   The distance between two towns is 255 km correct to the nearest 5 km.

  What is the upper bound of the distance?

**4**   Anne's weight is 66 kg correct to the nearest half kilogram.

  What is the least Anne could possibly weigh?

**5**   These lengths are correct to the nearest half centimetre.

  What are the upper and lower bounds of each length?

  **i**   10.5 cm    **ii**   7.0 cm    **iii**   23.5 cm    **iv**   15.0 cm

**6**   A breakfast cereal packet says that the size of a serving of cereal is 37.5 g.

  Assuming that this is measured correct to the nearest half gram, what are the upper and lower bounds of the weight of a serving of this cereal?

**C**

**7** An adult's daily recommended intake of salt is 6 g.

Is an adult who takes 6.5 g of salt within the recommendation?

What assumption do you have to make to answer this question?

## Learn... 3.5 Calculating with bounds

It is important to consider possible inaccuracies in measurements when combining measurements. For example, a packet could contain 20 chocolate bars, each weighing 35 g to the nearest gram.

If all the bars weighed the least they possibly could, the lower bound of the total weight in the pack of 20 would be $20 \times 34.5$ g $= 690$ g

If all the bars weighed the most they possibly could, the upper bound of the total weight in the pack of 20 would be $20 \times 35.5$ g $= 710$ g which is quite a difference!

**Example:** (k) Cartons contain 75 ml of fruit juice correct to the nearest half ml.

What are the maximum and minimum amounts of juice in a pack of 12 cartons of juice?

**Solution:** The least possible volume of juice in a carton is 74.75 ml and the maximum is 75.25 ml.

The minimum volume of juice in the pack is $12 \times 74.75$ ml $= 897$ ml

The maximum volume of juice in the pack is $12 \times 75.25$ ml $= 903$ ml

**Example:** A small bolt for a computer must be 5 mm long with a tolerance of 10%. What is the maximum possible length of the bolt?

**Solution:** A tolerance of 10% means that the bolt can be up to 10% less than 5 mm and up to 10% more than 5 mm.

So the maximum possible length is 5 mm + 10% of 5 mm = 5 mm + 0.5 mm = 5.5 mm

In calculating the maximum or minimum value of a quantity you have to think carefully about which bound to use: the upper bound or the lower bound.

If you need the **maximum** value:

maximum of $(a + b)$ = maximum of $a$ + maximum of $b$

maximum of $(a - b)$ = maximum of $a$ - minimum of $b$

maximum of $a \times b$ = maximum of $a$ × maximum of $b$

maximum of $\dfrac{a}{b} = \dfrac{\text{maximum of } a}{\text{minimum of } b}$

If you need the **minimum** value:

minimum of $(a + b)$ = minimum of $a$ + minimum of $b$

minimum of $(a - b)$ = minimum of $a$ - maximum of $b$

minimum of $a \times b$ = minimum of $a$ × minimum of $b$

minimum of $\dfrac{a}{b} = \dfrac{\text{minimum of } a}{\text{maximum of } b}$

**Example:** Find the minimum number (the number you can be sure of getting) of short pieces of string of length 33 cm that can be cut from a long piece of length 453 cm. Lengths are rounded to the nearest centimetre.

**Solution:** You need to use the minimum possible length of the long string and the maximum possible length of the short pieces (the 'worst case scenario') in the calculation.

$452.5 \div 33.5 = 12.7$, so the minimum number of short pieces that can be cut is 12.

> **Study tip**
>
> Normally 12.7 rounded to the nearest integer would be 13, but here you have to ignore any amount less than 1 to work out the number of pieces with the required length. (You cannot make 12.7 pieces into 13 whole pieces because the 13th piece would be too short.)

**B**

**A**

**A\***

## Practise... 3.5 **Calculating with bounds**

**1** A rectangle has length 10.5 cm and width 7.0 cm, both correct to the nearest half centimetre.
What is the maximum length of the perimeter of the rectangle?

**2** Alfie says 'If a length is 93 cm to the nearest cm, the maximum possible length is 93.49 cm.'

Is Alfie correct? Explain your answer.

**3** An athlete runs 100 m (measured to the nearest 5 cm) in a time of 13.1 seconds (measured to the nearest tenth of a second).

What is the maximum value of the athlete's average speed for this run?

**4** Keith drives a distance of 120 miles, correct to the nearest 10 miles, at an average speed of 45 miles per hour, correct to the nearest 5 miles per hour.

What is the maximum length of time the journey will take?

**5** A packet of breakfast cereal contains 450 grams of cereal, correct to the nearest 5 grams. What is:

**a** the maximum    **b** the minimum

number of 35 g servings, correct to the nearest 5 grams, that you can serve from this packet?

**6** 15 cartons each weighing 12.5 kg correct to the nearest 0.5 kg are to be lifted by a hoist that can take a maximum load of 190 kg.

Is it safe to use this hoist to lift these cartons?

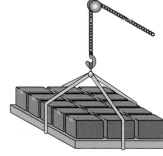

**7** Choco bars weigh 53 g to the nearest gram.
Toffo bars weigh 72 g to the nearest gram.

Calculate the maximum and minimum differences between the weights of the two types of bars.

**8** $a$, $b$, $c$ and $d$ are four positive numbers, each rounded to the nearest whole number. $a > b$ and $c > d$.

Mina has to find the maximum possible value of the answer to the calculation
$$\frac{a-b}{c-d}$$
Which of the numbers $a$, $b$, $c$ and $d$ should she give their maximum possible value and which should she give their minimum possible value?

> **Hint**
> Try it out with some easy numbers.

**9** A ball bearing has a diameter of 5.3 mm with a 5% tolerance. (It could be 5% more or 5% less.) The ball bearing's diameter must be correct to the nearest 0.5 mm. Does this ball bearing fit the specification?

**10** A cylindrical bar has to fit into a circular tube. The diameter of the bar is 5.3 mm correct to the nearest tenth of a millimetre and the diameter of the tube is 5.4 mm with a 10% tolerance.

Is it certain that the bar will fit into the tube?

**11** Kathryn's weight is 53.8 kg to the nearest 100 g. 1 kg = 2.20 pounds correct to three significant figures. What is the upper bound of Kathryn's weight in pounds?

# 3  Assess ⓚ

D

**1**  A train arrived at a station 30 minutes late.
What fraction is this of the journey time of $2\frac{1}{2}$ hours?

**2**  Catriona buys a car costing £3500.

There is a reduction of one-fifth of the price.
She pays three-eighths of the reduced price as deposit.

How much is the deposit?

**3**  The table shows the mean temperature in degrees Celsius each month in
Anchorage, Alaska, USA.

| Jan | Feb | Mar | Apr | May | Jun | Jul | Aug | Sep | Oct | Nov | Dec |
|-----|-----|-----|-----|-----|-----|-----|-----|-----|-----|-----|-----|
| −10 | −7 | −4 | 2 | 8 | 12 | 15 | 14 | 9 | 1 | −6 | −9 |

**a**  For what fraction of the months is the mean temperature above zero?

**b**  For what fraction of the months is the mean temperature more than 5 degrees below
zero?

**4**  The bar chart shows the percentage of national income spent on education by
EU countries in 2002.

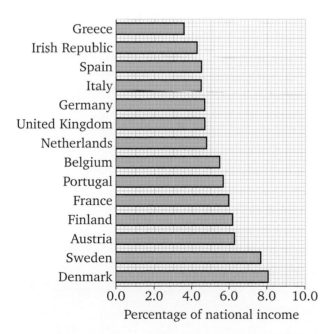

Source: Education at a Glance 2002,
Organisation for Economic
Co-operation and Development

**a**  What fraction of countries spent less than 5% of their national income on education?

**b**  What fraction of countries spent more on education than the United Kingdom?

**5**  Work out:

**a**  one-third of four-fifths of £30

**b**  $2\frac{2}{9} + 4\frac{1}{2}$

**c**  the number that, when reduced by one-third, becomes 14

**d**  the price that, when increased by one-quarter, becomes £26.50.

**C**

**6** Write down three numbers that:

   **a**    to one significant figure round to    **i**   100    **ii**   0.01

   **b**    to two significant figures round to    **i**   120    **ii**   0.12

**7** An amount of money is £49 to the nearest pound.

What is the greatest amount it could be? What is the least?

**8** Which of these numbers is/are the reciprocal of $\frac{b}{8}$?

0.625,    $\frac{8}{5}$,    $1\frac{3}{8}$,    $1\frac{3}{5}$,    $\frac{5}{8}$,    1.6

**9** Show that the product of a fraction and its reciprocal is 1.

**10** Write 0.8128 as a fraction in its simplest terms.

**11** Which of these fractions cannot be expressed as a terminating decimal?

$\frac{2}{3}, \quad \frac{3}{4}, \quad \frac{4}{5}, \quad \frac{5}{6}, \quad \frac{7}{8}, \quad \frac{8}{9}, \quad \frac{9}{10}, \quad \frac{10}{11}, \quad \frac{11}{12}$

**B**

**12** If a girl's age is correctly stated as 12, what is the maximum age she could be?

**13** A length $l$ cm is measured as 15 cm correct to the nearest half centimetre.

Copy and complete the statement ___ $\leqslant l <$ ___

**14** Rohan puts petrol in his car. Petrol is £0.98 a litre and he pays £49.90 to fill the tank.

How many litres does he buy?

How accurate is your answer?

**A**

**15** Lyra's height is 1.54 m and Louisa's is 1.61 m. Both heights are measured to the nearest centimetre.

What is the maximum possible difference between Lyra's height and Louisa's height?

**16** Bags of sweets are supposed to weigh 100 g correct to the nearest 5 grams.
They are filled with sweets that weigh 8 g correct to the nearest gram.

If 13 sweets are put into each bag can you be sure the weight is enough?

**17** The maximum weight of people that can safely travel in a lift is exactly 350 kilograms.

Four people are already in the lift. Their weights to the nearest kilogram are 63 kg, 65 kg, 72 kg and 75 kg.

   **a**    What is the maximum total weight of the people in the lift?

Rob wants to join them in the lift. Rob weighs 70 kg to the nearest 10 kilograms.

   **b**    Can Rob safely join them in the lift? Give reasons for your answer.

**A\***

**18** An athlete completes a mile (1760 yards, measured to the nearest tenth of a yard) in a race in 4 minutes, measured to the nearest tenth of a second. A yard is 0.914 m to the nearest millimetre.

What is the maximum possible value of the speed of the athlete in metres per second?

# Practice questions ⓚ

1    A book has a front and back cover and 100 pages.
The front and back cover are each 0.8 millimetres thick when measured to one decimal place.
Each page is 0.15 millimetres thick when measured to two decimal places.

Calculate the minimum thickness of the book.
You **must** show your working.                                                    *(2 marks)*

AQA 2007

2    Each fraction in this wall is the sum of the two supporting fractions in the wall below.
Complete the wall.

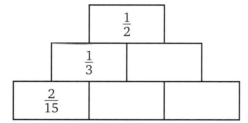

                                                                                   *(3 marks)*

AQA 2008

3    The cost of staying in a hostel is £13.50 for the first day.
The cost for each extra day is £10.50.
Eli has £75 to spend on accommodation.
He says that he can afford to stay in this hostel for seven days.

Is he correct?
You **must** show your working.                                                    *(3 marks)*

AQA 2009

# 4 Probability

## Objectives

Examiners would normally expect students who get these grades to be able to:

### D

use a two-way table to find a probability

understand mutually exclusive events

identify different mutually exclusive events and know, if they cover all the possibilities, then the sum of their probabilities is 1

### C

use probability to estimate outcomes for a population

understand and use relative frequency

### B

draw tree diagrams

### A

understand independent and non-independent events

find probabilities of successive independent events

### A*

find probabilities of successive dependent events.

## Key terms

mutually exclusive event
random
theoretical probability
experimental probability
trial
relative frequency

fair
biased
independent events
tree diagram
dependent events
conditional probability
two-way table

## Did you know?

### Lightning

In the UK around five people are killed by lightning each year. This means that the probability that you will be killed by lightning is approximately $\frac{1}{12\,000\,000}$

In fact, you are more likely to die falling off a ladder (probability $\frac{1}{2\,300\,000}$) or falling out of bed (probability $\frac{1}{2\,000\,000}$) than being killed by lightning.

## You should already know:

✔ how to cancel a fraction to its simplest form using a calculator

✔ how to add, subtract and multiply fractions and decimals

✔ how to convert between fractions, decimals and percentages

✔ how to calculate simple probabilities

✔ how to find outcomes systematically

✔ how to use a two-way table to find a probability.

# Learn... 4.1 Mutually exclusive events

**Mutually exclusive events** are events that cannot happen at the same time.

The sum of all the probabilities of mutually exclusive events = 1.

For example, the following events are mutually exclusive.

- Getting a head and getting a tail when a coin is flipped once.
- Getting a three and getting an even number when a dice is rolled once.
- Sleeping and running the marathon at the same time.
- Flying a plane and swimming the Channel at the same time.

For mutually exclusive events, A and B:

P(A or B) = P(A) + P(B). This is known as the OR rule.

P(A) is just a quick way of saying the probability of A, and so on.

So, for example P(Head or Tail) = P(Head) + P(Tail)

Other events are not mutually exclusive and can happen at the same time.

For example, the following events are not mutually exclusive.

- Getting a four and getting an even number when a dice is rolled.
- Getting a red card and getting an ace when a card is taken from a pack (e.g. you could get the ace of hearts).
- Driving a car and listening to the radio.
- Eating a meal and watching TV.

> **Study tip**
>
> In the examination the words 'mutually exclusive' will not be used.
>
> However, you need to understand how events happening at the same time affect probabilities.

**Example:**   10 discs are placed in a bag.

They are labelled X1, X2, X3, X4, Y1, Y2, Y3, Y4, Z1 and Z2.

One disc is picked at **random**.

Work out the probability of picking the following.

**a**   A disc with an X on it

**b**   A disc without an X on it

**c**   A disc with a 3 on it

**d**   A disc without a 3 on it

**e**   A disc with an X or a 3 on it

**Solution:**   **a**   Probability of an event happening = $\dfrac{\text{number of outcomes for that event}}{\text{total number of possible outcomes}}$

Probability of picking an X = $\dfrac{4}{10}$ ⟵ there are 4 discs with an X on
⟵ there are 10 discs altogether

**b**   Probability of an event happening = $\dfrac{\text{number of outcomes for that event}}{\text{total number of possible outcomes}}$

Probability of not picking an X = $\dfrac{6}{10}$ ⟵ there are 6 discs without an X on
⟵ there are 10 discs altogether

Here every disc has to be either an X or **not** an X.

The sum of all mutually exclusive probabilities = 1.

The probability of picking an X + the probability of not picking an X = 1.

So, the probability of not picking an X = 1 − the probability of picking an X.

Probability of not picking an X = $1 - \dfrac{4}{10} = \dfrac{6}{10}$

**c**    Probability of an event happening = $\dfrac{\text{number of outcomes for that event}}{\text{total number of possible outcomes}}$

Probability of picking a 3 = $\dfrac{2}{10}$ ⟵ there are 2 discs with a 3 on
⟵ there are 10 discs altogether

**d**    $1 - \dfrac{2}{10} = \dfrac{8}{10}$ (probability of not picking a 3 is 1 − probability of picking a 3)

**e**    The probability of picking a disc with an X or a 3 on is **not** $\dfrac{4}{10} + \dfrac{2}{10}$

This would count the X3 disc twice!

This shows that only mutually exclusive probabilities can be added.

Here you must use the list; there are 5 discs with either an X or a 3 on them. i.e. X1, X2, X3, X4, Y3.

So the probability is $\dfrac{5}{10}$

### Study tip

None of the answers in the example are simplified, as simplest form was not asked for.

If the exam question asks you to give an answer in its simplest form, then you must simplify.

## Practise... 4.1 Mutually exclusive events

**D**

**1**    Which of these pairs of dice events could not happen at the same time?

**a**    Roll a 1 and roll a number less than 5

**b**    Roll a 2 and roll an odd number

**c**    Roll an even number and roll an odd number

**d**    Roll a number more than 3 and a number less than 4

**2**    The probability that Georgina will wear black on a Sunday is 0.95

What is the probability that Georgina will not wear black on a Sunday?

**3**    The probability that Mike will have fish and chips for dinner is $\dfrac{7}{100}$

What is the probability that Mike will not have fish and chips for dinner?

**4**    The probability that Toni will not drink tea at work is 0.001

What is the probability that Toni will drink tea at work?

**5**    Losalot Town are playing in a football tournament.

Here are some probabilities for the outcome of their opening match.

Complete the table.

| Probability of winning | Probability of drawing | Probability of losing |
|---|---|---|
| $\dfrac{1}{10}$ | $\dfrac{1}{5}$ | |

**C**

**6**    A bag contains coloured discs.

Each disc also has a letter on it.

There are 5 red discs D, E, F, G and H.

There are 8 blue discs D, E, F, G, H, I, J and K.

There are 2 yellow discs D and E.

Work out the probability of picking a disc that:

**a**  is red                          **d**  is red or has an E on it

**b**  has an E on it                  **e**  is yellow or has an F on it

**c**  does not have an E on it        **f**  is blue or has an H on it.

**7**  The table shows the probabilities that a student will choose a certain drink.

| Lemonade | Cola | Orange | Other |
|----------|------|--------|-------|
| 0.3 | 0.2 | | 0.1 |

What is the probability that the student will choose:

**a**  orange                         **b**  cola or lemonade?

**⚠ 8**  Of the people attending a festival, one is chosen at random to win a prize.

The probability the chosen person is male is 0.515

The probability the chosen person is married is 0.048

The probability the chosen person is a married male is 0.029

What is the probability the chosen person is an unmarried female?

**⚠ 9**  In a game you choose to throw either one or two ordinary dice.

Your score is the number (if one dice) or sum of the numbers (if two dice).

You need to score a 4 to win the game.

Should you choose to roll 1 dice or 2 dice? Justify your choice.

**❓ 10**  A bag contains shapes which are coloured.

The probability of a red square is 0.2

The probability of a red shape is 0.2

Write down what you know about the red shapes in the bag.

## Learn...  4.2  Relative frequency

The probabilities so far have all been theoretical probabilities.

**Theoretical probability** is the probability of an event based on expectation (or theory).

**Experimental probability** is the probability of an event based on testing (or experiment).

A probability experiment is a test in which a number of **trials** are performed.

The experimental probability is also called the **relative frequency.**

$$\text{Relative frequency of an event} = \frac{\text{number of times an event has happened}}{\text{total number of trials}}$$

*Example:*   Niles rolls an ordinary dice 600 times.

His results are shown in the table.

| Score | 1 | 2 | 3 | 4 | 5 | 6 |
|-------|---|---|---|---|---|---|
| Frequency | 92 | 107 | 103 | 99 | 97 | 102 |

**a**  Work out the relative frequency for each score.

**b**  How many of each score would you expect if the dice was **fair**?

**c**  Do you think the dice is **biased**? Explain your answer.

**Solution:**  **a**  Relative frequency of an event = $\dfrac{\text{number of times an event has happened}}{\text{total number of trials}}$

In each case, the total number of trials is 600.

The relative frequencies are shown in the table.

| Score | 1 | 2 | 3 | 4 | 5 | 6 |
|---|---|---|---|---|---|---|
| Frequency | 92 | 107 | 103 | 99 | 97 | 102 |
| Relative frequency | $\frac{92}{600}$ | $\frac{107}{600}$ | $\frac{103}{600}$ | $\frac{99}{600}$ | $\frac{97}{600}$ | $\frac{102}{600}$ |

**b**  You would expect **about** 100 of each number if the dice is fair ($\frac{1}{6} \times 600$).

**c**  The dice does not look as though it is biased.

The relative frequencies are reasonably close to the theoretical probabilities.

| Score | 1 | 2 | 3 | 4 | 5 | 6 |
|---|---|---|---|---|---|---|
| Frequency | 92 | 107 | 103 | 99 | 97 | 102 |
| Relative frequency | $\frac{92}{600}$ | $\frac{107}{600}$ | $\frac{103}{600}$ | $\frac{99}{600}$ | $\frac{97}{600}$ | $\frac{102}{600}$ |
| Theoretical probability | $\frac{100}{600}$ | $\frac{100}{600}$ | $\frac{100}{600}$ | $\frac{100}{600}$ | $\frac{100}{600}$ | $\frac{100}{600}$ |

Throwing the dice 600 times is a large number so getting values close to 100 (600 ÷ 6) is a sign of no bias.

**Study tip**

Relative frequencies should always be given as fractions or decimals. Giving the frequencies will often score zero.

**Example:**  When Niles rolled the dice, he kept a record of the number of 4s in every 10 throws.

Here are his results.

| Number of throws | 10 | 20 | 30 | 40 | 50 | 60 | 70 | 80 | 90 | 100 | 110 | 120 |
|---|---|---|---|---|---|---|---|---|---|---|---|---|
| Number of 4s | 1 | 5 | 8 | 10 | 10 | 12 | 13 | 13 | 15 | 15 | 16 | 18 |

**a**  Find the relative frequency after every 10 throws.

**b**  Draw a line graph to show these results.

**c**  What does the graph show about the relative frequency values?

**Solution:**  **a**  After 10 throws there had been one 4 giving a relative frequency of $\dfrac{1}{10} = 0.1$

After 20 throws there had been five 4s giving a relative frequency of $\dfrac{5}{20} = 0.25$

**Study tip**

Use decimals to make graph plotting and comparison easier.

| Number of throws | 10 | 20 | 30 | 40 | 50 | 60 | 70 | 80 | 90 | 100 | 110 | 120 |
|---|---|---|---|---|---|---|---|---|---|---|---|---|
| Number of 4s | 1 | 5 | 8 | 10 | 10 | 12 | 13 | 13 | 15 | 15 | 16 | 18 |
| Relative frequency | $\frac{1}{10}$ | $\frac{5}{20}$ | $\frac{8}{30}$ | $\frac{10}{40}$ | $\frac{10}{50}$ | $\frac{12}{60}$ | $\frac{13}{70}$ | $\frac{13}{80}$ | $\frac{15}{90}$ | $\frac{15}{100}$ | $\frac{16}{110}$ | $\frac{18}{120}$ |
| Relative frequency | 0.1 | 0.25 | 0.27 | 0.25 | 0.2 | 0.2 | 0.19 | 0.16 | 0.17 | 0.15 | 0.15 | 0.15 |

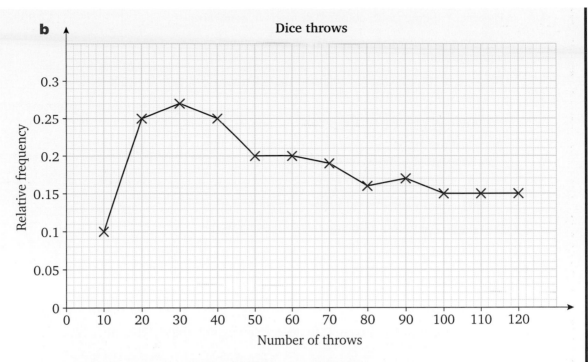

**b**

**Dice throws**

*Relative frequency* (y-axis)

*Number of throws* (x-axis)

**c**    Early on in the experiment the line is unpredictable.
This shows that using only a few results would be unreliable.

After a while the plotted values are all very similar.
This shows that more results leads to better estimates of probability.

## Practise... 4.2 Relative frequency     D C B A A*

**1**    Ruth flips a coin 240 times.

**a**    How many times would she expect to get a tail?

**b**    She actually gets 109 tails.
Do you think the coin is biased?
Give a reason for your answer.

**2**    Over a long time it is found that the probability of a faulty light bulb is 0.01

**a**    How many light bulbs would you expect to be faulty in a batch of 800?

**b**    One day, a light bulb checker finds 17 faulty bulbs.
Estimate how many bulbs she has checked that day.

**3**    The table shows the frequency distribution after drawing a card from a pack 40 times. The card is put back after each draw.

| Results from 40 draws | | | |
|---|---|---|---|
| | Club | Heart | Diamond | Spade |
| Frequency | 9 | 9 | 12 | 10 |

**a**    What is the relative frequency of getting a heart?

**b**    What is the relative frequency of getting a red card?

**c**    What is the theoretical probability of getting a club?

**d**    Ciaron says 'If you drew a card out 80 times you would probably get twice as many of each suit.' Explain why Ciaron is wrong.

D

C

**C**

**4**   Pete has a spinner with coloured sections of equal size.

He wants to know the probability that his spinner lands on blue.

He spins it 100 times and calculates the relative frequency of blue after every 10 spins.

His results are shown on the graph.

**a**   Use the graph to calculate the number of times the spinner landed on blue:

    **i**    after the first 20 spins

    **ii**   after the first 70 spins.

**b**   From the graph, estimate the probability of the spinner landing on blue.

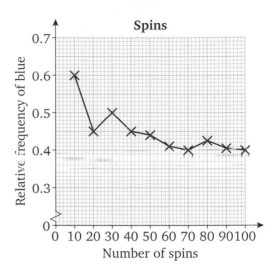

**5**   Izzy is rolling a dice.

After every 10 rolls she works out the relative frequency of a score of 1.

The diagram shows the relative frequency throughout the experiment.

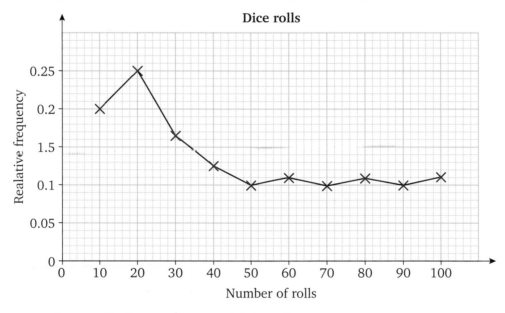

**a**   After 20 rolls, how many times did she roll a 1?

**b**   How many times did she roll a 1 between the 21st and 50th rolls?

**c**   Do you think this dice is biased? Explain your answer.

**⚠ 6**   The table shows the frequency distribution after rolling a dice 270 times.

| Results from 270 rolls of dice | | | | | |
|---|---|---|---|---|---|
| **1** | **2** | **3** | **4** | **5** | **6** |
| Frequency 52 | 56 | 41 | 37 | 45 | 39 |

**a**   What is the relative frequency of getting a 2?

**b**   What is the relative frequency of getting a score greater than 4?

**c**   What is the relative frequency of getting an even number?

**d**   Ellie says the relative frequency of getting a score less than 3 is $\frac{149}{270}$

    Is this correct? Explain your answer.

**e**   Which one of the frequencies is the same as the result you would expect from theoretical probability?

**7** Archie has a bag of counters.

Inside there are red, green, blue and yellow counters.

He thinks there is the same number of each colour in the bag.

He collects data by picking counters one at a time from the bag.
He replaces each counter in the bag before picking again.

Here are his results.

After 50 picks

| Colour | Red | Green | Blue | Yellow |
|---|---|---|---|---|
| Frequency | 20 | 8 | 6 | 16 |

After 100 picks

| Colour | Red | Green | Blue | Yellow |
|---|---|---|---|---|
| Frequency | 30 | 22 | 20 | 28 |

After 200 picks

| Colour | Red | Green | Blue | Yellow |
|---|---|---|---|---|
| Frequency | 57 | 55 | 43 | 45 |

After 400 picks

| Colour | Red | Green | Blue | Yellow |
|---|---|---|---|---|
| Frequency | 104 | 99 | 105 | 92 |

**a** Draw the relative frequencies for each colour all on the same chart.

**b** What evidence is there to support Archie's opinion after:

**i** 50 picks **ii** 100 picks **iii** 200 picks **iv** 400 picks

## Learn...   4.3 Independent events and tree diagrams

**Events** are **independent** if the outcome of one event does not affect the outcome of the other.

If two events are independent, then the probability that they will both happen is found by multiplying their probabilities together.

This can be written as P(A and B) = P(A) × P(B). This is known as the AND rule.

So, a dice showing an even number and a coin showing a head **are** independent events. Getting a six on successive throws of a fair dice are also independent events.

A **tree diagram** is a useful tool for showing probabilities.

The probabilities are written on the branches of the tree.

*Example:* A red dice and blue dice are rolled at the same time.
Find the probability that both dice show a six.

*Solution:* The scores on the two dice are independent.

The probability of a six on both dice

= the probability of a six on a red dice AND a six on the blue dice.

$$= \frac{1}{6} \times \frac{1}{6}$$

$$= \frac{1}{36}$$

*Example:* **k** The probability that Jeff is late for work on any particular day is 0.05

    **a**    Draw a tree diagram to show the possible outcomes for the two days.

    **b**    Use the tree diagram to find the probability that on two consecutive days:

        **i**    Jeff is late on both days

        **ii**    Jeff is late just once.

*Solution:*    **a**    L = late    N = not late

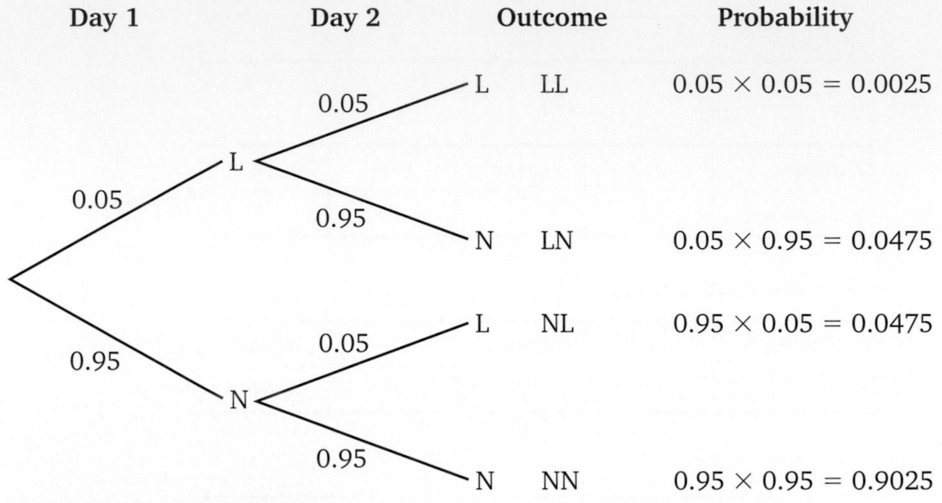

| Day 1 | Day 2 | Outcome | Probability |
|---|---|---|---|
| | 0.05 → L | LL | $0.05 \times 0.05 = 0.0025$ |
| 0.05 → L | 0.95 → N | LN | $0.05 \times 0.95 = 0.0475$ |
| 0.95 → N | 0.05 → L | NL | $0.95 \times 0.05 = 0.0475$ |
| | 0.95 → N | NN | $0.95 \times 0.95 = 0.9025$ |

**Study tip**

The probabilities on any given pair of branches must add up to 1.
The total probability of all the final outcomes should also be 1.

    **b**    **i**    To be late on both days means being late on day 1 **AND** being late on day 2.

        The events are independent so these probabilities can be multiplied.

        Probability of being late on both days = $0.05 \times 0.05 = 0.0025$

      **ii**    Probability of being late once = late on day 1 **AND** not late on day 2

                      **OR** not late on day 1 **AND** late on day 2

                = $(0.05 \times 0.95) + (0.95 \times 0.05)$

                = $0.0475 + 0.0475$

                = $0.095$

Remember that:

AND can be associated with multiplying probabilities of independent events.

OR can be associated with adding probabilities of mutually exclusive events.

**Practise…**

## 4.3 Independent events and tree diagrams

D C B A A*

B

**1**   State whether these events are independent.
Give a reason for your answers.

    **a**   You roll a fair six-sided dice.

        Event A: scoring a 3 on the dice

        Event B: scoring an odd number on the dice

    **b**   You pick a card from a normal pack and roll a dice.

        Event A: you get a heart

        Event B: you roll a 4

**2**   Complete the tree diagram.

    Use the tree diagram to find the probabilities of all possible outcomes.

    A bag has 10 balls, 3 with a letter A and 7 with a letter B.

    One ball is taken out at random, replaced and then a second is taken out at random.

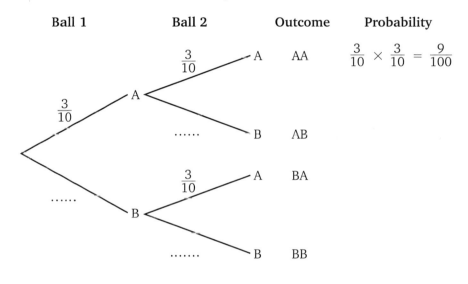

**3**   The probability that Mike takes a bus to work is 0.8

    Days are independent of each other.

    Work out the probability that Mike takes the bus on Monday and Tuesday.

A

**4**   Lorraine has a packet of crisps and a fruit juice for lunch every day.

    The probability that she has roast chicken crisps is 0.2

    The probability that she has orange juice is 0.4

    **a**   What is the probability that she has roast chicken crisps and orange juice?

    **b**   What is the probability that she does **not** have roast chicken crisps and does **not** have orange juice?

**5**   The probability that Katie has an argument with her husband on a given day is 0.4

    Days are independent of each other.

    **a**   Draw a tree diagram to show all the probabilities and outcomes for two days.

    **b**   Use the tree diagram to find the probability that Katie and her husband:

        **i**   argue on both days

        **ii**   argue on neither day

        **iii**   argue on exactly one day

        **iv**   argue on at least one day.

B

**6**    The probability that Jody stays up late on a night before school is 0.15

The probability that Jody stays up late on a night not before school is 0.37

What is the probability that Jodie does not stay up late for 7 consecutive days during a school term?

**7**    A fair coin is flipped 3 times.

**a**    Draw a tree diagram showing the possible outcomes

**b**    Use your tree diagram to find the probability that:

     **i**     at least two of the coins land on heads

     **ii**    no more than one tail occurs.

**8**    32% of British people can speak a foreign language.

**a**    Two British people are chosen at random.

Use a tree diagram to find the probability that:

     **i**     both can speak a foreign language

     **ii**    exactly one can speak a foreign language.

**b**    Janet and Mavis are British twins.
Why is it unlikely that the probability they both speak a foreign language is the answer to part **a i**?

**c**    98% of people born in Luxembourg can speak a foreign language.
What is the probability that 5 randomly chosen people born in Luxembourg can all speak a foreign language?

**9**    The probability that Kels works 7 days in a week is $x$.

Weeks are independent of each other.

The probability that Kels works 7 days for two consecutive weeks is 0.1764

Find $x$.

**10**    Explain why the probability of two independent events happening is always less than or equal to the individual probabilities.

## Learn...   4.4 Dependent events and conditional probability

**Events** are **dependent** if the outcome of one event affects the outcome of the other. This is also known as **conditional probability**.

Many examples of conditional probability involve choosing items and not replacing them, e.g. counters from bags, students from classes, etc.

Again, a tree diagram is a useful tool for showing probabilities.

As before, the probabilities are written on the branches of the tree.

**Study tip**

The examination uses the term 'without replacement' to indicate that the first item is not put back before the second item is chosen.

*Example:*    A bag contains 10 red discs and 8 blue discs.

One disc is chosen at random and **not** replaced.

A second disc is then chosen at random.

**a**    Work out the probability that both discs are blue.

**b**    Use a tree diagram to show all the possible events and their probabilities.

**Solution:**    **a**    The probability that both discs are blue

= probability 1st disc is blue AND 2nd disc is blue

= probability 1st disc is blue × probability 2nd disc is blue

$= \dfrac{8}{18} \times \dfrac{7}{17}$ ◄── only 7 blue discs left as the 1st one is not replaced

               ◄── only 17 discs left altogether as the 1st one is not replaced

$= \dfrac{56}{306} = \dfrac{28}{153}$

> **Study tip**
>
> If the exam question asks you to give an answer in its simplest form, then you must cancel. Always show the original fraction in case you make a mistake cancelling down.

**b**

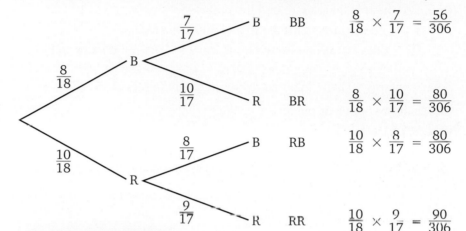

| Disc 1 | Disc 2 | Outcome | Probability |
|---|---|---|---|

Branches:

- Disc 1: B ($\frac{8}{18}$) → Disc 2: B ($\frac{7}{17}$), outcome BB, $\frac{8}{18} \times \frac{7}{17} = \frac{56}{306}$
- Disc 1: B → Disc 2: R ($\frac{10}{17}$), outcome BR, $\frac{8}{18} \times \frac{10}{17} = \frac{80}{306}$
- Disc 1: R ($\frac{10}{18}$) → Disc 2: B ($\frac{8}{17}$), outcome RB, $\frac{10}{18} \times \frac{8}{17} = \frac{80}{306}$
- Disc 1: R → Disc 2: R ($\frac{9}{17}$), outcome RR, $\frac{10}{18} \times \frac{9}{17} = \frac{90}{306}$

> **Study tip**
>
> The probabilities on any given pair of branches must add up to 1. The total probability of all the final outcomes should also be 1.

**Practise...**

## 4.4 Dependent events and conditional probability

D C B A A*

**1**    A set of cards is numbered 1, 2, 3, 4, 5, 6, 7, 8, 9 and 10.

Given that the first card picked is even, work out the probability of:

**a**   a 7      **b**   an 8      **c**   a 7 or an 8      **d**   not an 8      **e**   not a 7

**2**    A bag contains 10 counters; 6 are black, 4 are white.
Two counters are chosen at random without replacement.

Draw a tree diagram and use it to work out the probability that:

**a**   both counters are black      **c**   the counters are of different colours.

**b**   both counters are white

**3**    A box contains 3 red pencils and 8 blue pencils.
Two pencils are taken from the box without replacement.

Draw a tree diagram and use it to find:

**a**   the probability that both pencils are red

**b**   the probability that both pencils are green

**c**   the probability that one pencil is red and one is green.

**A***

**4** The cards from Question 1 are face down on the table and in a random order.

One card is picked at random.
It is then put back and the cards are shuffled.
A second card is then picked at random.

**a** Work out the probability that one card is a 7 and the other is even.

Starting again from the same set of cards, two cards are now picked at random without replacement.

**b** What is the probability that one card is a 7 and the other is even?

**5** The probability that Mr Metcalf sleeps through his alarm is 0.09

If he sleeps through his alarm the probability he will miss breakfast is 0.72

If he does not sleep through his alarm the probability he will miss breakfast is 0.26

**a** Draw a tree diagram to show these probabilities.

**b** Use the tree diagram to find the probability that Mr Metcalf:

  **i** sleeps through his alarm and misses breakfast

  **ii** does not sleep through his alarm and does not miss breakfast.

**6** A bag contains 90 balls coloured red or green in the ratio $4:5$

Two balls are drawn at random.

Using a tree diagram, find the probability that one ball of each colour is picked.

**7** The National Lottery is played by choosing 6 numbers from the values 1–49 inclusive.

What is the probability of choosing all 6 numbers correctly?

Give your answer correct to 3 s.f.

**8** The histogram shows the time taken for customer calls to be answered at a call centre.

Two of these customers are chosen at random to answer a survey.

**a** Work out the probability that:

  **i** both customers waited for more than 4 seconds to be answered

  **ii** one customer waited less than 4 seconds and one customer waited for more than 4 seconds.

**b** Given that both customers actually had to wait under 3 seconds, what is the probability they both had to wait under 2 seconds?

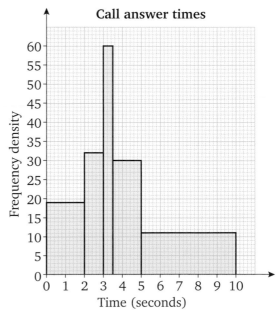

**9** The **two-way table** shows information about the gender of performers in a school show.

Two of the performers are chosen at random to talk to the local newspaper.

What is the probability that they are both:

**a** boys          **b** dancers?

|  | Boys | Girls |
|---|---|---|
| **Singers** | 4 | 12 |
| **Dancers** | 10 | 16 |

**10** Jack has some socks in his drawer. Some of them are black.

If he chooses two socks at random, the probability he gets a black pair is $\frac{132}{380}$

How many socks were in the drawer and how many of them were black?

# 4  Assess

**1**  In the UK the probability of being left handed is about 0.11

How many left-handed people would you expect to find in the following?

**a**  a class of 33 children.

**b**  a street of 132 people.

**c**  a town of 55 000 people.

**2**  Two pentagonal spinners, each with the numbers 1 to 5, are spun.
Their outcomes are added together to give a score.

**a**  Draw a two-way table for the two spinners.

**b**  Use your diagram to find:

    **i**  the probability of a score of 4    **iii**  the probability of a score of 9

    **ii**  the probability of a score of 5    **iv**  the most likely score.

**c**  Repeat parts **a** and **b** for a score that is the outcomes **multiplied** together.

**3**  A fair six-sided dice is thrown 250 times and the following results obtained.

| Score | 1 | 2 | 3 | 4 | 5 | 6 |
|---|---|---|---|---|---|---|
| Frequency | 45 | 48 | 43 | 40 | 38 | 36 |

**a**  What is the relative frequency of a score of 1?

**b**  What is the relative frequency of a score of 6?

**c**  What is the relative frequency of scoring more than 3?

**d**  How does this data confirm that the dice is fair?

**e**  Draw a new table with possible frequencies if this dice was thrown 6000 times.

**4**  The table below shows the probabilities of selecting tickets from a bag.

The tickets are coloured yellow, black or green and numbered 1, 2, 3 or 4.

| | 1 | 2 | 3 | 4 |
|---|---|---|---|---|
| Yellow | $\frac{1}{20}$ | $\frac{1}{16}$ | $\frac{3}{40}$ | $\frac{1}{8}$ |
| Black | $\frac{1}{10}$ | $\frac{3}{40}$ | 0 | $\frac{3}{40}$ |
| Green | 0 | $\frac{1}{8}$ | $\frac{3}{16}$ | $\frac{1}{8}$ |

A ticket is taken at random from the bag.

Calculate the probability that:

**a**  it is black and numbered 4    **c**  it is not black

**b**  it is green    **d**  it is yellow or numbered 3

**5**  The probability Callum has to work overtime on a given day is 0.12

**a**  What is the probability that he has to work overtime on two consecutive days?

**b**  What assumption did you make to answer part **a**?

**A**

**6**  The relative frequency of rain for the last 100 hundred years in London is 0.42 for any given day.

    **a**  Use a tree diagram to show the outcomes for two consecutive days and their probabilities.

    **b**  Using this data, what is the probability that it will rain on two consecutive days?

    **c**  Why is this probability unlikely to be correct?

**A\***

**7**  Maria plays tennis better on grass courts than any other.

On grass courts she has a 75% chance of winning.

On other courts she has a 60% chance of winning.

She plays 45% of her games on grass courts.

Use a tree diagram to find the probability that she will win the next game she plays.

**8**  At a party there are 40 balloons for the children to take home.

The table shows the number of each colour.

The balloons are given out at random.

Linda and Natalie are the first two to get a balloon.

Find the probability that neither Linda nor Natalie get a red balloon.

| Colour | Number |
|--------|--------|
| Blue   | 12     |
| Green  | 6      |
| Orange | 10     |
| Red    | 7      |
| Yellow | 5      |

**9**  There are 12 sandwiches left in a cabinet at a café.

Six are meat sandwiches, four are fish, and the other two are vegetarian.

Earl chooses two sandwiches. His choices are independent. He likes all the choices.

    **a**  Draw a tree diagram to show the possible outcomes and their probabilities.

    **b**  What is the probability that exactly one of his sandwiches is a fish sandwich?

# Practice questions ⓚ

1  At the end of a training course candidates must take a test in order to pass the course.
The probability of passing the test at the first attempt is 0.8
Those who fail re-sit once.
The probability of passing the re-sit is 0.5
No further attempts are allowed.

    **a**  **i**  Complete the tree diagram, which shows all the possible outcomes.

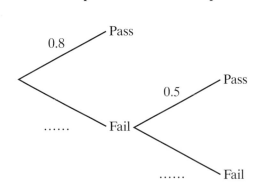

        **ii**  What is the probability that a candidate fails both attempts and so fails the course?  *(2 marks)*

    **b**  What is the probability that a candidate passes the course?  *(1 mark)*

    **c**  Hassan and Louise both take the training course.
What is the probability that one of them passes and one of them fails?  *(3 marks)*

AQA 2008

## Objectives

Examiners would normally expect students who get these grades to be able to:

**D**

substitute numbers into formulae such as
$$C = \frac{(A + 1)D}{9}$$

derive complex expressions and formulae

distinguish between an expression, an equation, an identity and a formula

**C**

rearrange linear formulae such as $p = 3q + 5$

**B**

rearrange formulae involving brackets, indices, fractions and square roots

**A**

rearrange formulae where the variable appears twice.

### Key terms

formula
expression
substitute
equation
identity
term
subject

I used the formula: cooking time = 20 per pound weight + 20 to work out how long the chicken needed. Perhaps the time should have been in minutes not hours!

*Did you know?*

## Formulae can be very useful

Formulae are used in everyday life, for example in cooking instructions. Be careful to check that the units you are working with make sense!

## You should already know:

✔ order of operations (BIDMAS)

✔ the four rules applied to negative numbers

✔ the four rules applied to fractions

✔ how to calculate the squares, cubes and other powers of numbers

✔ how to write simple formulae using letters and symbols

✔ how to simplify expressions

✔ how to expand brackets such as $4(x + 2)$

✔ how to factorise expressions

✔ how to solve linear equations.

# Learn... 5.1 Substitution and writing formulae

When you write **formulae** you need to remember the following.

If $a$ stands for a number then $2 \times a$ can be written as $2a$. Write the number in front of the letter.

The **expression** $3x + 5$ means multiply $x$ by 3 then add 5.

The expression $5(y - 2)$ means subtract 2 from $y$ then multiply the answer by 5.

To **substitute** numbers into a formula, always write down the formula first. Then replace the letters with the values you are given, and write this down. Then start the working out.

**Study tip**

You can use brackets to help you do calculations in the correct order.

Remember BIDMAS applies to algebra as well as arithmetic.

**Study tip**

Be careful when you choose your own letters in problems. Some letters are easily confused with numbers.

$Z$ and 2 can get confused.

$I$ and 1 can get confused.

$b$ and 6 can get confused.

$q$ and 9 can get confused.

$S$ and 5 can get confused.

---

**Example:**    Georgia is using the formula $s = ut + \frac{1}{2}at^2$ in science. She needs to find $s$ when

     **a**    $u = 2, t = 3, a = 0.5$          **b**    $u = 5, a = -1, t = 6$

**Solution:**    **a**    $s = ut + \frac{1}{2}at^2$          Write the formula down first.

             $s = 2 \times 3 + \frac{1}{2} \times 0.5 \times 3^2$      Replace the letters by their values.

             $s = 6 + 2.25$

             $s = 8.25$

     **b**    $s = ut + \frac{1}{2}at^2$

             $s = 5 \times 6 + \frac{1}{2} \times (-1) \times 6^2$      Using brackets can help with signs.

             $s = 30 - 18$

             $s = 12$

**Study tip**

Remember to show all stages of your working; you gain method marks for this in an examination.

---

**Example:**    A rectangle is 5 cm longer than it is wide. The width is $c$.
             Show that the area of the rectangle can be found using the formula $A = c^2 + 5c$

**Solution:**    For a rectangle, area is length multiplied by width.

           The width is $c$.

           The length is $c + 5$.

           Area $=$ length $\times$ width

           Area $= (c + 5) \times c$

           Area $= c^2 + 5c$

---

**Example:**    The instructions for cooking a lamb joint are as follows.

           Allow 60 minutes for each kg plus an extra 30 minutes.

     **a**    Write a formula for this rule. Use $w$ for the weight in kg and $t$ for the time needed in minutes.

     **b**    How much time is needed to cook a lamb joint weighing 750 g?

     **c**    Rachel is cooking a lamb joint. It has already been in the oven for 90 minutes. She correctly works out that it needs a further 45 minutes. How much does the lamb joint weigh?

**Solution:**

**a**    $t = 60w + 30$

> **Study tip**
>
> Make sure that units are consistent. If you are working in pounds then make sure all prices/costs are in pounds. If you are working in kg, then make sure that all 'weights' are in kg, and so on.

**b**    $750\,g = 0.75\,kg$ (as $1\,kg = 1000\,g$)

| | |
|---|---|
| $t = 60w + 30$ | Write down the formula. |
| $t = 60 \times 0.75 + 30$ | Replace the letters by numbers. |
| $t = 45 + 30$ | Work out one step at a time. |
| $t = 75$ minutes | Remember to state units clearly. |

> **Study tip**
>
> If there are units in your answer, but no units on the answer line in your exam, then there will be a mark just for writing in the correct units.

**c**    Total cooking time is $90 + 45 = 135$ minutes

| | |
|---|---|
| $t = 60w + 30$ | |
| $135 = 60w + 30$ | Subtract 30 from each side. |
| $105 = 60w$ | |
| $\dfrac{105}{60} = w$ | Divide both sides by 60. |
| $1.75 = w$ | |
| So $w = 1.75\,kg$ | |

## Practise... 5.1 Substitution and writing formulae  k  D C B A A*

**1**    A particular type of coach has 56 seats.

   **a**    How many seats are there on 2 coaches?

   **b**    How many seats are there on 3 coaches?

   **c**    Write down a formula showing how to work out the number of seats from the number of coaches. Use $S$ for the number of seats and $C$ for the number of coaches.

**2**    Write down a formula for the total cost of:

   **a**    $x$ lollies at 70p each and $y$ lollies at 80p each

   **b**    $c$ cakes at 90p each and $b$ biscuits at 20p each.
      Use $T$ for the total cost.
      Why is it not a good idea to use $C$ for the total cost in part **b**?

**3**    A cookery book gives this rule to roast a chicken.

> **Total time = 40 minutes per kilogram plus 20 minutes**

Write a formula for the time needed to roast a chicken using this rule.
Use $w$ for the weight in kg and $t$ for the time in minutes.

**4**    Kate has £2 to spend. She buys $x$ biros at $y$ pence each.

   **a**    Write down an expression for the total amount she spends.

   **b**    Write down a formula for the amount of change she receives. Use $C$ to stand for her change in pence.

D

**D**

**5** Phil bought $x$ cups of tea and $y$ cups of coffee from his local cafe for himself and his friends. The tea cost 80p per cup, and the coffee cost 90p per cup.

Which one of the following could be a formula for the total cost in pence, $C$?

$C = 90x + 80y$

$C = 80x + 90y$

$C = 80x90y$

Explain your answer, and state why the other formulae are not correct.

**6** PizzaQuick works out its delivery charge with the following formula.

Delivery charge (£) = number of pizzas × 0.75 + 1.50

**a** Work out the delivery charge for three pizzas.

**b** Richard pays a delivery charge of £6. How many pizzas did he order?

**c** Mary is charged £8 for delivery. Explain how you know that Mary was not charged correctly?

**7** Mrs Bujjit is working out the wages at the factory. She uses the following formula.

Wages equal hours worked multiplied by rate per hour.

**a** Write this formula in algebra.

**b** How much does Ellen earn if she is paid £7 an hour and she works for 30 hours?

**c** How much does Francis earn if he works for 25 hours and is paid £8 an hour?

**d** How many hours did Ruth work if her hourly rate is £12.50 and she earned £475?

**8** In geography, Fiona is converting degrees Fahrenheit into degrees Celsius.

She uses the formula: $C = \dfrac{5(F - 32)}{9}$

Find $C$ if:

**a** $F = 77$     **b** $F = 32$     **c** $F = -31$     **d** $F = -13$

**9** The rule for finding out how far away thunderstorms are is:

'Count the number of seconds between the lightning and the thunder. Divide the answer by 5. The answer gives the distance in miles.'

**a** Write a formula for this rule.
Use $s$ to stand for the number of seconds and $d$ to stand for the distance in miles.

**b** In a thunderstorm, Jan counts 12 seconds between lightning and thunder. How far away is the thunderstorm?

**c** Jamie counts for 8 seconds. A thunderstorm is 3.5 miles away. How many more seconds does he have to wait before he hears the thunder?

**10** Rachel is doing an experiment in science. She uses the following formula.

$$\text{Average speed} = \frac{\text{Total distance travelled}}{\text{Total time taken}}$$

She uses this formula to work out that if an object has an average speed of 20 m/s and travels for 10 seconds then it must have travelled 2 m.

What mistake has Rachel made?

**C**

**11** Sean and Dee organise a quiz evening.

A quiz team is made up of four people.

Each team is charged £8 to enter the quiz.

Sean and Dee spend £20 on prizes and £25 on food and drink.

There are $x$ teams at the quiz evening.

On average, each team member spends £3 on refreshments.

Write down an expression in $x$ for the profit they make.

**12** Use the formula $v = ut - \frac{1}{2}at^2$ to find $v$ when:

**a** $u = 2, t = 3, a = 4$

**b** $u = 12, t = 2, a = -6$

**c** $u = 1, t = 3, a = -2$

**⚠ 13** Tom is calculating the interest on some savings.

He uses $I$ to stand for interest in the formula $I = \frac{PTR}{100}$

**a** If the principal $(P) = £300$, the time $(T) = 2$ years and the rate $(R) = 0.5\%$, calculate the interest.

**b** How long would he have to save if he wanted £45 interest?

**⚠ 14** Natland Taxis use the formula $C = 3m + 4.5$ to work out the cost of journeys for customers.

$C$ is the total charge in pounds and $m$ is the number of miles for the journey.

Every journey has a minimum charge and a charge for each mile.

**a** What is Natland Taxis' minimum charge?

**b** What is the cost per mile?

 **15** Sedgwick Tool Hire charge £18 to hire a cement mixer for 1 day.
They charge £9 for every extra day.

Harry says the formula for the total charge is $C = 18d + 9$
He uses $d$ for the number of days and $C$ for the total charge.

**a** Explain why Harry's formula is not correct.

**b** Write down what Harry's formula should be.

**c** Use the internet to find some costs for tool hire.
Write down some formulae for the cost of tool hire.

---

## Learn... 5.2 Changing the subject of a formula

You need to be able to identify whether an algebraic statement is a **formula**, an **equation**, an **expression** or an **identity**.

A **formula** tells you how to work something out. It can be written using words or symbols and will always have an equals sign. There will be at least two letters involved.

For example: **Area of a rectangle is equal to length multiplied by width** is a formula in words.

$A = L \times W$ is the same formula in symbols, where $A$ stands for area, $L$ for length and $W$ for width.
From this formula, you can work out the area of any rectangle if you know its length and width. $L$ and $W$ can have any value.
You can tell this is a formula, it tells you what to do with $L$ and $W$ to work out, $A$. There is an equals sign, and there are more than 2 two letters being used.

An **equation** is two expressions separated by an equals sign. You are often asked to solve an equation, in which case there will be only one letter, but it may appear more than once.

For example: $x + 3 = 7$ is an equation, $x$ is equal to 4. This is the only possible value of $x$ as any other number added to 3 does not equal 7.

You can tell this is an equation, there is an expression on each side of the equals sign. There is only one letter involved. It can be solved to find a value of $x$.

Formulae and equations can sometimes look very similar.

An **expression** is just a collection of **terms**. An expression does not have an equals sign.

For example: $3x + 2y - 5$ is an expression.

You can tell this is an expression as it is just a collection of terms. There is no equals sign.

An **identity** is a statement that is true whatever the value of the symbols.
For example: $3x + 4x \equiv 7x$ is always true ($\equiv$ is the identity symbol).

## Changing the subject of a formula

The **subject** of a formula is the letter on the left-hand side of the equals sign.

$P$ is the subject of the formula $P = 3L + 2$

You can change the subject of this formula to make $L$ the subject.
You will then have a formula telling you what to do to $P$ to work out $L$.
You use the same strategies that you learned when you solved equations.

**Hint**

Remember that what you do to one side of an equation, you must also do to the other side.

**Example:**

**a** Make $L$ the subject of the formula $P = 3L + 2$

**b** Make $r$ the subject of the formula $M = nr^2$

**c** Make $x$ the subject of each of the following formulae.

    **i**    $c(5 - x) = e$      **ii**    $f = \sqrt{\dfrac{h + i}{x}}$      **iii**    $\dfrac{a + bx}{cx} = d$

**Solution:**

**a**

| | |
|---|---|
| $P = 3L + 2$ | Write the formula down first. |
| $P - 2 = 3L + 2 - 2$ | Subtract 2 from both sides. |
| $P - 2 = 3L$ | |
| $\dfrac{P - 2}{3} = \dfrac{3L}{3}$ | Divide both sides by 3. |
| $\dfrac{P - 2}{3} = L$ | |
| $L = \dfrac{P - 2}{3}$ | Put $L$ on the left hand side as the subject of the formula. |

**b**

| | |
|---|---|
| $M = nr^2$ | Write the formula down first. |
| $\dfrac{M}{n} = r^2$ | Divide both sides by $n$. |
| $\pm\sqrt{\dfrac{M}{n}} = r$ | Take the square root of both sides (remember the square root of a number can be + or −). |
| $r = \pm\sqrt{\dfrac{M}{n}}$ | Rewrite the formula with $r$ as the subject. |

**c**   **i**

| | |
|---|---|
| $c(5 - x) = e$ | Write the formula down first. |
| $5c - cx = e$ | Multiply out the brackets. |
| $5c = e + cx$ | Add $cx$ to both sides (to get a positive term involving $x$). |
| $5c - e = cx$ | Subtract $e$ from both sides. |
| $\dfrac{5c - e}{c} = x$ | Divide both sides by $c$. |
| $x = \dfrac{5c - e}{c}$ | Rewrite with $x$ as the subject. |

**ii**    $f = \sqrt{\dfrac{h + i}{x}}$    Write the formula down first.

$f^2 = \dfrac{h + i}{x}$    Square both sides.

$f^2 x = h + i$    Multiply both sides by $x$.

$x = \dfrac{h + i}{f^2}$    Divide both sides by $f^2$.

**iii**    $\dfrac{a + bx}{cx} = d$    Write the formula down first.

This formula is different to the others, as the 'new' subject, $x$, appears twice.

$a + bx = dcx$    Multiply both sides by $cx$.

$a = dcx - bx$    Subtract $bx$ from both sides. (This gathers all the terms in $x$ on one side of the equal sign.)

$a = x(dc - b)$    Factorise (you only take the $x$ out as common factor here. It is important to get the $x$ on its own.)

$\dfrac{a}{(dc - b)} = x$    Divide both sides by the contents of the bracket (leaving just x on its own).

$x = \dfrac{a}{(dc - b)}$    Rewrite to make $x$ the subject.

## Practise...

## 5.2 Changing the subject of a formula

D  C  B  A  A*

**1**    In this chapter you will have met these words:

*expression, formula, equation, identity.*

Choose the correct word to describe each of the following.

**a**    $p = a + b + c + d$          **e**    $5 = 1 - 2q$

**b**    $2x + 5y - 4z$              **f**    $9k - 3$

**c**    $7m + 3m \equiv 10m$        **g**    $c = 25h - 9$

**d**    $3h = 6$                    **h**    $3z + 5 = 26$

**2**    Rearrange the formula $M = n + 42$ to make $n$ the subject.

**3**    Rearrange each of these formulae to make $y$ the subject.

   **a**    $5 + y = c$    **b**    $64 + 2y = f$    **c**    $d = 24 + 3y$    **d**    $j = 4y - 3k$

**4**    Rearrange each of these formulae to make $x$ the subject.

   **a**    $gx + t^2 = s^2$              **c**    $kx - 19 = n$

   **b**    $m = 7x - 49$                **d**    $y - x = 50$

**5**    Which of the following is a correct rearrangement of $m = 4x - 3$?

   **A**    $x = \dfrac{m - 3}{4}$        **C**    $x = \dfrac{m - 4}{3}$        **E**    $x = \dfrac{3 - m}{4}$

   **B**    $x = \dfrac{m + 3}{4}$        **D**    $x = m + \dfrac{3}{4}$        **F**    $x = \dfrac{m + 4}{3}$

D

C

**C**

**6** Sam rearranges the formula $y = \dfrac{3}{x}$ to make $x$ the subject.

She gets the answer $x = \dfrac{y}{3}$

Is she correct? Give a reason for your answer.

**7** The formula for finding the speed of an object is $s = \dfrac{d}{t}$ where $s$ stands for speed, $d$ for distance and $t$ for time.

**a** Rearrange the formula to make $d$ the subject.

**b** Rearrange the formula to make $t$ the subject. (It may be easier to use your answer to part **a** as your starting point.)

**B**

**8** Rearrange each of these formulae to make $x$ the subject.

**a** $x^2 - b = 9$

**b** $ax^2 = y$

**c** $gx^2 - c = d$

**9** Anne is using the formula $V = \pi r^2 h$ to find $r$.

She rearranges the formula and gets $r = \dfrac{\sqrt{V}}{\pi h}$

Is she correct?

Give a reason for your answer.

**B**
**A**

**10** Rearrange these formulae to make $x$ the subject.

**a** $f(x + g) = h$      **c** $r + s = t\sqrt{x}$

**b** $l = m(n - x)$      **d** $a = 3x + bx$

**11** The formula to find the length of the diagonal, $d$, of a rectangle $l$ units long and $w$ units wide is $d = \sqrt{l^2 + w^2}$

**a** Make $l$ the subject of the formula.

**b** Find the length of $l$ when $d = 30\,\text{cm}$ and $w = 18\,\text{cm}$.

**12** Rearrange the formula $y = \dfrac{x + a}{x - a}$ to make $x$ the subject.

**13** Brian and Amy are rearranging the formula $T = 2\pi\sqrt{\dfrac{l}{g}}$ to make $l$ the subject.

Brian gets $l = \dfrac{T^2 g}{2\pi}$ for his answer and Amy gets $l = \dfrac{T^2 g}{4\pi}$

Is either of them correct? Give a reason for your answer.

**14** Make the letter in square brackets the subject of the formula.

**a** $x(a - b) = b(a - x)$     $[x]$

**b** $E = \frac{1}{2}m(v^2 - u^2)$     $[u]$

**15** **a** Find a formula for the sum $(S)$ of three consecutive whole numbers $n, n + 1,$ and $n + 2$.

**b** Rearrange the formula to make $n$ the subject.

**c** Find the three consecutive whole numbers whose sum is 369.

**? 16** Choose a 2 × 2 square from the grid.
Draw the square and add opposite corners.

For example:

| 1 | 2 | 3 | 4 | 5 | 6 |
|---|---|---|---|---|---|
| 7 | 8 | 9 | 10 | 11 | 12 |
| 13 | 14 | 15 | 16 | 17 | 18 |
| 19 | 20 | 21 | 22 | 23 | 24 |
| 25 | 26 | 27 | 28 | 29 | 30 |
| 31 | 32 | 33 | 34 | 35 | 36 |

| 14 | 15 |
|---|---|
| 20 | 21 |

14 + 21 = 35

15 + 20 = 35

Try some more 2 × 2 squares from this grid.

This square

| $n$ | |
|---|---|
| $n+6$ | |

is from this grid.

Fill in the missing numbers. Write down a formula for the diagonal sum, $d$, in terms of $n$.

What happens for 3 × 3 squares?

4 × 4 squares?

Try this for a larger grid such as this one.

| 1 | 2 | 3 | 4 | 5 | 6 | 7 |
|---|---|---|---|---|---|---|
| 8 | 9 | 10 | 11 | 12 | 13 | |
| 15 | 16 | 17 | | | | |

Extend this to a grid $g$ units wide.

# Assess

**1** The formula for a sequence is $t_n = 5n - 3$, where $t_n$ is the $n$th term.

**a** Use this formula to find the 7th term in the sequence.

**b** Which term in the sequence is equal to 92?

**2** A cup of coffee costs £1.80 and a cup of tea costs £1.20 at Strickland's snack bar.

**a** Write a formula for the total cost, $T$, of $x$ coffees and $y$ teas.

**b** Janet buys 3 coffees and 4 teas. Use your formula to find the total cost of these drinks.

**3** Jessica is $x$ years old.
Paul is 2 years older than Jessica.

**a** Write down an expression for Paul's age.

**b** Nick is three times as old as Paul.

Write down an expression for Nick's age.

**4** Wooden joists are used in houses to support ceilings and floors.

The safety rule for joists 2 inches wide is:

'find depth in inches by dividing the span in feet by two, then add two to the result'

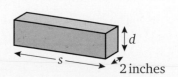

Lynn is a builder.

**a** Write down a formula that Lynn could use showing depth in terms of span.

**b** Find $d$ when $s$ is 16 feet.

**c** If $d$ is 8 inches what is the largest span this rule allows?

D
C

**C**

**5** George is using the formula $K = \dfrac{5(F - 32)}{9} + 273$

   **a** Find $K$ if $F = 41$

   **b** Find $F$ if $K = 303$

   **c** Make $F$ the subject of the formula.

**B**

**6** Rearrange the formula $m = 4(3c + d) - 1$ to make $c$ the subject.

**7** Make $y$ the subject of the straight-line equation $3x + 4y = 12$

**8** Make $c$ the subject of the formula $E = mc^2$

**B**
**A**

**9** Make $x$ the subject of the following formulae.

   **a** $y - x^2 = 9$

   **b** $y = \sqrt{x}$

   **c** $3y = 2x^2 + 3$

   **d** $5y - 2x = mx + 4$

**10** A shop uses the following formula to work out the total cost when customers pay by instalments.

$d = 0.1C$

$C = d + 36m$

$C$ is the total cost in pounds.
$d$ is the deposit in pounds.
$m$ is the monthly payment in pounds.

The total cost of a chair is £800.

Work out the monthly payments.

## Practice questions  ⓚ

**1** A shopkeeper uses this formula to calculate the total cost when customers pay by monthly instalments.

$$C = d + 24 \times m$$

$C$ is the total cost in pounds.
$d$ is the deposit in pounds.
$m$ is the monthly instalment in pounds.

   **a** The deposit for a wardrobe is £16.
      The monthly payments are £10.
      What is the total cost?            *(2 marks)*

   **b** How many years does it take to finish paying for goods using this formula?    *(1 mark)*

   **c** The total cost of a sofa is £600.
      The deposit is £120.
      Work out the value of the monthly instalment.    *(3 marks)*

AQA 2009

2    A teacher sets an extended task.
     Any task that is handed in late has the original mark reduced using this formula.

$$R = \frac{(N + 9) \times M}{40}$$

$R$ is the reduction.
$N$ is the number of days late.
$M$ is the original mark.

   a    Adam hands in his task one day late.
        His original mark is 32.
        Work out his new mark.                                      *(3 marks)*

   b    Belinda hands in her task 5 days late.
        Her mark is reduced by 7 marks.
        Work out her original mark.                                 *(3 marks)*

                                                                    AQA 2008

# 6 Enlargements

## Objectives

Examiners would normally expect students who get these grades to be able to:

**D**

enlarge a shape by a positive scale factor from a given centre

compare the area of an enlarged shape with the original area

**C**

find the ratio of corresponding lengths in similar shapes and identify this as the scale factor of enlargement

use ratios in similar shapes to find missing lengths

**B**

enlarge a shape by a fractional scale factor

**A**

enlarge a shape by a negative scale factor

compare lengths, areas and volumes of enlarged shapes

use the effect of enlargement on perimeter, area and volume in calculations.

### Key terms

| | |
|---|---|
| enlargement | similar |
| transformation | ratio |
| image | scale factor |
| object | centre of enlargement |
| congruent | vertex, vertices |

## Did you know?

### Ancient columns

This impressive building is the Colosseum in Rome built in ACE 70–82. It has always been recognisable by its shape. It is formed of layers that contain many striking columns.

Did you know that the three layers contain different types of columns? Did you know that for a column to be classed as Doric, Ionic or Corinthian requires a certain approximate height to width ratio?

| | | |
|---|---|---|
| Doric columns | 8 : 1 | strongest layer (bottom) |
| Ionic columns | 9 : 1 | |
| Corinthian columns | 10 : 1 | most slender layer (top) |

Nelson's column in Trafalgar square is a Corinthian column. The height of the column itself is 46 m and the base diameter is 4.6 m.

More Corinthian columns can be found in the Pantheon in Rome. The columns are much smaller with heights of approximately 46 feet and base diameters of 4 feet 11 inches.

This means that all Corinthian columns are approximate enlargements of each other.

## You should already know:

✔ how to plot coordinates in all four quadrants

✔ about units of length and how to use them

✔ about ratio and how to simplify a ratio

✔ how to use the vocabulary of transformations: object and image

✔ how to recognise and use corresponding angles

✔ how to find the area of simple shapes including a rectangle and a triangle.

**Learn...    6.1 Enlargement and scale factor**

**Enlargements** are a type of **transformation**.

They are the only transformations learned at GCSE that change the size of a shape.

All the other transformations (reflections, rotations and translations) keep the **image** the same size as the **object** (the original shape). The shapes are **congruent**.

An enlargement changes the size of the object but not the shape.

All the lengths will be changed but all the angles will stay the same. The object and the image are **similar**.

The **ratios** of corresponding sides in similar shapes are all equal and are equivalent to the **scale factor** of enlargement.

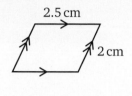 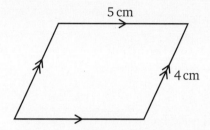

Not drawn accurately

$$\text{scale factor of enlargement} = \frac{\text{length on the enlarged shape (image)}}{\text{corresponding length on the original shape (object)}}$$

$\frac{5}{2.5} = 2$ and $\frac{4}{2} = 2$

The scale factor of enlargement is 2.

*Example:*    The two doors are drawn on centimetre grids.
The doors are similar. One is an enlargement of the other.
All corresponding angles are equal.
All corresponding sides are in the same ratio.

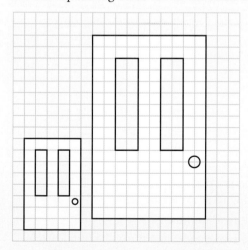

   **a**    What is the scale factor of enlargement?

   **b**    What is the area of one pane of glass in the small door (object)?

   **c**    What is the area of one pane of glass in the enlarged door (image)?

*Solution:*    **a**    To find the scale factor, you need to take two corresponding sides: one on the original (object) and one on the new one (image).

$$\text{scale factor} = \frac{\text{length of door on enlargement}}{\text{length of door on the original}} = \frac{16}{8} = 2$$

   **b**    Area of pane of glass on the object = $1 \times 4 = 4\,\text{cm}^2$

   **c**    Area of pane of glass on the image = $2 \times 8 = 16\,\text{cm}^2$

**D**

## Practise... 6.1 Enlargement and scale factor

**1** In these diagrams, *A* has been enlarged to give *B*.

**a** What is the scale factor of each enlargement?

**b** Work out the areas of the object (original) and the image (enlargement).

**c** What do you notice about the areas?

**i**          **ii**

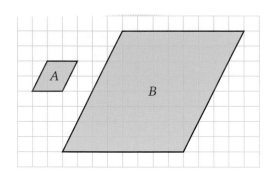 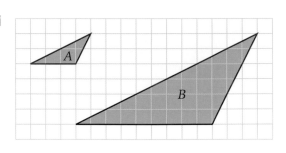

**C**

**2** Triangle *A* is enlarged with scale factor 3 into triangle *B*.

**a** One side of the triangle *B* has length 7.5 cm.
What is the length of the corresponding side of triangle *A*?

**b** One angle of the triangle is 45°.
What is the size of the corresponding angle in triangle *A*?

**3** Enlarge this shape by a scale factor of:

**a** 1.5

**b** 2.25

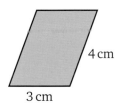

4 cm   Not drawn accurately

3 cm

**⚠ 4** The diagram shows a plan for a garden.
Quadrants of circles have been dug up to make a flower bed and a pond with a path beside it.
The radius of the pond is 2 metres.

> **Hint**
>
> A quadrant is a quarter of a circle.

3.6 m

lawn   10 m

? 2 m

← 5 m →

**a** To form the enlarged quadrant (the pond and path), the pond has been enlarged with scale factor 1.5

   **i** What is the radius of this enlarged quadrant?

   **ii** Find the area of each of these two quadrants to two decimal places.

   **iii** Using these two answers and the scale factor of enlargement, show that your answers are correct. Work to two decimal places.

**b** The flower bed is also an enlargement of the quadrant for the pond.

   **i** What is the scale factor of enlargement?

   **ii** Find the area of the flower bed.

**c** Find the area of the lawn.

**d** The gardener wants to copy this design for use in another garden. The new garden has dimensions that are exactly double this garden.

What will the area of the lawn be in the new garden?

> **Study tip**
>
> When you are working with areas or volumes, be careful that you are stating the units correctly, for example:
>
> length cm   area cm²   volume cm³

**5** **a** Julie has a photograph of her cat. She wants to have the photograph enlarged to put on the cover of her portfolio.

She wants the picture to fill the cover of the portfolio.

What is the scale factor of the enlargement she needs?

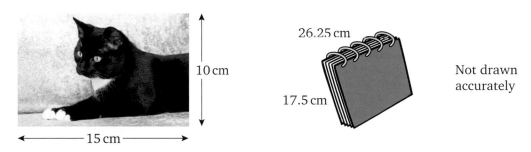

10 cm

15 cm

26.25 cm

17.5 cm

Not drawn accurately

**b** Julie also wants to enlarge the photograph to fit a frame to go on her wall. The frame is 82.5 cm wide.

**i** Find the scale factor to be used to enlarge the original photograph to fit the frame.

**ii** Find the height of the frame.

**iii** If the photograph on the folder was enlarged to fit the frame, find the scale factor.

**6** The area diagrams show a single square which has been enlarged by scale factor 2 and scale factor 3.

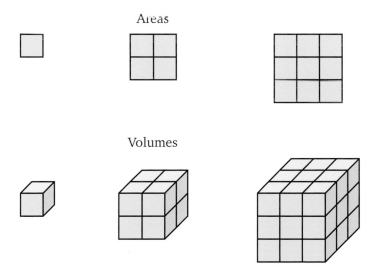

Areas

Volumes

**a** **i** Calculate the area of each of these shapes.

**ii** What do you notice about the areas compared with the original square?

**b** Now look at the diagrams for the volumes.

**i** Calculate the volume of each cube.

**ii** What do you notice about the volumes compared with the original cube?

# Learn... 6.2 Centres of enlargement

When drawing enlargements you need some extra information.

An enlargement is defined by its **centre of enlargement** and **scale factor**.

The centre of enlargement can be outside, on the edge of, or even inside the object.

In each diagram the same scale factor has been used but the centre of enlargement, marked with a cross, is different.

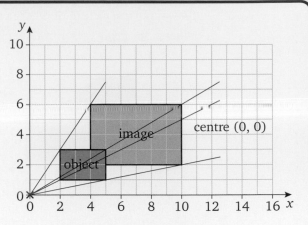

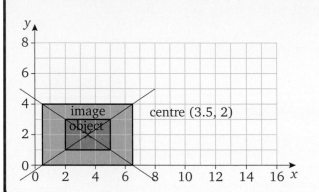

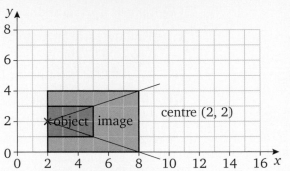

*Example:*    Enlarge the rectangle *A* by scale factor 2, centre of enlargement (1, 1).

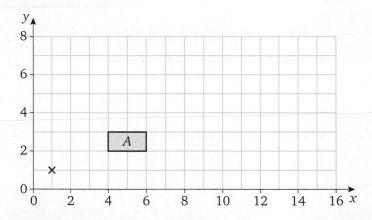

To enlarge a shape:

1   Plot the centre of enlargement on the grid with a cross.

2.  Choose a **vertex** (corner) of the shape. Join the centre of enlargement to this vertex and extend the line past the vertex.

3.  Measure the distance from the centre of enlargement to the vertex and multiply this by the scale factor. In this case, the scale factor is 2.

4.  This is the new distance from the centre of enlargement to the corresponding vertex on the new shape. Measure this distance along the line you have drawn and mark the new point.

5.  Repeat this for all the other **vertices**.

When the enlargement is finished, the distance from each vertex to the centre of enlargement will be twice as long as it was before.

*Study tip*

Always use a sharp pencil and a ruler. Make sure that the lines are drawn exactly through the intersection of the lines of the grid.

*Study tip*

There are usually two vertices that are easier to draw because the construction lines do not cross over the shape itself. Do these first!

Every length on the new rectangle will be twice as long as it was before.

The original rectangle was 2 by 1 units. The enlarged rectangle is now 4 by 2 units.

The rectangles are similar.

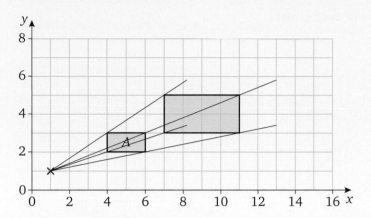

An alternative method would be to count the horizontal and vertical distance from the centre of enlargement to a vertex.

The new vertex would be at a point twice the horizontal distance and twice the vertical distance from the centre of enlargement.

**Hint**

You will know from the scale factor what the dimensions of the new rectangle should be. You can use this fact to help you draw an accurate diagram and to check your enlargement.

**Study tip**

Don't forget that you can use either of these methods to find the new position of a vertex. You can even use a combination of both!

*Example:*   Enlarge triangle $ABC$ with scale factor $\frac{1}{2}$ using $O$ as the centre of enlargement.

*Solution:*   A fractional scale factor, between 0 and 1, makes the object smaller rather than larger.

It reduces the size, but mathematically it is still called an enlargement.

Join each vertex in turn, from the object to the centre of enlargement.

$OA'$ must be $\frac{1}{2}$ of the original distance $OA$, so measure $OA$ and position $A'$ accordingly.

Repeat for $B$ and $C$.

If you have constructed this accurately, then the sides of $A'B'C'$ should be half the length of the sides of $ABC$.

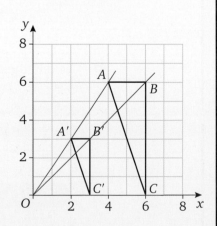

**Example:**   The trapezium *RSTU* has been enlarged to give trapezium *VWYZ*.

Find:

  **a**   the scale factor of enlargement

  **b**   the centre of enlargement.

**Solution:**

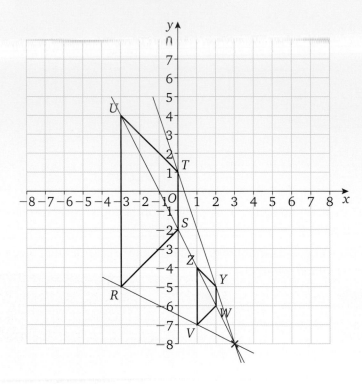

  **a**   Measure a side on the object *RSTU* (the original shape) and a corresponding side on the image *VWYZ* (the enlarged shape).

For example, $RU = 9$ units and $VZ = 3$ units

The scale factor $= \dfrac{VZ}{RU} = \dfrac{3}{9} = \dfrac{1}{3}$

Scale factor is $\frac{1}{3}$

The scale factor $= \dfrac{WY}{ST} = \dfrac{1}{3}$

> **Hint**
>
> It is a good idea to do this for two lengths on the object so that one can be used as a check.

  **b**   To find the centre of enlargement, join corresponding vertices *R* and *V*, and extend the line.

Repeat with the other three vertices.

The point where they meet is the centre of enlargement.

Centre of enlargement is $(3, -8)$.

> **Study tip**
>
> Once you have identified the centre of enlargement, choose a vertex.
>
> Then check that:
>
> the distance of the vertex on the image from the centre of enlargement = (scale factor) × distance of corresponding vertex on the object from the centre of enlargement.

## Practise... 6.2 Centres of enlargement

**1**   Copy the shape onto squared paper.

Enlarge the shape by a scale factor of 2.
Use the cross as the centre of enlargement.

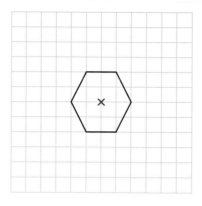

**2**   In this diagram, *A* has been enlarged to give *B*.

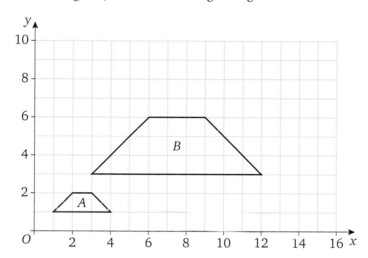

Find the scale factor and centre of enlargement.

**3**   **a**   **i**   Draw a pair of axes with *x*-values from 0 to 16 and *y*-values from 0 to 8.

  **ii**   Plot and label rectangle *E* with vertices at (6, 2), (6, 4), (10, 4) and (10, 2).

**b**   Draw the image of rectangle *E* after an enlargement of scale factor 1.5 with centre (0, 0).
Label the image *F*.

**c**   What are the coordinates of the vertices of *F*?

**4**   Copy each shape onto squared paper.

Enlarge **a** by a scale factor of $\frac{1}{2}$.

Enlarge **b** by a scale factor of $\frac{1}{4}$.

**a**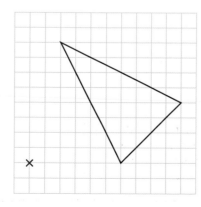

**b**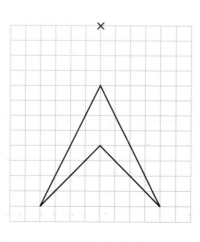

**5**  **a**  **i**  Draw a pair of axes with *x*-values from −2 to 12 and *y*-values from −4 to 6.

  **ii**  Plot and label parallelogram *ABCD* with vertices at (6, −1), (10, 1) and (10, 4) and (6, 2).

 **b**  Draw the image of *ABCD* after an enlargement of scale factor $\frac{1}{2}$ with centre (−2, −4).
Label the image *A′B′C′D′*.

 **c**  What are the coordinates of the vertices of the image?

 **d**  **i**  Measure the diagonals *AC* and *A′C′*.

  **ii**  What do you notice about these lengths?

 **e**  Repeat the process with the diagonals *BD* and *B′D′*.

 **f**  Relate your findings to the scale factor.

**6**  A jewellery designer was asked to make a pendant which perfectly matched a pair of earrings. In order for them to look similar, he decided that the pendant should be an enlargement of the earrings. He worked out that a scale factor of 3 would be most suitable.

Here is the plan of one of the earrings.
Each square represents a square
0.5 cm by 0.5 cm.

Copy this diagram onto squared paper and use this to draw the plan for the pendant.

The centre of enlargement is marked by a cross on the diagram.

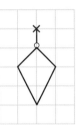

**7**  **a**  On an A4 piece of plain paper, construct an equilateral triangle of side 2 cm in the centre of the paper. Then construct another five similar triangles to form a regular hexagon. Label this *ABCDEF*.

 **b**  Using the cross as the centre of enlargement and scale factor 1.5, draw the image of *ABCDEF*.
Label your image $A^1B^1C^1D^1E^1F^1$.

 **c**  Enlarge $A^1B^1C^1D^1E^1F^1$ with the same centre and scale factor to give $A^2B^2C^2D^2E^2F^2$.

 **d**  Repeat this process, always enlarging the latest shape you have drawn to get the next one.
Your diagram will then consist of several hexagons, each one outside the previous one.

 **e**  What do you notice about these hexagons?
Comment on their sizes. Give reasons for your answer.

> **Hint**
> When the second enlargement is formed, from $A^1B^1C^1D^1E^1F^1$ to $A^2B^2C^2D^2E^2F^2$, you were not enlarging the original. What would the scale factor of enlargement be for *ABCDEF* to $A^2B^2C^2D^2E^2F^2$?

 **f**  Find the scale factors for each enlargement when *ABCDEF* is always used as the object.

## Learn... 6.3 Negative scale factors

If the scale factor of an enlargement is negative, the object and the image are on opposite sides of the centre of enlargement.

*Example:* Copy the diagram onto squared paper. Enlarge the shape by a scale factor of −2, using the point marked with a cross as the centre of enlargement.

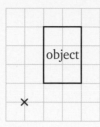

*Solution:* Label the object *ABCD*.

Join *A* to *X* and extend the line through *X* to the other side of the centre of enlargement.

Measure the distance *XA* and position *A′* on this extended line such that *XA′* = 2 × *XA*

Repeat this for all other vertices *B*, *C* and *D*.

Join *A′*, *B′*, *C′* and *D′* to form the image rectangle.

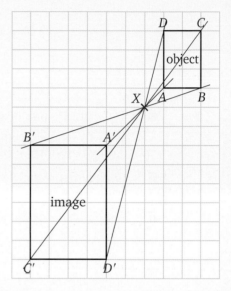

> **Hint**
>
> Do not forget that it can sometimes be helpful to use the patterns on the grid. To get from *X* to *A*, you move 1 to the right and 1 up. So to get from *X* to *A′* you move 2 to the left and 2 down.

*Example:* Draw and label the *x*-axis from −8 to 12 and the *y*-axis from −6 to 10.

Draw the triangle *ABC* with coordinates (1, 2), (1, −4) and (10, −4).

Enlarge triangle *ABC* with centre (−2, 5) and scale factor $-\frac{1}{3}$

*Solution:* Draw the triangle and then join *A* to *X*, the centre of enlargement.

Extend this line through the point of enlargement, to form a line on the opposite side to *A*.

The scale factor is $-\frac{1}{3}$. The negative scale factor shows you to extend the line using the method shown in the previous example. The image point *A′* will be a third of the distance from *X* as the object point *A* was from *X*.

You could also use the patterns on the grid. *X* to *A* involves moving 3 to the right and 3 down, so *X* to *A′* will involve a journey of $\frac{1}{3}$ of this; 1 to the left and 1 up.

Repeat this process for *B* and *C*.

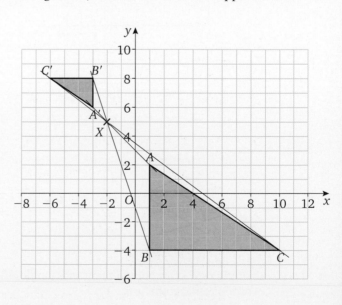

> **Study tip**
>
> An enlargement with scale factor $-\frac{1}{3}$ is equivalent to a rotation of 180° about the centre of enlargement, followed by an enlargement about the same centre, scale factor $+\frac{1}{3}$. Use this as a check.

## Practise... 6.3 Negative scale factors

**A**

**1** Copy the axes and shape shown in the diagram.

Enlarge the shape from the centre (5, 5) with scale factor −3.

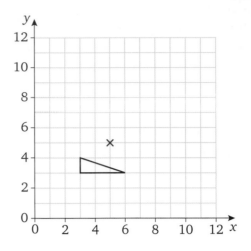

**2** **a** **i** Draw a pair of *x*- and *y*-axes from −9 to 9.

**ii** Draw the rectangle with coordinates (1, 1), (4, 1), (4, 3) and (1, 3).

**b** Enlarge the rectangle with centre (0, 2) and scale factor −2.

**c** Enlarge the original rectangle with centre (1, −2) and scale factor $-1\frac{1}{3}$

Both parts of the question can be drawn on one set of axes.

> **Hint**
>
> For part **b**, use the pattern of squares as well as measuring the distance along the line.

**3** The shape *ABCDEF* has been enlarged to make the shape *A'B'C'D'E'F'*.

Find the scale factor and centre of enlargement.

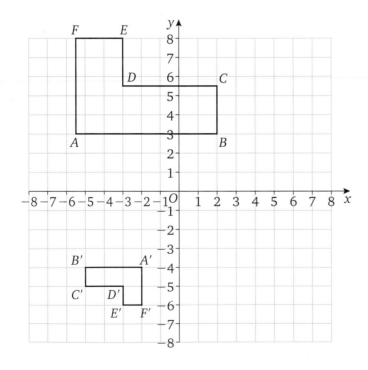

**4** Triangle *DEF* is an enlargement of triangle *ABC*, centre of enlargement *X*.

**a** If *BX* = 2*EX*, what is the scale factor of enlargement?

**b** If *FE* = 2.9 cm and *AB* = 8.2 cm, find the lengths of *DE* and *BC*.

Not drawn accurately

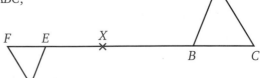

**5**    **a**    **i**    Draw a pair of $x$- and $y$-axes from $-8$ to $8$.

**ii**    Plot the trapezium $ABCD$ with these points: $A(2, 2)$, $B(5, 2)$, $C(5, 5)$, $D(2, 4)$.

**b**    Enlarge $ABCD$ with scale factor $-2$ and centre $(1, 1)$.
Label the image $A^1B^1C^1D^1$.

**c**    Enlarge $A^1B^1C^1D^1$ with scale factor $-1$ and centre $(-4, -2)$.
Label the image $A^2B^2C^2D^2$.

**d**    Translate $A^2B^2C^2D^2$ with vector $\begin{pmatrix} 9 \\ 0 \end{pmatrix}$ to form $A^3B^3C^3D^3$.

**e**    Find the transformation that takes $A^3B^3C^3D^3$ back to the original $ABCD$.

 **6**    The following diagram shows a plan for making a two-ended measuring spoon.
The centre of the enlargement is marked with a cross.

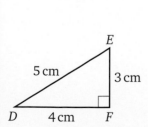

**a**    Find the scale factor of the enlargement.

**b**    Both spoons are the same depth but have the cross-sectional areas as shown.
The smaller spoon can contain 2.5 ml of liquid.
Explain why the larger spoon contains 10 ml.

**c**    If the depth of the 2.5 ml spoon was also enlarged by the same scale factor to make
the larger spoon, what would be the capacity of the larger spoon in ml?

## **Learn...**    **6.4 Similar shapes and scale factors**

The following triangles are **similar**.

Triangle $ABC$ is an enlargement of triangle $DEF$ with a scale factor of 2.

This means that **every** side on triangle $ABC$ is twice the length of the corresponding length on triangle $DEF$.

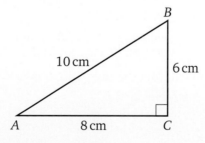

Not drawn accurately

The corresponding sides are all in the same ratio $2:1$

$$AC:DF = 8:4 = 2:1$$
$$BC:EF = 6:3 = 2:1$$
and    $$AB:DE = 10:5 = 2:1$$

Note that the perimeters are also in the same ratio.

perimeter of $ABC = 24$ cm    perimeter of $DEF = 12$ cm

perimeter of $ABC$ : perimeter of $DEF$
$$= 24:12$$
$$= 2:1$$

This is because perimeter is a 'length'. In similar shapes the perimeters will be in the same ratio as any other lengths.

Now look at the areas of the triangles:

area of triangle $ABC = \frac{1}{2} \times 8 \times 6 = 24\,\text{cm}^2$      area of triangle $DEF = \frac{1}{2} \times 4 \times 3 = 6\,\text{cm}^2$

area of triangle $ABC$ : area of triangle $DEF$

$$
\begin{aligned}
&= 24\,\text{cm}^2 : 6\,\text{cm}^2 \\
&= \quad 24 : 6 \\
&= \quad\ \ 4 : 1 \\
&= \quad\ \ 2^2 : 1^2
\end{aligned}
$$

In similar figures, the ratio of areas $=$ (ratio of length)$^2$

or scale factor of enlargement for area $=$ (scale factor of enlargement for length)$^2$

This can be extended into three dimensions.

In similar solids, the ratio of volumes $=$ (ratio of length)$^3$

or scale factor of enlargement for volume $=$ (scale factor of enlargement for length)$^3$

---

**Example:**    Rectangles *ABCD* and *EFGH* are similar.

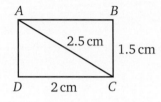 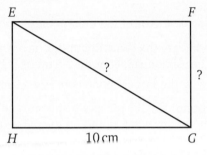

Not drawn accurately

a    Write down the ratio of $DC : HG$ in its simplest form.

b    What is the scale factor of the enlargement?

c    Find the length of *FG*.

d    Find the length of the diagonal *EG*.

**Solution:**   
a    $DC = 2\,\text{cm}$      $HG = 10\,\text{cm}$

$DC : HG = 2 : 10$

$\qquad\qquad = 1 : 5$

The ratio $1 : 5$ is not the same as $5 : 1$. Order matters.
Here the smallest side is written first so it must be $1 : 5$

b    The scale factor is taken from the ratio once it is in the form $1 : n$ or $n : 1$
Scale factor of the enlargement $= 5$

c    $BC = 1.5\,\text{cm}$
$FG = 1.5 \times 5 = 7.5\,\text{cm}$

d    $AC = 2.5\,\text{cm}$
$EG = 2.5 \times 5 = 12.5\,\text{cm}$

---

**Example:**    These cuboids are similar.

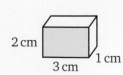 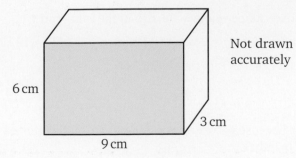

Not drawn accurately

**a**   What is the ratio of the lengths and then the widths of the facing (shaded) rectangles?

**b**   Show that the ratio of the perimeters of these rectangles is the same as the ratio of the lengths.

**c**   Find the ratio of the depths of the cuboids.

**d**   Find the ratio of areas of the two facing rectangles.

**e**   Find the ratio of the volumes of the cuboids.

*Solution:*   **a**   Length of small facing rectangle = 3 cm

Length of large facing rectangle = 9 cm

So ratio of lengths = 3 cm : 9 cm

$$= \quad 1 : 3$$

As long as the units, for example, cm, are the same on both sides of a ratio, they can be left out of the following working.

Width of small facing rectangle = 2 cm

Width of large facing rectangle = 6 cm

So ratio of widths = 2 : 6

$$= 1 : 3$$

When a ratio is in the form $1 : n$ or $n : 1$, the scale factor of enlargement $n$ can be read off easily.

Here the scale factor is 3.

**b**   Perimeter of small rectangle = 2(3 + 2) cm = 10 cm

Perimeter of large rectangle = 2(9 + 6) cm = 30 cm

So ratio of perimeters = 10 : 30

$$= \quad 1 : 3 \text{ as required}$$

**c**   Depth of small cuboid = 1 cm

Depth of large cuboid = 3 cm

So ratio of depths        = 1 : 3

These depths are also in the same ratio, which confirms that the cuboids are similar.

**d**   Area of small rectangle = 2 × 3 = 6 cm²

Area of large rectangle = 9 × 6 = 54 cm²

So ratio of areas = 6 : 54

$$= 1 : 9$$

Note that    $1 : 9 = 1^2 : 3^2$

In similar figures, the ratio of areas = (ratio of lengths)²

or scale factor of enlargement for area = (scale factor of enlargement for length)²

**e**   Volume of small cuboid = 3 × 2 × 1 = 6 cm³

Volume of large cuboid = 9 × 6 × 3 = 162 cm³

So ratio of volumes = 6 : 162

$$= 1 : 27$$

Note that      $1 : 27 = 1^3 : 3^3$

In similar figures, the ratio of volumes = (ratio of lengths)³

or scale factor of enlargement for volume = (scale factor of enlargement for length)³

**Example:** Two similar glasses have heights of 15 cm and 5 cm. When full, the larger glass contains 540 ml of liquid.

How much liquid does the smaller glass contain when full?

**Solution:** Height of large glass = 15 cm

Height of small glass = 5 cm

The heights are both lengths.

Ratio of lengths = 15 : 5

$\qquad\qquad\qquad = 3 : 1$

The capacity of something is a measure of volume.

Because ratio of volumes = (ratio of lengths)³

$\qquad$ then ratio of capacities = (ratio of lengths)³

$$= 3^3 : 1^3$$

$$= 27 : 1$$

This means that:

the capacity of the larger glass is 27 times the capacity of the smaller glass

or

the capacity of the smaller glass is $\frac{1}{27}$ of the capacity of the larger glass.

Capacity of large glass = 540 ml

Capacity of small glass = $\frac{1}{27}$ × 540 ml

$$= 20 \, ml$$

**Study tip**

Always re-read the question again at the end. Were you asked to find the smaller or larger value of something? Did your answer come out smaller or larger? Should you have multiplied or divided?

**Practise... 6.4 Similar shapes and scale factors** ⓚ  D C B A A*

**1** Triangles *ABC* and *DEF* are similar.

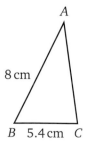
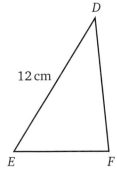

8 cm

*A*

*B* 5.4 cm *C*

12 cm

*D*

*E*        *F*

Not drawn accurately

**a** Work out the ratio of the corresponding lengths *AB* and *DE*.

**b** Simplify the ratio into the form 1 : *n*

**c** Find the length of the side *EF*.

**2**    One triangle is an enlargement of the other.

Find the missing lengths.

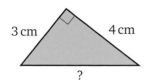
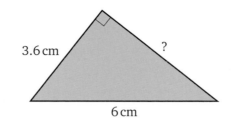

Not drawn accurately

**3**    The larger trapezium is an enlargement of the smaller one.

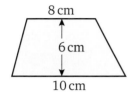
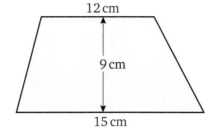

Not drawn accurately

**a**    Find the ratio of lengths.

**b**    **i**    Find the area of each trapezium.

**ii**    From these, find the ratio of areas.

**iii**    Now rewrite this ratio in the form $1 : n$

**iv**    What is the scale factor of enlargement for area?

**4**    These cylinders are similar.

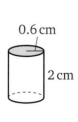
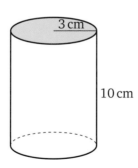

Not drawn accurately

**a**    Find the ratio of heights.

**b**    Find the ratio of radii.

**c**    **i**    Find the area of each cross-section shaded in the diagrams.

**ii**    From these, find the ratio of the areas.

**d**    Find the ratio of the volumes of the cylinders.

> **Hint**
>
> Area of circle = $\pi r^2$
> Volume of cylinder = $\pi r^2 h$

**B**

**5** In each of the following pairs of diagrams, decide whether the shapes shown are similar or not similar.

**a**

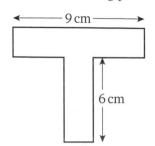 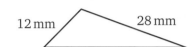

Not drawn accurately

**b**

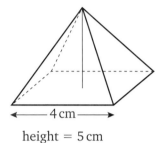

Not drawn accurately

**c**

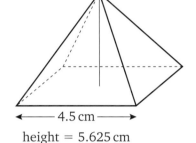

height = 5 cm    height = 5.625 cm

Not drawn accurately

**d**

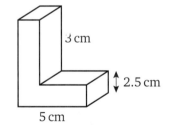

Not drawn accurately

**A**

**6** The area of a shape is 7 cm². Each side of the shape is enlarged by a scale factor of 5.

What is the area of the enlarged shape?

**7** The volume of a shape is 4 cm³. Each side of the shape is enlarged by a scale factor of 5.

What is the volume of the enlarged shape?

**8** A cuboid is enlarged. The original length was 3 cm and the enlarged length is 18 cm.

If the original volume was 24 cm³, what is the volume of the enlarged cuboid?

**9** Two similar flower vases have heights of 18 cm and 28.8 cm.
It takes 0.5 litre of water to fill the smaller vase.

How much water does it take to fill the larger one?

**10** A supermarket sells tinned fruit in two different sizes. The containers are similar.
The larger catering-size tin contains 4 kg of fruit and the smaller tin contains
500 g of fruit.

If the height of the smaller tin is 14 cm, what is the height of the larger tin?

**11** Two ice-cream cones are similar. The curved surface area of the large cone is
65 π cm² and the curved surface area of the smaller cone is 16.25 π cm².

If the volume of the small cone is 12.5 cm³, find the volume of the large cone in cm³.

⚙ **12**  **a**  Twenty-seven small steel spheres are melted down and recast into one larger one.
The original radius of each sphere was 1 cm. What is the radius of the new steel sphere?

**b**  This new steel sphere is now compared with an even larger one. These two spheres have curved surface areas of $36\pi\,\text{cm}^2$ and $144\pi\,\text{cm}^2$ respectively.
Write down in ascending order the ratio of the radii of all three different-sized spheres.

# Assess ⓚ

**1**  Copy this shape and enlarge it with scale factor 2, using the centre of enlargement shown.

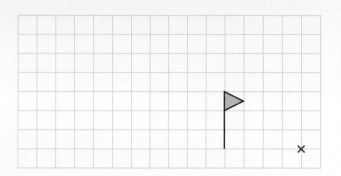

**2**  **a**  **i**  Draw a pair of axes with $x$- and $y$-values from 0 to 16.

  **ii**  Plot and label triangle $A$ with vertices $(6, 7)$, $(6, 11)$ and $(10, 11)$.

**b**  Draw the image of triangle $A$ after an enlargement of scale factor 3.
The centre of enlargement is $(7, 10)$.
Label this triangle $B$.

**c**  What are the coordinates of the vertices of $B$?

⚙ **3**  The diagram below shows two different sizes of wheels. The dimensions labelled are the diameters of the alloy and of the wheel plus the alloy. These are still measured in inches. An alloy is sometimes referred to as the hub cap.

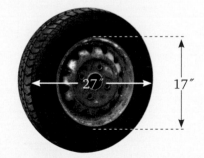

**a**  What is the ratio of the corresponding diameters of the alloys?
Give the ratio in the form $1 : n$. Give your answer to two decimal places.

**b**  What is the ratio of the corresponding external diameters? (alloy + tyre)

**c**  Is the larger wheel an enlargement of the smaller one?

**4**  The following are similar triangles.

**a**  Find the ratio of the corresponding sides in the form $1 : n$

**b**  Find the missing lengths.

**c**  Find the area of each of the triangles.

Not drawn accurately

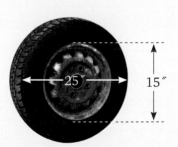

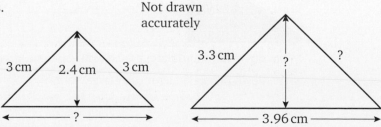

**d**  What is the ratio of areas in the form $1 : n$
Give your answer to two decimal places.

**B**

**5** **a** **i** Draw a pair of axes with $x$- and $y$-values from $-10$ to 6.

**ii** Plot and label triangle $A$ with vertices at $(-4, -2)$, $(-4, -10)$ and $(-8, -2)$.

**b** Draw the image of triangle $A$ after an enlargement of scale factor $\frac{1}{4}$ with centre $(4, 2)$.

Label the image $B$.

**c** What are the coordinates of the vertices of $B$?

**A**

**6** **a** **i** Draw a pair of axes with $x$-values from $-10$ to 5 and $y$-values from $-6$ to 5.

**ii** Plot and label triangle $A$ with vertices $(1, 2)$, $(3, 2)$ and $(3, 3)$.

**b** Draw the image of triangle $A$ after an enlargement of scale factor $-3$.
The centre of enlargement is $(0, 1)$.

Label this triangle $B$.

**c** What are the coordinates of the vertices of $B$?

**7** The area of a trapezium is $12\,\text{cm}^2$. It is enlarged by a scale factor for length of 4.

What is the area of the enlarged trapezium?

# Practice questions  *k*

1 In the diagram, shape $B$ is an enlargement of the shaded shape $A$.

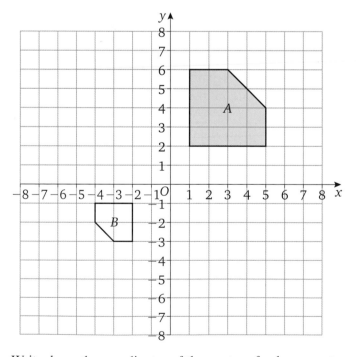

**a** Write down the coordinates of the centre of enlargement. *(1 mark)*

**b** Write down the scale factor of enlargement. *(1 mark)*

AQA 2005

**2**   Triangle *PQR* is an enlargement of triangle *ABC* with scale factor $\frac{5}{4}$

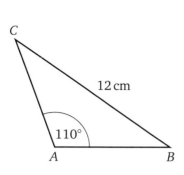 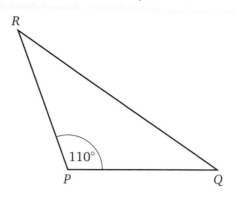

Not drawn accurately

Calculate the length of *RQ*.

*(2 marks)*

AQA 2007

**3**   The diagram shows three mathematically similar containers.

Not drawn accurately

small                medium                large

The table shows some information about the containers.

|  | Height (cm) | Area of top of container (cm²) | Volume (cm³) |
|---|---|---|---|
| **small** | 12 | *X* | 400 |
| **medium** | 24 | 500 |  |
| **large** | 36 |  | *Y* |

Calculate the missing entries *X* and *Y*.

*(4 marks)*

**Study tip**

Make sure that you show all the working on the answer page. Don't be tempted to write just the answers for *X* and *Y* in the table.

AQA 2007

## Objectives

Examiners would normally expect students who get these grades to be able to:

### B

use sine, cosine and tangent to calculate a side in a right-angled triangle

use sine, cosine and tangent to calculate an angle in a right-angled triangle

### A/A*

use trigonometry to solve problems, including those involving bearings

use trigonometry to find sides and angles in three dimensions.

## Key terms

trigonometry
hypotenuse
opposite side
adjacent side
tangent
cosine
sine
angle of elevation

## Did you know?

### The Katoomba railway

This railway line in Australia is the steepest in the world. It was originally used for mining, but still runs as a tourist attraction.

The line is 415 m long, and the end is 178 m lower than the start.

At its steepest, it makes an angle of 52° with the horizontal.

## You should already know:

✔ the sum of the angles in a triangle

✔ the sum of angles round a point

✔ symmetry and angle properties of isosceles triangles

✔ how to measure angle bearings

✔ ratio properties of similar triangles

✔ Pythagoras' theorem

✔ how to solve equations when the unknown is the denominator of a fraction.

## Learn...

# 7.1 Calculating the side of a right-angled triangle using trigonometry

**Trigonometry** is the study of the relationship between sides and angles in triangles.

All **right-angled triangles** that contain the same angle (in addition to the right angle) are similar. For example, all right-angled triangles with an angle of 30° are similar.

This means their sides are in the same ratio (or proportion) regardless of the actual size of the triangle.

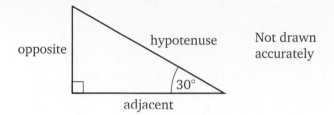

The longest side, opposite the right angle, is called the **hypotenuse**.

The side opposite the known angle is called the **opposite side**.

The side next to the known angle is called the **adjacent side**.

The length of the opposite side divided by the length of the adjacent side is called the **tangent** of the angle.

This is usually abbreviated to tan$x$, where $x$ is the size of the angle.

$$\tan x = \frac{\text{opposite}}{\text{adjacent}}$$

The length of the adjacent side divided by the length of the hypotenuse is called the **cosine** of $x$, or cos$x$.

$$\cos x = \frac{\text{adjacent}}{\text{hypotenuse}}$$

The opposite side divided by the hypotenuse is called the **sine** of $x$, or sin$x$.

$$\sin x = \frac{\text{opposite}}{\text{hypotenuse}}$$

For an angle $x$:

$$\sin x = \frac{\text{opposite}}{\text{hypotenuse}}, \quad \cos x = \frac{\text{adjacent}}{\text{hypotenuse}}, \quad \tan x = \frac{\text{opposite}}{\text{adjacent}}$$

Trigonometry questions will always involve two sides and an angle.

Identify the two sides, and then choose the ratio (sin, cos or tan) that includes those two sides.

**Example:**   Calculate the length of *BC*.

Give your answer to an appropriate degree of accuracy.

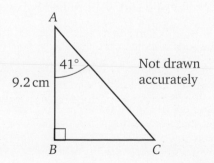

**Solution:** Copy and label the diagram with hyp, opp and adj.

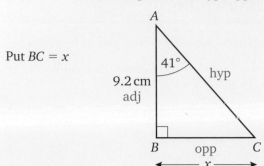

Put $BC = x$

> **Study tip**
>
> Once you know which acute angle you are using (41°), mark the opposite side to that angle 'opp'. The side opposite the right angle is 'hyp', which leaves the remaining side 'adj'.

$$\sin = \frac{\text{opp}}{\text{hyp}}, \cos = \frac{\text{adj}}{\text{hyp}}, \tan = \frac{\text{opp}}{\text{adj}}$$   Identify the known side (adjacent) and the required side (opposite) to choose sin, cos or tan. You know adj and want to find opp, so choose tan.

$\tan = \dfrac{\text{opp}}{\text{adj}}$   Start with the formula.

$\tan 41° = \dfrac{x}{9.2}$   Substitute known information.

$9.2 \times \tan 41° = x$   Multiply both sides by 9.2

$x = 7.997437988\ldots$   Choose an appropriate degree of accuracy; in the question, $AB$ was given to 2 s.f. (9.2 cm), so give the answer to the

$BC = 8.0 \text{ cm (to 2 s.f.)}$   same degree of accuracy.

---

**Example:** Calculate the length of $AB$, giving your answer to an appropriate degree of accuracy.

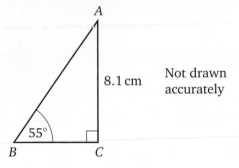

8.1 cm   Not drawn accurately

**Solution:** Copy and label the diagram.

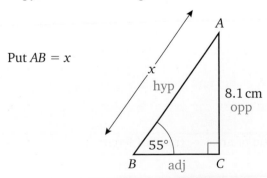

Put $AB = x$

> **Study tip**
>
> Always complete the algebraic manipulation before using your calculator.

$$\sin = \frac{\text{opp}}{\text{hyp}}, \cos = \frac{\text{adj}}{\text{hyp}}, \tan = \frac{\text{opp}}{\text{adj}}$$   You know opp and want to find hyp, so choose sin.

$\sin = \dfrac{\text{opp}}{\text{hyp}}$   Start with the formula.

$\sin 55° = \dfrac{8.1}{x}$   Substitute known information.

$x = \dfrac{8.1}{\sin 55°}$   Make $x$ the subject of the equation.
   Divide 8.1 by $\sin 55°$.

$\quad = 9.888274169\ldots$

$AB = 9.9 \text{ cm (to 2 s.f.)}$

**Practise...**

## 7.1 Calculating the side of a right-angled triangle using trigonometry

D C B A A*

C

B

The shapes in these exercises are not drawn accurately.

**1** In the diagrams below, identify the opposite side, the adjacent side and the hypotenuse.

**a**

**b**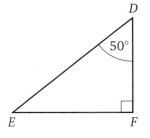

**c**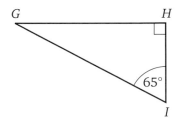

**2** Copy these diagrams and label them.

Calculate the length marked $x$, giving your answers correct to one decimal place.

**a**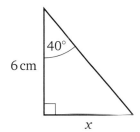

**c**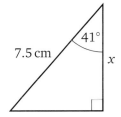

**e**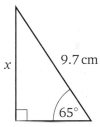

**b**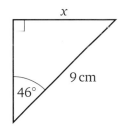

**d**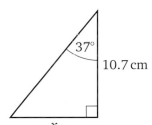

**f**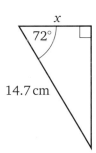

**3** Copy these diagrams and label them.

Calculate the length marked $x$, giving your answers correct to one decimal place.

**a**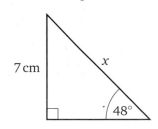

**c**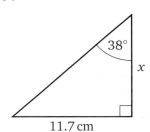

**e**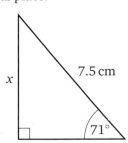

**b**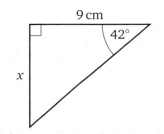

**d**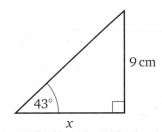

**f**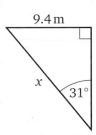

**4** *ABCDE* is a pentagon made up of three similar right-angled triangles.

*AB* = 10 cm

Calculate *AE*.

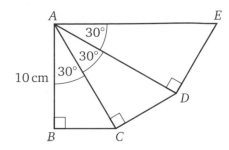

**5** A 5 m ladder leans against a vertical wall, making an angle of 73° with the horizontal ground.

How far up the wall does it reach?

**6** A shed roof has sloping sides at an angle of 30°. Each edge is 3 m long.

Calculate, *x*, the width of the shed.

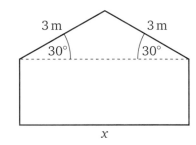

**7** An aerial runway is to be built in an adventure playground.
It needs to have a slope of 5° to the horizontal.
The lower end must be 2 m high.
The runway is 30 m long.

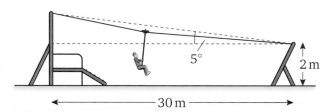

How high should the starting post be?

**8** Dave is making some trestles.
Here is his design.

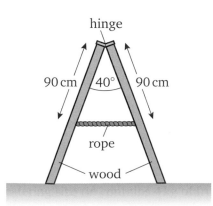

He wants the trestles to open to an angle of 40°.
The horizontal rope support needs to be fixed 90 cm away from the hinge.

How long should the rope be?

**9** Holly is working out with a punchbag.
The distance from the end of the punchbag to its support is 130 cm.
It swings so it is 20° from the vertical.

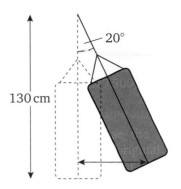

**a** How far has the bottom moved in a horizontal direction (shown in red)?

**b** How far would it move horizontally if it swings at an angle of 40°?

**c** How far would it move horizontally if it swings at an angle of 100°?

130 cm

---

**Learn...** **7.2 Calculating angles using trigonometry**

Your calculator can change the sine, cosine or tangent back to an angle.

The reverse of sin is written as $\sin^{-1}$, or inverse sin or arc sin.

On many calculators, you access it by pressing SHIFT, INV or 2ND FUNCTION before the sin key.

Using your calculator, $\sin 60° = 0.8660254038...$, and $\sin^{-1} 0.8660254038... = 60°$

Remember you can type in $\sin 60°$ to get the answer of $0.8660254038...$ and then SHIFT sin ANS to get back to 60°.

In the same way, SHIFT cos and SHIFT tan convert cosines and tangents into angles.

In the diagram, $\sin = \dfrac{\text{opp}}{\text{hyp}}$

$\sin x = \dfrac{6}{8} = 0.75$

So $x = \sin^{-1} 0.75$

SHIFT sin $0.75 = 48.59037789...°$

Or $x = 48.6°$ (1 d.p.)

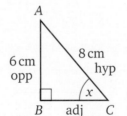

Not drawn accurately

**Study tip**

Make sure your calculator is in degree mode.

---

**Example:** *ABCD* is a rectangle.

Calculate the size of angle *BAC* in this diagram.

Not drawn accurately

A        7.5 cm        B

5.8 cm

D                        C

**Solution:** First, copy and label the diagram.

Use *x* for angle *BAC*, and mark on 'opp', 'hyp' and 'adj'.

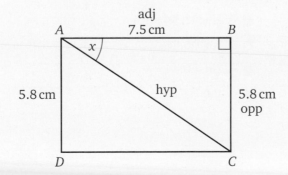

$$\sin = \frac{\text{opp}}{\text{hyp}}, \cos = \frac{\text{adj}}{\text{hyp}}, \tan = \frac{\text{opp}}{\text{adj}}$$

$$\tan x = \frac{\text{opp}}{\text{adj}}$$ The two known sides are opposite and adjacent to angle $x$, so choose tan.

$$\tan x = \frac{5.8}{7.5}$$ Substitute.

$$x = \tan^{-1}\left(\frac{5.8}{7.5}\right)$$
$$= 37.71597635...°$$ Calculate $\tan^{-1}$.

Angle $BAC = 37.7°$ (1 d.p.)

**Example:** Bayston is 8 km due west of Greenmore. Greenmore is 7 km due north of Sliddow.

Calculate the bearing of Bayston from Sliddow.

**Solution:** First, draw a sketch. Bearings are measured clockwise from north.

Identify the required bearing (marked in red).

Identify angle $x$.

Label the sides as hypotenuse, opposite and adjacent.

$$\sin = \frac{\text{opp}}{\text{hyp}}, \cos = \frac{\text{adj}}{\text{hyp}}, \tan = \frac{\text{opp}}{\text{adj}}$$ You know the opposite and adjacent, so choose tangent.

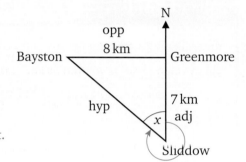

To calculate angle $x$,

$$\tan x = \frac{\text{opp}}{\text{adj}}$$

$$\tan x = \frac{8}{7}$$

$$x = \tan^{-1}\left(\frac{8}{7}\right)$$

$$x = 48.81407483...°$$

$$x = 48.8°$$ (1 d.p.)

So the bearing is $360° - 48.8° = 311.2°$

## 7.2 Calculating angles using trigonometry

**Practise...**

**B**

**1** Write the angles given below to one decimal place.

a $\sin^{-1}0.65$     e $\cos^{-1}0.59$

b $\cos^{-1}0.7$     f $\sin^{-1}0.56$

c $\tan^{-1}0.86$     g $\sin^{-1}0.44$

d $\cos^{-1}0.234$     h $\tan^{-1}1.2$

**2** Calculate the angles marked with letters in the diagrams below.

**a**
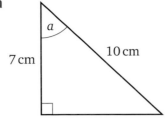
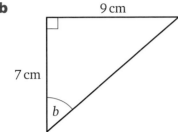
7 cm, 10 cm, angle a

**b**
9 cm, 7 cm, angle b

**c**
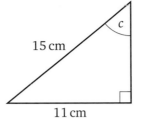
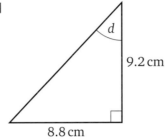
15 cm, 11 cm, angle c

**d**
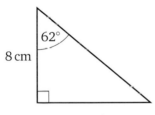
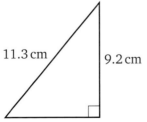
9.2 cm, 8.8 cm, angle d

**e**
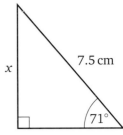
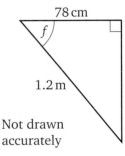
7.5 cm, 71°, x

**f**
78 cm, 1.2 m, angle f

Not drawn accurately

**Study tip**

When you calculate the size of a missing angle, always check that your answer makes sense. The smallest angle is always opposite the smallest side; checking for this can indicate you have made an error.

**3** In the triangles below, calculate all the missing sides and angles.

**a** 62°, 8 cm

**b**
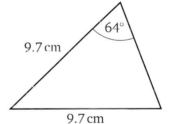
11.3 cm, 9.2 cm

**c**
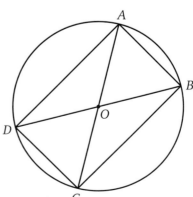
64°, 9.7 cm, 9.7 cm

Not drawn accurately

 **4** *ABCD* is a rectangle inscribed in a circle with centre *O* and radius 8 cm.

*AD* = 11 cm

Calculate angle *ABD*.

**5** A ship sails 12 km due east, then 8 km due south. It then sails straight back to the starting point.

**a** On what bearing does it sail back?

**b** How far is the total journey?

**6** **a** A train is climbing a hill with a gradient of 1 in 14.

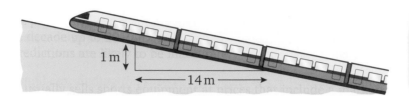

Calculate the angle of elevation.

**b** When the gradient is measured, it is easier to measure the distance along the surface rather than the horizontal distance.
The real measurements taken are as shown.

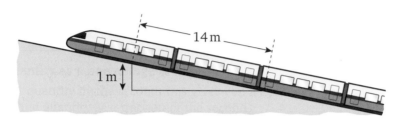

Calculate the angle of elevation now.

**7** What angle has a cosine equal to sin 30°?

What angle has a cosine equal to sin 40°?

Write a general rule for this relationship.

 **Learn...** **7.3 Trigonometry in three dimensions**

Look at the cuboid *ABCDEFGH*.

It contains many right angles, for example angles *ADE*, *ADC* and *CDE*.

It is not always easy to tell whether angles are right angles.

For example, look at angles *ADH* and *FDH*.

Imagine turning the cuboid so that the face *DCHE* is at the bottom.

*DH* is then horizontal. *AD* is vertical. So *ADH* must be a right angle.

It is not possible to arrange the cuboid so that *DH* is horizontal and *DF* is vertical, so *FDH* cannot be a right angle.

Identifying right-angled triangles enables you to apply trigonometry and Pythagoras' theorem to three-dimensional problems.

**The angle between a line and a plane**

Look at the diagonal *AH*.

When questions ask about the angle between *AH* and the base *EFGH* it means the angle *AHF*.

Then the shortest distance from *A* to the base is *AF*.

*AHF* is a right-angled triangle, so trigonometry can be used.

Sometimes, it is necessary to use Pythagoras' theorem first.
For example, if you knew the lengths of *EH* and *EF*, you could use Pythagoras' theorem to calculate *FH*.

**Study tip**

Always draw out the right-angled triangle you are going to use, in this case triangle *AFH*.

**Example:**   A pyramid has a square base with sides of 8 cm and a perpendicular height of 6 cm.

Calculate the angle between *DE* and the base.

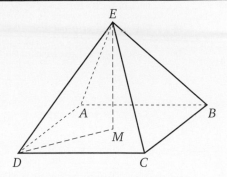

**Solution:**   The view of the base from above looks like this.

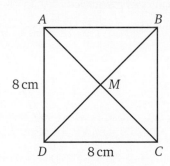

It is very important to draw two-dimensional diagrams to show the right-angled triangles correctly.

Using Pythagoras' theorem,

$DC^2 + BC^2 = DB^2$

$8^2 + 8^2 = DB^2$

$64 + 64 = DB^2$

$DB^2 = 128$

$DB = \sqrt{128} = 8\sqrt{2}$ cm $(= 11.3137...)$   Using surds avoids any errors due to rounding.

$DM = \frac{1}{2}DB = 4\sqrt{2}$ cm $(= 5.6568...)$

Now consider triangle *EDM*.

$\tan x = \dfrac{\text{opp}}{\text{adj}}$

$\tan x = \dfrac{6}{4\sqrt{2}}$

$x = \tan^{-1}\left(\dfrac{6}{4\sqrt{2}}\right)$

$= 46.6861...°$

Angle *EDM* = 46.7° (1 d.p.)

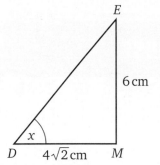

**Practise...**   **7.3 Trigonometry in three dimensions**

**1**   A 4 m flagpole leans at an angle of 84° with the ground.

Calculate the distance between the top of the flagpole and the ground.

**B**

**2**   A cone has a radius of 7 cm and a perpendicular height of 12 cm.

Calculate the angle *ABC*.

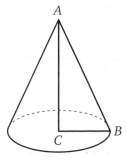

**A\***

**3**  A cuboid is 8 cm long, 6 cm wide and 5 cm high.

**a**  Calculate angle *DEF*.

**b**  Calculate angle *BFH*.

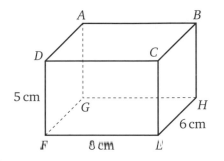

Not drawn accurately

**⚠ 4**  Four 3-metre bamboo canes are used to make a support for growing some runner beans.

One end of each cane is stuck in the ground at the corners of a square of side 1 m. The top ends are tied together.

**a**  Calculate the angle *BAC*.

**b**  Calculate the angle *BAD*.

> **Hint**
>
> Drawing in the line of symmetry in an isosceles triangle makes two congruent right-angled triangles.

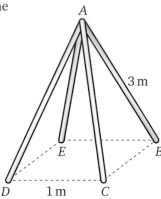

**⚙ 5**  A shed has a base that measures 6 m by 2 m.
The roof slopes so that the front edge is 2 m tall, and the slope is 30°.

Calculate the height of the back of the shed.

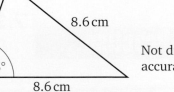

# Assess ⓚ

**B**

**1**  Calculate the sides marked *x* in the diagrams below.

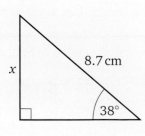

8.7 cm

*x*

38°

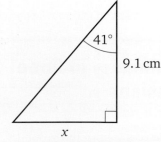

41°

9.1 cm

*x*

*x*

65°

8.6 cm

8.6 cm

Not drawn accurately

**2**  Calculate the angles marked *x* below.

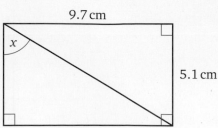

9.7 cm

*x*

5.1 cm

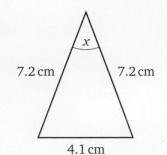

*x*

7.2 cm    7.2 cm

4.1 cm

Not drawn accurately

**A**

**3**   Ware is 8.3 km from Wye on a
bearing of 072°.
Hoo is due south of Ware, and
on a bearing of 162° from Wye.

Calculate the distance from
Wye to Hoo.

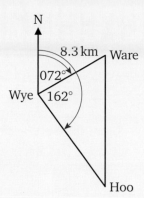

Not drawn
accurately

**4**   A pyramid has a square base *BCDE* with sides of 8.2 cm.
*X* is the centre of the base.
The vertical height, *AX*, is 11.6 cm.

Calculate the angle *ACE*.

Calculate the angle *BAD*.

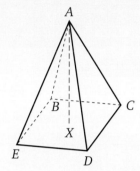

# Practice questions 🄚

**1**   The diagram shows two right-angled triangles.
*AD* − 15 cm.
*CD* = 6 cm.

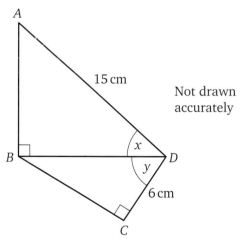

Not drawn
accurately

Given that $\cos x° = \frac{2}{3}$, work out the value of $\sin y°$.                    *(5 marks)*

AQA 2003

**2**   A prism *ABCDEF* with a right-angled triangular cross section has dimensions as shown.

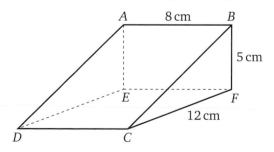

Not drawn
accurately

**a**   Calculate the length *BD*.                                                      *(3 marks)*

**b**   Hence, or otherwise, calculate the angle *BDF*.                          *(2 marks)*

AQA 2008

# 8 Percentages and ratios

## Objectives

Examiners would normally expect students who get these grades to be able to:

### D

increase or decrease by a given percentage

express one quantity as a percentage of another

use ratio notation, including reduction to its simplest form and its links to fraction notation

solve simple ratio and proportion problems, such as finding and simplifying a ratio

### C

work out a percentage increase or decrease

solve more complex ratio and proportion problems

solve ratio and proportion problems using the unitary method

### B

use a multiplier raised to a power to solve problems involving repeated percentage changes and exponential growth

### A

work out values and draw graphs in situations involving exponential growth. For example, draw a graph to show the way in which a population of bacteria grows

solve direct and indirect proportion problems

interpret graphs showing direct and indirect proportion problems.

## Key terms

percentage
depreciation
exponential growth
Value Added Tax (VAT)
discount

ratio
unitary ratio
unitary method
direct proportion
indirect proportion

---

### *Did you know?*

## The origin of mathematical symbols

| 15th century | 17th century | Now |
|---|---|---|
| p̴ō | o/o | % |

Did you know that the symbol % for per cent and : for ratio were not introduced until relatively recently. The % sign probably developed from the first symbol shown above. This appeared in an Italian manuscript dating from 1425. In Italian 'each hundred' is 'per cento', in French it is 'pour cent' and in English 'per cent'.

An Englishman, William Oughtred, was the first to use a colon : for ratios in his book, *Canones Sinuum,* in 1657.

Find out when other symbols such as $+$, $-$, $\times$, $\div$ and $=$ were introduced. What did people use before then?

### You should already know:

✔ about place values in decimals and how to put decimals in order of size

✔ how to simplify fractions with and without a calculator

✔ how to write a fraction as a decimal and vice versa

✔ how to change a percentage to a fraction or decimal and vice versa.

## Learn... 8.1 Increasing or decreasing by a percentage

There are a variety of different ways to increase or decrease a quantity by a **percentage** but the most efficient way on a calculator is to use a multiplier. For example, suppose a new car costs £17 500, but its value **depreciates** (goes down) by 20% in the first year after it is bought.

The value of the car after one year will be £17 500 × 0.8 = £14 000

After a 20% decrease, the value is 80% of the original value, so the multiplier is 0.80 or 0.8

This is very quick to do on a calculator.
The method is summarised below.

**To increase or decrease by a given percentage:**

* work out the new percentage (add a percentage increase to 100%; subtract a percentage decrease from 100%)

* divide the new percentage by 100 to find the **multiplier**

* **multiply the original quantity by the multiplier.**

Work out the multiplier in your head if you can.

Suppose the value of the car depreciates by another 20% in the following year.

You can find the value of the car after 2 years in a single calculation:
17 500 × 0.8 × 0.8 = 17 500 × 0.8² = £11 200

> **Study tip**
>
> Multiplying multipliers together is the quickest way to combine percentage changes.

If you just want to know the overall percentage fall in the value of the car, multiply the multipliers together:

0.8 × 0.8 = 0.8² = 0.64 so after 2 years the car is worth 64% of its original value.

Its value has depreciated by 36%          because 100% − 64% = 36%

Percentage increases can also be combined. If the same percentage increase is repeated again and again, it leads to **exponential growth**. This is what happens in the following example.

---

**Example:**     A population of bacteria increases by 60% every hour.

**a**    Copy and complete this table of values.

| Time (hours)      | 0    | 1 | 2 | 3 | 4 | 5 |
|-------------------|------|---|---|---|---|---|
| Number of bacteria | 1000 |   |   |   |   |   |

**b**    Draw a graph of the number of bacteria against time.

**Solution:**    **a**    At the end of each hour, the number of bacteria will be 160% of the number at the beginning of that hour.

The multiplier = 1.60 = 1.6 for each hour

After 1 hour there will be 1000 × 1.6 = 1600 bacteria.

After 2 hours there will be 1600 × 1.6 = 2560 bacteria.

At each stage, continue the working on your calculator rather than starting again.

After 3 hours there will be 2560 × 1.6 = 4096 bacteria and so on.

The table gives the number of bacteria after each hour, with values rounded to the nearest whole number where necessary.

| Time (hours)      | 0    | 1    | 2    | 3    | 4    | 5      |
|-------------------|------|------|------|------|------|--------|
| Number of bacteria | 1000 | 1600 | 2560 | 4096 | 6554 | 10 486 |

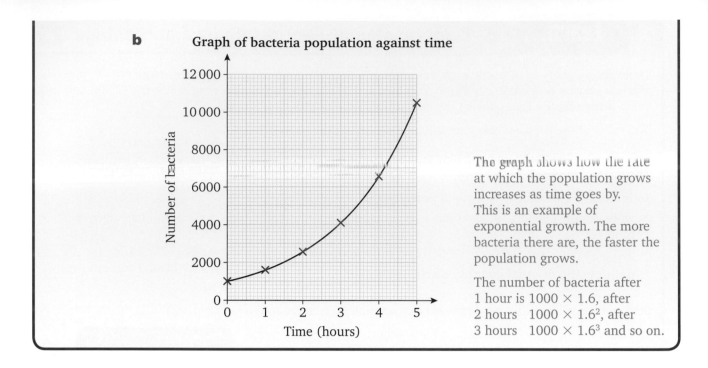

**b** Graph of bacteria population against time

The graph shows how the rate at which the population grows increases as time goes by. This is an example of exponential growth. The more bacteria there are, the faster the population grows.

The number of bacteria after 1 hour is $1000 \times 1.6$, after 2 hours $1000 \times 1.6^2$, after 3 hours $1000 \times 1.6^3$ and so on.

## **Practise...** 8.1 Increasing or decreasing by a percentage

**D C B A A***

**D**

**1** Use multipliers to:

**a** increase 250 m by 40%

**b** increase 80 kg by 70%

**c** decrease 24 miles by 5%

**d** decrease 37.5 litres by 12%

**e** increase £54.60 by 43%

**f** decrease £180 by 62.5%

Check your answers using a different method.

> **Hint**
>
> One way to check answers is to find the increase (or decrease) first, then add it to (or subtract it from) the original amount.

**2** The prices of each of these items are given **excluding Value Added Tax (VAT)**.

Find the cost of each item **including** VAT at the rate given.

**a**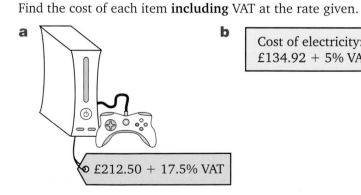

£212.50 + 17.5% VAT

**b** Cost of electricity: £134.92 + 5% VAT

**c**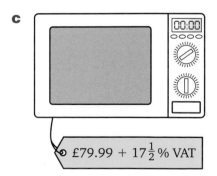

£79.99 + $17\frac{1}{2}$% VAT

**C**

**3** Zoe invests £2000 in shares. In the first year the shares go up in value by 9% In the second year they go down in value by 4%

How much is Zoe's investment worth after 2 years?

**4** The rate at which bacteria increase depends on the conditions in the laboratory or in the outside world. Three populations of bacteria, A, B and C, all start with 1000 bacteria but are then kept in different conditions.

**a** Population A doubles every hour.

   Find the number of bacteria in population A after two hours.

**b** Population B increases by 50% each hour.

   Find the number of bacteria in population B after two hours.

**c** Population C increases by 25% every hour.

   **i** Complete a table to show the number of bacteria in population C after 0, 1, 2, 3, 4, 5 and 6 hours.

   **ii** Draw a graph of the number of bacteria in population C against time.

   **iii** Describe the way in which this population grows.

**5** There are estimated to be 5000 trout in a lake. This number is expected to decrease by 8% per year.

*The way in which the number of trout decreases is called exponential decay. The next question gives another example of this.*

**a** How many trout are expected to be in the lake after:

   **i** 2 years  **ii** 5 years  **iii** 10 years  **iv** 20 years?

**b** Use your answers to part **a** to help you sketch a graph of the number of trout against time.

**6** A car worth £16 000 loses one quarter of its value every year.

**a** How much will the car be worth after 4 years?

**b** Sketch a graph of the value of the car against time.

**7** A young manager has a job with a starting salary of £19 000 increasing by 2.4% per year.

**a** What is her salary after:  **i** one year  **ii** two years  **iii** ten years?

**b** Your answer to part **a iii** may not be very realistic. Why?

**8** The radioactive substance bismuth-210 decays at a rate of 12.9% every day. There is 1 kilogram of bismuth-210.

**a** How much bismuth-210 will there be after two weeks?

**b** How many more days will it take for the bismuth-210 to decay to less than one-tenth of its original mass?

**9** **a** The organisers of a sponsored swim give 40% of all the money raised to a children's charity.
   They give 25% of the remaining money to an animal sanctuary and the rest to a local hospice.

   What percentage of all the money raised is given to the local hospice?

**b** The organisers aim to increase the amount raised by 20% each year.
   The treasurer says that it will take 5 years to double the amount raised.

   Do you agree? Explain your answer.

**10** Scientists estimate that the area of the Arctic polar ice cap varies during the course of a year from about 7 million $km^2$ to about 15 million $km^2$. They also say that the ice cap is melting at a rate of 10% per decade.

Assuming that this is true, predict the way in which the area of the ice cap will vary over the course of a year at the end of this century.

**11**   Between 2000 and 2010 the world's population increased from 6.1 billion to 6.9 billion.

Use this information to make predictions about how the world's population may grow in each decade up to 2050. Describe any assumptions you make and any reasons why your predictions are likely to be inaccurate.

**12**   A shop usually sells sports equipment at prices that include a markup of 40% for profit. The manager decides to have a sale, but still wants to make at least 5% profit on the equipment sold.

What is the maximum percentage by which the manager can reduce the usual prices of the equipment in the sale and still make 5% profit?

## Learn... 8.2 Writing one quantity as a percentage of another

**To write one quantity as a percentage of another:**

- divide the first quantity by the second; this gives you a decimal (or write the first quantity as a fraction of the second)
- then multiply by 100% to change the decimal or fraction to a percentage.

**To write an increase or decrease as a percentage:**

- find the difference between the old quantity and the new quantity; this gives the increase or decrease
- divide the increase (or decrease) by the **original** amount or write the increase (or decrease) as a fraction of the **original** amount
- then multiply by 100 to change the decimal or fraction to a percentage.

Sometimes you may need to write one part as a percentage of the whole amount (as in the first example below).

The quantities must always be in the **same units**.

You can also use this method to find a percentage profit or loss.

---

**Example:**   Last season a school's football team won 18 matches, drew 4 matches and lost 10 matches.

   **a**   What percentage of the matches were won?     **c**   What percentage were lost?

   **b**   What percentage were drawn?

**Solution:**   You must write each number as a percentage of the total number of matches.

The total number of matches = 18 + 4 + 10 = 32

or using the fraction key:

**a**   percentage of games won   $= \dfrac{18}{32} \times 100\% = 18 \div 32 \times 100\% = 56.25\%$    % won $= \dfrac{18}{32} \times 100\% = 56\frac{1}{4}\%$

**b**   percentage of games drawn   $= \dfrac{4}{32} \times 100\% = 4 \div 32 \times 100\% = 12.5\%$    % drawn $= \dfrac{4}{32} \times 100\% = 12\frac{1}{2}\%$

**c**   percentage of games lost   $= \dfrac{10}{32} \times 100\% = 10 \div 32 \times 100\% = 31.25\%$    % lost $= \dfrac{10}{32} \times 100\% = 31\frac{1}{4}\%$

Add the percentages to check: 56.25% + 12.5% + 31.25% = 100% ✓

---

**Example:**   Jack's pay rate has gone up by 45 pence to £8.55 per hour. Find the percentage increase.

To work in pence use £8.55 = 855 pence

**Solution:**   The increase in Jack's hourly pay rate = 45 pence

His **original** hourly pay rate was 855 − 45 = 810 pence

% increase $= \dfrac{45}{810} \times 100\% = 45 \div 810 \times 100\% = 5.555...\%$   or using the fraction key

The % increase in Jack's hourly pay rate = 5.6% (to 1 d.p.)    $\dfrac{45}{810} \times 100\% = 5\frac{5}{9}$

You get the same answer if you work in pounds:
% increase = 0.45 ÷ 8.10 × 100% = 5.6% (to 1 d.p.)

## 8.2 Writing one quantity as a percentage of another

**Practise...**

When answers are not exact, round them to one decimal place.

**1** A school's athletic team is made up of 16 girls and 19 boys.

What percentage of the team are:

**a** girls **b** boys?

**2** The table shows the amount of waste recycled by a local authority last year.

What percentage of the waste was glass?

| Type of waste | Amount (tonnes) |
|---|---|
| Paper & cardboard | 12 400 |
| Glass | 4100 |
| Metal (including cans) | 3500 |
| Green waste | 8200 |

**3** A garden centre buys plants for 56 pence each. It sells them for 99 pence each.

Work out the percentage profit.

> **Hint**
> The percentage profit is the percentage increase in price.

**4** Sharon buys a motor bike for £3400. She sells it a year later for £2900.

Work out her percentage loss.

> **Hint**
> The percentage loss is the percentage decrease in price.

**5** A furniture shop reduces its prices in a sale. Dan buys a table and four chairs.

Work out the percentage reduction in the total price.

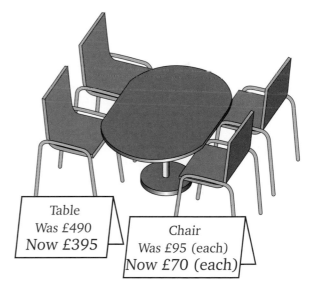

Table
Was £490
Now £395

Chair
Was £95 (each)
Now £70 (each)

**6** The cost of Greg's car insurance has gone up by £60 to £480.
Greg works out 60 ÷ 480 × 100.
He says the cost has increased by 12.5%

**a** What mistake has he made?

**b** What is the actual percentage increase in the cost of the insurance?

**7** Sara gets a 30% reduction on her car insurance because she has not made previous claims.
She gets a further 10% **discount** on the reduced price by agreeing to pay the first £100 of any claim.
Sara says the total reduction is 40%

Do you agree? Explain your answer.

**8** A manufacturer makes a rectangular rug that is 160 cm long and 120 cm wide.
The manufacturer decides to increase both dimensions of the rug by 25%

  **a** Find the percentage increase in:
    **i**    the perimeter of the rug      **ii**    the area of the rug.

  **b** Would the percentage increase in the perimeter and area have been the same if the rug was square?
    Explain your answer.

 **9** A manufacturer who sells muesli in 800 g bags wants to increase his profits.
One option is to increase the price of each bag by 5%
Another option is to keep the price the same but reduce the contents of each bag to 750 g.

Which option do you think would increase the profits more? Explain your answer.

 **10** Paul takes a maths test and a science test in December.
He takes another test in each subject the following June.
The table shows his scores.
Paul says 'I improved most in science.'
His teacher says 'Actually you improved most in maths.'
How did his teacher decide? How did Paul decide?
You must show your working to justify your answer.

| | December | June |
|---|---|---|
| Maths | 46% | 62% |
| Science | 53% | 71% |

## Learn...   8.3 Using ratios and proportion

**Ratios** are a good way of comparing quantities. To do this, the quantities must be in the same units.

Two (or more) ratios that simplify to the same ratio are called equivalent ratios. For example, $8:12$ and $100:150$ are equivalent because they both simplify to $2:3$.

To simplify a ratio, divide each part by the same number.

> £3 = 300 pence
> When the amounts are in the **same units**, you can omit the units.

For example, the ratio of £3 to 40 pence $= 300:40 = 30:4 = 15:2$
      Each number is divided by 10, then 2

> You can use the fraction key on your calculator to simplify ratios.

This is the **simplest form** of this ratio. It uses the smallest possible whole numbers.

Sometimes ratios are divided further until one side is 1. This gives the $1:n$ (or the $n:1$) form. These are called **unitary ratios**.

Dividing $15:2$ by 2 gives the ratio $7\frac{1}{2}:1$ or $7.5:1$    Dividing the original ratio $300:40$ by 40 also gives this.

The scale of maps and models are often given as unitary ratios.

The **unitary method** is based on working out what happens with **one** unit of something.
It can be used to solve a variety of different problems involving ratio and proportion.

There are some links between ratios and fractions.

For example, suppose a brother and sister share an inheritance in the ratio $3:4$

* This means that for every £3 the brother gets, the sister gets £4.
* The brother's share is $\frac{3}{4}$ of the sister's share. The sister's share is $\frac{4}{3}$ or $1\frac{1}{3}$ times the brother's share.
* The brother gets $\frac{3}{7}$ of the whole inheritance and the sister gets the other $\frac{4}{7}$

In the **multiplier method** you multiply the quantity by the fraction representing the ratio.

*Example:*    A model of a car is made using a scale of $1:50$

    **a** The model car is 9 centimetres long.
      How long is the real car in metres?

    **b** The real car is 2 metres wide.
      How wide is the model car in centimetres?

**Solution:**  **a**   The ratio 1 : 50 means that 1 cm on the model car represents 50 cm on the real car.

To find the length of the real car, multiply the length of the model car by 50.

Length of the real car = 9 cm × 50 = 450 cm

1 metre = 100 centimetres

Length of the real car in metres = 450 ÷ 100 = 4.5 m

You can change the units before or after using the scale.

**b**   The width of the real car = 2 m = 200 cm

To find the width of the model car, divide the width of the real car by 50.

Width of model = 200 ÷ 50 = 4 cm

---

**Example:**   Liam earns £97.20 for working 15 hours in a supermarket.

How much does he earn for 24 hours at ← the same rate of pay?

The amount Liam earns is **proportional** to the time he works. (If he works twice as long, he gets paid twice as much. If he works 3 times as long, he gets paid 3 times as much... and so on.)

**Solution:**   For 15 hours Liam earns £97.20.

For 1 hour he earns £97.20 ÷ 15 = £6.48.          Divide the pay for 15 hours by 15.

For 24 hours he earns £6.48 × 24 = £155.52.      Multiply the pay for 1 hour by 24.

You can do this all in one calculation:

£97.20 ÷ 15 × 24 = £155.52

find the pay     then the pay
for 1 hour       for 24 hours

Always check that your answer looks reasonable.

Here the pay for 24 hours is more than that for 15 hours.

**Multiplier method**

£97.20 × $\frac{24}{15}$ = £155.52

Multiplying by $\frac{24}{15}$ is the same as dividing by 15 and multiplying by 24.

---

**Example:**  **a**   Which jar of coffee gives the best value for money?

**b**   Give a reason why you might decide to buy one of the other jars.

**Solution:**   You can use the **unitary method** to solve 'best buy' problems.

**a**   Find the cost of **1 gram** in each jar. Working in pence gives easier numbers to compare.

Small jar:   Cost of 50 g  = 156 pence
             Cost of 1 g   = 156p ÷ 50
                           = 3.12 pence

Medium jar: Cost of 100 g = 229 pence
             Cost of 1 g   = 229p ÷ 100
                           = 2.29 pence

Large jar:   Cost of 200 g = 445 pence
             Cost of 1 g   = 445p ÷ 200
                           = 2.225 pence

There are sometimes other methods you could use. In this problem you could compare the cost of 100 g.

Small jar:    100 g (2 jars) costs 156p × 2 = 312 pence

Medium jar:  100 g costs 229 pence

Large jar:    100 g ($\frac{1}{2}$ jar) costs 445p ÷ 2 = 222.5 pence

This also shows that the large jar gives the best value for money.

The cost of 1 gram of coffee is **least** in the large jar. The large jar gives the best value for money.

**b**   You might buy a smaller jar if you only want a small amount of coffee (or if you do not have £4.45 to spend).

## Practise...    8.3 Using ratios and proportion

**D**

**1** A builder makes mortar by mixing cement and sand in the ratio 1 : 5

    **a** How many buckets of sand does he need to mix with 3 buckets of cement?

    **b** How many buckets of cement does he need to mix with 10 buckets of sand?

    **c** How many buckets of cement and sand does he need to make 30 buckets of mortar?

**2** The numbers $x$ and $y$ are in the ratio 3 : 4

    **a** If $x$ is 12, what is $y$?

    **b** If $y$ is 12, what is $x$?

    **c** If $x$ is 1, what is $y$?

    **d** If $y$ is 1, what is $x$?

    **e** If $x$ and $y$ add up to 35, what are $x$ and $y$?

**C**

**3** Ewan is paid £87.50 for 14 hours work.

    **a** How much should he be paid for 20 hours work?

    **b** He is paid £100. How many hours has he worked?

    **c** What assumption do you have to make to answer these questions?

**4**   **a** Amy and Bianca buy some euro before they go to Paris for the weekend. Amy gets 300 euro for £250.

      How many euro does Bianca get for £275?

    **b** When they return, they go back to the bank to sell the euro they have left. Amy gets £40 for 50 euro.

      How much does Bianca get for 105 euro?

**5** 5 miles is approximately equal to 8 kilometres.

    **a** The distance from Southampton to Sheffield is 195 miles. How far is this in kilometres?

    **b** The distance from Barcelona to Madrid is 628 kilometres. How far is this in miles?

**6** A box of chocolates contains milk chocolates, plain chocolates and white chocolates in the ratio 4 : 3 : 2

    **a** What fraction of the chocolates is:

      **i** milk    **ii** plain    **iii** white?

    **b** Show how you can check your answers to part **a**.

**7** The ratio of men to women on a holiday cruise is 3 : 5

What percentage of the people on the cruise are women?

 **8** The scale on a map is 1 : 50 000

    **a** The distance between two landmarks on the map is 12 centimetres. Find the actual distance in kilometres.

    **b** Kathy says that the distance between these landmarks on a map with a scale of 1 : 25 000 will be 6 cm.

      Is she correct? Explain your answer.

**9**    Road signs use ratios or percentages to give the gradients of hills.

Ratio of vertical distance : horizontal distance          Vertical distance as a % of the horizontal distance

Which of the hills described by these road signs is steeper? Explain your answer.

 **10**    When you enlarge a photograph, the ratio of the height to width must stay the same.
If the ratio is different, the objects in the photograph will look stretched or squashed.

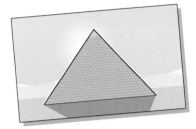    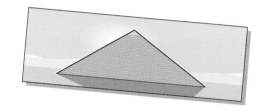

**a**    Chloe has a photo of her favourite pop group that is 15 cm wide and 10 cm high.
What is the ratio of width to height in its simplest form?

**b**    Chloe wants to put an enlarged copy of the photo in a frame on her bedroom wall.
The table gives the sizes of the frames she can buy.

Which of these frames is most suitable?
Explain your answer.

| Frame | Width (cm) | Height (cm) |
|---|---|---|
| A | 25 | 20 |
| B | 30 | 25 |
| C | 40 | 30 |
| D | 45 | 30 |
| E | 50 | 40 |

 **11**    The table on the right gives the ages of the children who are booked into a pre-school crèche. The crèche has three rooms: one for children under two years old, one for two-year olds and one for children aged three years and over.

The minimum adult : child ratios for crèches are given in the table below.

| Age (years) | Number of children | |
|---|---|---|
| | morning | afternoon |
| 0 | 2 | 1 |
| 1 | 4 | 2 |
| 2 | 6 | 9 |
| 3 | 5 | 8 |
| 4 | 2 | 1 |

| Age | Minimum adult : child ratio |
|---|---|
| Children under 2 years | 1 : 3 |
| Children aged 2 years | 1 : 4 |
| Children aged 3–7 years | 1 : 8 |

How many staff does the crèche manager need:

**a**    in the morning                    **b**    in the afternoon?

 **12**    **a**    Which size of shampoo bottle gives the best value for money?

You must show all your working and give a reason for your answer.

**b**    Why might someone buy a different size?

**Buy 1, get 1 free**          **20% extra free**          **10% off marked price**

**13** Students at a school can visit a theme park, a zoo or a safari park.
The table shows how many have chosen each place.

| Choice | Number of students |
|---|---|
| Theme park | 124 |
| Zoo | 76 |
| Safari park | 98 |

The school's policy is to have a maximum child : adult ratio of 8 : 1 on school visits.
There are 20 teachers available and some parents have offered to go on the visits if they are needed.

How many parent volunteers are needed?

## Learn... 8.4 Direct and indirect proportion

### Direct proportion

Two variables, $x$ and $y$, are in **direct proportion** if they have a constant ratio.

| $x$ | 2 | 4 | 6 |
|---|---|---|---|
| $y$ | 6 | 12 | 18 |

For the values in the table, the ratio $x:y = 1:3$ and the relationship between $x$ and $y$ is $y = 3x$

If one of the quantities is multiplied or divided by a number, then so is the other.
For example, if $x$ is doubled, so is $y$. If $x$ is divided by 3, so is $y$.

In general, $y$ **is directly proportional to** $x$ and can be written as $y \propto x$.
This means that $y = kx$ where $k$ is a constant. The graph of $y$ against $x$ is a **straight line through the origin**, (0, 0), with **gradient $k$**.

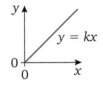

If $y = kx^2$, then the quantities $x^2$ and $y$ have a constant ratio (but $x$ and $y$ change at different rates).
This gives a different type of direct variation.

In this case $y$ is directly proportional to $x^2$.       written as $y \propto x^2$

Similarly, if $y = kx^3$, then $y$ is directly proportional to $x^3$       written as $y \propto x^3$

and if $y = k\sqrt{x}$, then $y$ is directly proportional to $\sqrt{x}$.       written as $y \propto \sqrt{x}$

$k$ is called the **constant of proportionality**.

### Indirect proportion

Two quantities, $x$ and $y$, are in **indirect proportion** if $xy = k$ where $k$ is a constant. As one quantity increases, the other decreases.

| $x$ | 2 | 4 | 6 |
|---|---|---|---|
| $y$ | 12 | 6 | 4 |

For the values in the table $xy = 24$
If $x$ is doubled, then $y$ is halved. If $x$ is divided by 3, then $y$ is multiplied by 3.

The equation $xy = k$ can be written as $y = \dfrac{k}{x}$ or $y = \dfrac{1}{x}$

So when $y$ is indirectly proportional to $x$, $y \propto \dfrac{1}{x}$

There are also other types of indirect variation.

For example, if $y = \dfrac{k}{x^2}$, then $y$ is indirectly proportional to $x^2$       written as $y \propto \dfrac{1}{x^2}$

and if $y = \dfrac{k}{\sqrt{x}}$, then $y$ is indirectly proportional to $\sqrt{x}$.       written as $y \propto \dfrac{1}{\sqrt{x}}$

*Example:*  $y \propto x^2$ and when $x = 2$, $y = 36$

     **a**  Find the value of $y$ when $x = 4$

     **b**  Find the value of $x$ when $y = 4$

**Solution:**    $y \propto x^2$    so $y = kx^2$

$x = 2$ when $y = 36$, so $36 = k \times 4$ and $k = 9$

the equation connecting $x$ and $y$ is $y = 9x^2$

**a**    When $x = 4$, $y = 9 \times 16$

$y = 144$

**b**    When $y = 4$, $4 = 9x^2$

$\frac{4}{9} = x^2$

$x = \pm\frac{2}{3}$

---

**Example:**    $y$ is directly proportional to $\sqrt{x}$.

Work out the missing value in the table.

| $x$ | 400 | |
|---|---|---|
| $y$ | 10 | 12 |

**Solution:**    $y \propto \sqrt{x}$ and so $y = k\sqrt{x}$

When $x = 400$, $y = 10$, so $10 = k \times 20$ and $k = 0.5$

The equation connecting $x$ and $y$ is $y = 0.5\sqrt{x}$

When    $y = 12$

$12 = 0.5 \times \sqrt{x}$        $\sqrt{x}$ means the

$\sqrt{x} = 24$                       positive square

$x = 24^2$                           root of $x$.

$x = 576$

---

**Example:**    Which of these formulae indicate that the quantities $x$ and $y$ are inversely proportional to each other? ($k$ is a constant.)

**a**  $x = \dfrac{k}{y}$    **b**  $xy = k$    **c**  $x = yk$    **d**  $y = \dfrac{x}{k}$    **e**  $x + y = k$    **f**  $xy = \dfrac{1}{k}$

**Solution:**    Those formulae that can be written as $xy = $ a constant are those in which $x$ and $y$ are inversely proportional to each other

**a**  Yes    **b**  Yes    **c**  No    **d**  No    **e**  No    **f**  Yes, because $\dfrac{1}{k}$ is a constant.

---

**Example:**    The length, $l$ cm, and width, $w$ cm, of a rectangle vary in such a way that its area is a constant $20$ cm$^2$.

**a**    Show that $l \propto \dfrac{1}{w}$ and write down the constant of proportionality.

**b**    Draw a graph of $l$ against $w$.

**Solution:**    **a**    The area of a rectangle is given by the product of its length and width.

In this case $lw = 20$ which can be rearranged to give $l = \dfrac{20}{w}$

So $l \propto \dfrac{1}{w}$ ($l$ is inversely proportional to $w$) and the constant of proportionality is 20.

**b**    Here is a table of some possible values for $l$ and $w$.

| $w$ | 1 | 2 | 4 | 5 | 10 | 20 |
|---|---|---|---|---|---|---|
| $l$ | 20 | 10 | 5 | 4 | 2 | 1 |

The graph of $l = \dfrac{20}{w}$ is a curve (called a rectangular hyperbola).

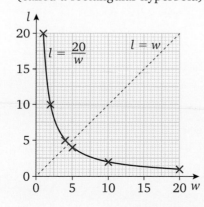

All inverse proportion graphs have this shape. The line $l = w$ is the line of symmetry.

The graph never touches the $w$- and $l$-axes but gets closer and closer to them as $w$ gets larger and as $l$ gets closer to zero.

The length and width of a rectangle cannot be negative. However, if $w$ and $l$ represent just numbers, they can be negative.

For example, in $l = \dfrac{20}{w}$, $w$ could be $-1$ and $l$ could be $-20$, or $w$ could be $-10$ and $l$ could be $-2$.

This means that there is another part of the graph of $l$ against $w$, where both $w$ and $l$ are negative. This is a 180° rotation about the origin of the curve shown above.

The complete graph of an indirectly proportional relationship is of the form shown here.

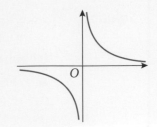

**Study tip**

Make sure that you can recognise proportional relationships and their graphs.

## Practise...    8.4 Direct and indirect proportion ⓚ

**A**

**1**    $y$ is directly proportional to the square of $x$. When $x = 5$, $y = 100$

    **a**    Work out an equation connecting $y$ and $x$.

    **b**    Draw a graph of $y$ against $x$ for $0 \leqslant x \leqslant 5$

**2**    $T$ is inversely proportional to $V$. When $V = 60$, $T = 4$

    **a**    Obtain an equation connecting $T$ and $V$.

    **b**    Work out the value of $V$ when $T = 12$

**3**    A triangle has a fixed area of $15\,\text{cm}^2$.

    **a**    Express the formula connecting the base, $b$ cm, and the perpendicular height, $h$ cm, in the form $b = \dfrac{k}{h}$, and find the value of the constant of proportionality, $k$.

    **b**    Find three possible pairs of values for $b$ and $h$.

    **c**    Sketch a graph of $b$ against $h$.

**4**    You are given that $x \propto \dfrac{1}{\sqrt{y}}$ and when $y = 2.25$, $x = 3.2$

    **a**    Find an equation connecting $x$ and $y$.

    **b**    Work out the value of $x$ when $y = 0.25$

    **c**    Work out the value of $y$ when $x = 1.2$

**5**    A glass company makes hemispherical paperweights of different sizes. The price of each paperweight is proportional to the cube of the diameter of the paperweight. The price of a paperweight of diameter 8 cm is £16.

What is the price of a smaller paperweight of diameter 6 cm?

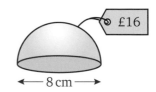

**6**   In each part, say which of the following relationships apply and find the constant of proportionality.

$$y \propto x \qquad y \propto x^2 \qquad y \propto \frac{1}{x} \qquad y \propto \frac{1}{x^2}$$

**a**   Diameter of a circle $= x$ cm, circumference of the circle $= y$ cm

**b**   Radius of a circle $= x$ cm, area of the circle $= y$ cm

**c**   Price of bananas $= x$ pence per kilogram, the weight of bananas you can buy for £2 $= y$ kg

**d**   Average speed of a car $= x$ mph, the time taken to travel 250 miles $= y$ hours

**e**   Distance between two landmarks on a map with a scale of $1 : 50\,000 = x$ cm, actual distance between the landmarks $= y$ km

**f**   Mass of each biscuit made at a factory $= x$ grams, number of biscuits the factory can make from 10 kilograms of biscuit dough $= y$

**7**   For each of these graphs, say whether it shows $y \propto x$ or $y \propto \frac{1}{x}$ or neither.

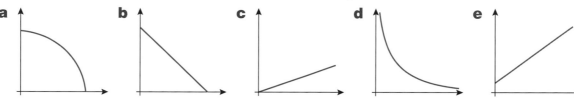

a     b     c     d     e

**8**   You can use Body Mass Index (BMI) to work out whether your weight is underweight, healthy, overweight or obese. It is worked out from your weight ($W$ kilograms) and height ($h$ metres) using

$$\text{BMI} = \frac{W}{h^2}$$

**a**   Sketch a graph of BMI against $W$ (assuming a constant height $h$).

**b**   Sketch a graph of BMI against $h$ (assuming a constant weight $W$).

**9**   Peter and Carly work in a supermarket. Peter earns £8.75 an hour and Carly earns £10 per hour.

**a**   Write down a formula to show:

   **i**   the relationship between Peter's pay and the hours worked

   **ii**   the relationship between Carly's pay and the hours worked.

**b**   Sketch a graph to compare Peter's and Carly's earnings.

**10**   Calls on a mobile phone cost 25 pence per minute during peak periods and 15 pence per minute in off-peak periods.

**a**   Draw a graph to show the cost of peak calls and the cost of off-peak calls for times up to 200 minutes.

**b**   Find:

   **i**   the difference between the peak and off-peak cost of a call that lasts 45 minutes

   **ii**   the number of extra minutes you get for £15 during off-peak periods.

**c**   A contract phone costs £15 per month. For this you get 60 minutes of 'free' calls and pay for all other calls at 20 pence per minute.

   **i**   Draw another line on your graph to show this.

   **ii**   Is the cost of calls on this mobile phone contract proportional to the length of the calls in minutes?
Give a reason for your answer.

**11**   $z$ is inversely proportional to $y^2$ and $y$ is directly proportional to $\sqrt{x}$.

Describe the relationship between $z$ and $x$ and sketch a graph of $z$ against $x$.

# 8  Assess (k)

**1** A school buys 10 bottles of milk for drinks at a parents evening.
Each bottle holds enough for 25 drinks.
They make 235 drinks.

Calculate the percentage of milk used.

**2** What percentage of this shape is blue?

5 cm
2 cm
2 cm
2 cm   4 cm

Not drawn accurately

**3** 168 men and 210 women book a holiday cruise.

Write the ratio of the number of men to the number of women:

**a** in its simplest form

**b** in the form $1 : n$

**4** The table shows the amounts needed to make 24 fruit biscuits.

| Ingredient | Amount for 24 biscuits (g) |
|---|---|
| Flour | 300 |
| Butter | 150 |
| Sugar | 100 |
| Fruit | 120 |

Calculate the amount of each ingredient needed to make 36 fruit biscuits.

**5** In the 1908 Olympic Games, Reggie Walker won the 100 metres in a time of 10.8 seconds.
A century later, in the 2008 Olympics, Usain Bolt won the 100 metres in 9.69 seconds.

Calculate the percentage decrease in the winning time.

**6** It costs £259.80 for 20 m² of carpet.

How much does it cost for 36 m² of the same carpet?

**7** Sun tan lotion is sold in two different sizes: small and large.

**a** Which bottle gives the best value for money?

**b** Give one reason why you might prefer to buy the other bottle.

£8.99

£11.99

TOP-SUN TANNING LOTION  SF15   125 ml

TOP-SUN TANNING LOTION  SF15   200 ml

**8** A company has spent £25 000 on new equipment.
The value of the equipment falls by 18% in the first year and 12% in the second year after it is bought.

**a** How much is the equipment worth when it is two years old?

**b** The manager says that the value of the equipment has fallen by 30% in two years.

Is she correct? Explain your answer.

D
D
C
C
B

**9** In a flu epidemic, the number of people who have flu is increasing at a rate of 10% per week.
It is estimated that 3200 people have flu this week.

**a** Predict, to the nearest hundred, the number of people who will have flu 8 weeks from now.

**b** Sketch a graph of the number of people who have flu against time.

**c** Describe this growth and give a reason why it cannot continue in the long term.

**10** $P$ and $Q$ are both positive quantities. $P$ is inversely proportional to $Q$.
When $Q = 12$, $P = 15$

**a** Express $P$ in terms of $Q$.

**b** What is the value of $P$ when $Q = 10$?

**c** What is the value of $Q$ when $P = 10$?

**d** Sketch a graph of $P$ against $Q$.

**11** Here are sketches of three graphs.

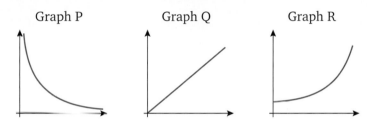

Graph P        Graph Q        Graph R

Copy and complete the following statements.

**a** $y = 20x$ matches Graph …

**b** $y = \dfrac{20}{x}$ matches Graph …

**c** $y = 20 \times 1.5^x$ matches Graph …

# Practice questions ⓚ

1 The size of the North Sea cod stock in 2008 was estimated at 250 000 tonnes.
Because of over-fishing it is decreasing at the rate of 11% per annum.
How many years will it be before the North Sea cod stock falls below the critical level of 70 000 tonnes?
You must show your working and justify your answer fully. *(4 marks)*

AQA 2008

2 75 scientists are trapped in the Antarctic.
They have enough food for 30 days on full rations.
After 16 days on full rations, a rescue party of 9 people arrives.
The rescue party brings enough food to increase existing supplies by 60%
The weather then gets worse and both the scientists and the rescue party are trapped.
They decide to go on half rations.
How many more days before the food runs out? *(4 marks)*

AQA 2008

# 9 Quadratics

## Objectives

Examiners would normally expect students who get these grades to be able to:

### C

draw graphs of quadratics such as $y = x^2 + 2x + 1$

use a graph to estimate $x$- and $y$-values, giving answers to an appropriate degree of accuracy

draw graphs of harder quadratics such as $y = 2x^2 - 7x + 5$

### B

factorise an expression such as $x^2 - 5x + 14$ or $x^2 - 9$

solve an equation such as $x^2 - 5x + 14 = 0$

### A

factorise an expression such as $3x^2 + 7x + 2$ or $3x^2 - 27$

simplify an expression such as $\dfrac{x^2 + 3x + 2}{x^2 - 1}$ by factorising

solve an equation such as $3x^2 + 7x + 2 = 0$ by factorising

solve problems using equations such as $2x^2 - 6x + 1 = 0$ by using the quadratic formula

solve problems using equations such as $x^2 + 3x + 2 = 5$ by graphical methods

### A*

solve an equation such as $\dfrac{3}{x - 2} + \dfrac{4}{x - 1} = 2$

solve an equation such as $x^2 - 8x + 11 = 0$ by completing the square.

### Key terms

quadratic expression
factorise
expand
quadratic equation
surd

coefficient
consecutive
quadrant
parabola

*Did you know?*

## Quadratic equations

The history of algebra began in ancient Egypt and Babylon. People there learned to solve linear ($ax = b$) and quadratic ($ax^2 + bx = c$) equations, as well as equations such as $x^2 + y^2 = z^2$. The use of quadratic equations can be traced back to 2000 BCE when they were solved by methods like the ones used today.

## You should already know:

✔ how to collect like terms

✔ how to multiply brackets by a single term

✔ how to multiply two brackets together

✔ how to solve a linear equation

✔ how to simplify algebraic fractions.

**Learn...** **9.1 Factorising quadratic expressions**

A **quadratic expression** is always in the form $ax^2 + bx + c$

**Factorising** is the inverse operation to **expanding**.

**Example:**   If the answer is $x^2 + 5x + 6$, what was in the brackets?

**Solution:**

| × | $x$ | ? |
|---|---|---|
| $x$ | $x^2$ | |
| ? | | +6 |

To get $x^2$, the brackets must start with $x$ and $x$.

To get $+6$, the second terms must multiply to $+6$, so could be:

$\quad + 1$ and $+ 6$

or $+ 2$ and $+ 3$

or $- 1$ and $- 6$

or $- 2$ and $- 3$

Possible factors:   $(x + 1)(x + 6)$

$\qquad\qquad\qquad\quad (x + 2)(x + 3)$

$\qquad\qquad\qquad\quad (x - 1)(x - 6)$

$\qquad\qquad\qquad\quad (x - 2)(x - 3)$

Each pair of brackets multiplies to $x^2 \ldots\ldots + 6$ but only one multiplies to $x^2 + 5x + 6$

Check them by multiplying out.

Notice that the brackets with negative numbers will not produce a middle term of $+ 5x$

The factors are $(x + 2)(x + 3)$.

**Example:**   If the answer is $y^2 + 3y - 10$, what was in the brackets?

**Solution:**

| × | $y$ | ? |
|---|---|---|
| $y$ | $y^2$ | |
| ? | | $-10$ |

To get $y^2$, the brackets must start with $y$ and $y$

To get $-10$, the second terms must multiply to $-10$, so could be:

$\quad + 1$ and $- 10$

or $+ 2$ and $- 5$

or $- 1$ and $+ 10$

or $- 2$ and $+ 5$

Possible factors:   $(y + 1)(y - 10)$

$\qquad\qquad\qquad\quad (y + 2)(y - 5)$

$\qquad\qquad\qquad\quad (y - 1)(y + 10)$

$\qquad\qquad\qquad\quad (y - 2)(y + 5)$

> **Study tip**
>
> If you can multiply out brackets correctly, then you can factorise correctly too.
>
> Always check your answer by multiplying out to see if you arrive back at the quadratic.

Each pair of brackets multiplies to $y^2 \ldots\ldots - 10$ but only one multiplies to $y^2 + 3y - 10$

Check them by multiplying out.

The factors are $(y - 2)(y + 5)$.

### The difference of two squares

These are quadratic expressions like $a^2 - 9$, $b^2 - 25$, $x^2 - y^2$

They have no $bx$ term.

*Example:* Factorise $a^2 - 9$

*Solution:* $a^2 \quad 9 \quad a^2 \quad 9$

To get $a^2$, the brackets must start with $a$ and $a$.

To get $-9$, the second terms must multiply to $-9$.

so could be:

$+ 1$ and $- 9$

or $- 1$ and $+ 9$

or $+ 3$ and $- 3$

If the term in $a$ has vanished, it must have been made up from $+ 3a$ and $- 3a$.

The factors are $(a + 3)(a - 3)$.

## Practise... 9.1 Factorising quadratic expressions (k) D C B A A*

**B**

Factorise:

**1** $a^2 + 9a + 20$

**2** $b^2 + 10b + 24$

**3** $c^2 - 9c + 18$

**4** $d^2 - 7d + 12$

**5** $e^2 + 8e - 20$

**6** $f^2 + 4f - 21$

**7** $m^2 - 2m - 15$

**8** $n^2 - n - 20$

**9** $p^2 + 6p + 9$

**10** $q^2 - 4q + 4$

**11** $r^2 - 4$

**12** $v^2 - 49$

**13** $w^2 - 5w - 24$

**14** $x^2 + 10x - 24$

**15** $y^2 + y - 30$

**16** $t^2 - 4t - 32$

**17** $h^2 + 7h - 18$

**18** $k^2 - 13k + 22$

**19** $x^2 + 23x + 42$

**20** $y^2 + 2y - 63$

**21** Factorise:

**a** $x^2 - 5xy + 4y^2$ **b** $p^2 + pq - 12q^2$ **c** $a^2 - b^2$ **d** $4c^2 - 25d^2$

**22** Use your knowledge of the difference of two squares to work out:

**a** $31^2 - 30^2$ **b** $57^2 - 43^2$

**23** The factors of $x^2 + kx + 12$ are $(x + a)(x + b)$ where $a$ and $b$ are positive integers.

Show that there are three possible values of $k$.

**24** The factors of $y^2 + nx - 15$ are $(y + c)(y + d)$ where $c$ and $d$ are integers.

Show that there are four possible values of $n$.

**Learn...**   **9.2 Factorising harder quadratic expressions**

In this section, the **coefficient** of $x^2$ is not equal to 1, so the brackets will not both start with $x$. There may be many possible pairs of brackets.

*Example:*   Factorise $2x^2 + 15x + 7$

*Solution:*

| × | 2x | ? |
|---|-----|-----|
| x | $2x^2$ | |
| ? | | +7 |

To get $2x^2$, the brackets must start with $2x$ and $x$.

To get $+7$, the second terms must multiply to $+7$, so could be:

$+1$ and $+7$.

or $-1$ and $-7$

However, $-1$ and $-7$ will not give $+15x$ as the middle term.

Possible factors:   $(2x + 1)(x + 7)$
$(2x + 7)(x + 1)$

Each pair of brackets multiplies to $2x^2 + \ldots\ldots + 7$ but only one multiplies to $2x^2 + 15x + 7$

Check them by multiplying out.

The factors are $(2x + 1)(x + 7)$.

*Example:*   Factorise: $6y^2 - 5y - 4$

*Solution:*

| × | 2y | ? |
|---|-----|-----|
| 3y | | |
| ? | | −4 |

or

| × | y | ? |
|---|-----|-----|
| 6y | | |
| ? | | −4 |

To get $6y^2$, the brackets could start with $2y$ and $3y$, or with $y$ and $6y$.

To get $-4$, the second terms must multiply to $-4$, so could be:

$+2$ and $-2$

or $+1$ and $-4$

or $-1$ and $+4$

Possible factors:   $(2y + 2)(3y - 2)$          $(y + 2)(6y - 2)$
$(2y - 2)(3y + 2)$          $(y - 2)(6y + 2)$
$(2y + 1)(3y - 4)$          $(y + 1)(6y - 4)$
$(2y - 1)(3y + 4)$          $(y - 1)(6y + 4)$
$(2y + 4)(3y - 1)$          $(y + 4)(6y - 1)$
$(2y - 4)(3y + 1)$          $(y - 4)(6y + 1)$

Each pair of brackets multiplies to $6y^2 + \ldots\ldots - 4$ but only one multiplies to $6y^2 - 5y - 4$

Check them by multiplying out.

The factors are $(2y + 1)(3y - 4)$.

**Example:** Factorise completely $6z^2 - 26z - 20$

**Solution:** This quadratic has the factor 2.

$6z^2 - 26z - 20 = 2(3z^2 - 13z - 10)$

The factors of $3z^2 - 13z - 10$ are $(3z + 2)(z - 5)$.

The factors of $6z^2 - 26z - 20$ are $2(3z + 2)(z - 5)$.

### Study tip

You will be told to 'factorise completely' when there are three factors. Don't forget to write all three factors in your answer.

## 9.2 Factorising harder quadratic expressions

**Practise...**

D C B A A*

**A**

Factorise:

**1** $2a^2 + 7a + 3$

**2** $3b^2 + 5b + 2$

**3** $2c^2 - 5c + 3$

**4** $5d^2 - 2d + 7$

**5** $7e^2 - 2e - 5$

**6** $3f^2 + f - 2$

**7** $2x^2 - 7x - 4$

**8** $3y^2 + 7y - 6$

**9** $5m^2 - 11m - 12$

**10** $3n^2 - 28n + 9$

**11** $5p^2 + 13p + 6$

**12** $2q^2 + 15q + 18$

**13** $4t^2 - 12t + 9$

**14** $9u^2 + 30u + 25$

**15** $4v^2 + 8v + 3$

**16** $4w^2 - 21w + 5$

**17** $4x^2 - 9$

**18** $9y^2 - 25$

Factorise completely:

**19** $2x^2 + 10x + 8$

**20** $3y^2 - 9y + 6$

**21** $5z^2 - 45$

**22** $3b^2 - 27$

Factorise:

**23** $2x^2 + 7xy - 15y^2$

**24** $4p^2 + pq - 5q^2$

**25** One of the factors of $3x^2 + kx + 8$ is $(x + 2)$.

Find the value of $k$.

**26** One of the factors of $5y^2 - y - n$ is $(5y + 1)$.

Find the value of $n$.

## Learn... 9.3 Simplifying algebraic fractions

To simplify algebraic fractions, you should factorise the numerator and/or the denominator. Then divide the numerator and denominator by common factors.

**Example:** Simplify $\dfrac{x^2 + 3x + 2}{x^2 - 1}$

**Solution:**

Factorise the numerator $\quad x^2 + 3x + 2 = (x + 1)(x + 2)$

Factorise the denominator $\quad x^2 - 1 = (x - 1)(x + 1)$

Rewrite the fraction as $\quad \dfrac{(x + 1)(x + 2)}{(x - 1)(x + 1)}$

Divide top and bottom by the common factor $\quad \dfrac{\cancel{(x + 1)}(x + 2)}{(x - 1)\cancel{(x + 1)}} = \dfrac{x + 2}{x - 1}$

> **Study tip**
>
> If there is no common factor in a question like this you are likely to have made an error.

## Practise... 9.3 Simplifying algebraic fractions  D C B A A*

Simplify:

**1** $\dfrac{c^2 + 2c + 1}{4c + 4}$

**2** $\dfrac{y^2 - 4}{3y - 6}$

**3** $\dfrac{w^2 - 4w + 4}{5w - 10}$

**4** $\dfrac{t^2 + 11t + 18}{t^2 + 9t + 14}$

**5** $\dfrac{x^2 + 3x - 4}{x^2 + 7x + 12}$

**6** $\dfrac{y^2 - 2y - 3}{y^2 - 6y + 9}$

**7** $\dfrac{x^2 + 3x - 4}{x^2 - 1}$

**8** $\dfrac{3z^2 + 5z - 2}{9z^2 - 1}$

**9** $\dfrac{2x^2 + x - 6}{x^2 - 4}$

**10** $\dfrac{5a^2 + 7a + 2}{5a^2 - 13a - 6}$

**11** $\dfrac{4m^2 - 9}{2m^2 - 3m - 9}$

Simplify:

**12** $\dfrac{x^3 + x^2 - 2x}{x - 1}$

**13** $\dfrac{a^2 + 9a + 20}{3a - 15} \times \dfrac{a^2 - a - 20}{a^2 + 8a + 16}$

**14** $\dfrac{c^2 - 2c - 3}{c^2 - 5c + 6} \times \dfrac{2c - 6}{c^2 - 1}$

## Learn... 9.4 Solving quadratic equations by factorising

If $p \times q = 0$, then either $p$ or $q$ (or both of them) must be 0.

$\quad 7 \times 0 = 0$

$\quad 0 \times 4 = 0$

$\quad 0 \times 0 = 0$

This is the basis for solving quadratic equations by factorising.

If $(x - 2) \times (x + 5) = 0$ then either $(x - 2) = 0$ or $(x + 5) = 0$ and $x$ can be either 2 or $-5$.

**Example:** Solve the equation $x^2 - 5x - 14 = 0$

**Solution:** Factorising gives $(x - 7)(x + 2) = 0$

Either $(x - 7) = 0$ or $(x + 2) = 0$

$x = 7$  $x = -2$

The solutions are $x = 7$ or $-2$

---

**Example:** Solve the equation $x^2 - 3x = 0$

**Solution:** Factorising gives $x(x - 3) = 0$  Here the 'first bracket' is just $x$.

Either $x = 0$ or $(x - 3) = 0$

$x = 3$

The solutions are $x = 0$ or $3$

---

**Example:** Solve the equation $2x^2 - 9x - 5 = 0$

**Solution:** Factorising gives $(2x + 1)(x - 5) = 0$

> **Hint**
>
> If $(2x + 1) = 0$ then $2x = -1$
>
> so $x = -\frac{1}{2}$

Either $(2x + 1) = 0$ or $(x - 5) = 0$

$x = -\frac{1}{2}$  $x = 5$

The solutions are $x = -\frac{1}{2}$ or $5$

---

**Example:** A rectangular garden is $y$ metres wide.
The length of the garden is 7 metres more than the width.
The area of the garden is 120 m².

Form a quadratic equation in $y$ and solve it to find the dimensions of the garden.

**Solution:** Width $= y$ metres, so length $= y + 7$ metres

Area of garden $=$ width $\times$ length

$= y(y + 7)$  Expand the brackets.
$= y^2 + 7y$

> **Study tip**
>
> Rearrange a quadratic equation in the form
>
> .................... $= 0$
>
> before you factorise.

Area of the garden $= 120$ m²
So $y^2 + 7y = 120$

$y^2 + 7y - 120 = 0$  Take 120 from both sides.
$(y + 15)(y - 8) = 0$  Then factorise.

Either $(y + 15) = 0$ or $(y - 8) = 0$

$y = -15$ or $y = 8$  Reject the negative value as $y$ is a length.

So $y = 8$

Length $= 8 + 7 = 15$ m and width $= 8$ m

Check:  area $= 15 \times 8 = 120$ m² ✓

## 9.4 Solving quadratic equations by factorising

**Practise...**

D C B A A*

Solve these equations.

**1**   $(m - 3)(m + 2) = 0$

**2**   $(n + 1)(2n - 5) = 0$

**3**   $x^2 - 5x + 4 = 0$

**4**   $y^2 - 2y - 15 = 0$

**5**   $b^2 + 5b - 84 = 0$

**6**   $c^2 - c - 12 = 0$

**7**   $p^2 + 5p = 14$

**8**   $q^2 + 27 = 12q$

**9**   $t^2 = 100$

**10**   $a^2 + 7a = 0$

> **Study tip**
>
> Rearrange a quadratic equation in the form .......... = 0 before you factorise.

**11**   $2b^2 - 8b = 0$

**12**   $2x^2 - 9x - 5 = 0$

**13**   $3y^2 + 8y - 3 = 0$

**14**   $5z^2 + 12z + 4 = 0$

**15**   $5t^2 - 3t - 14 = 0$

**16**   $2p^2 + 13p = 7$

**17**   The quadratic equation $x^2 + 2x - p = 0$ has a solution $x = -5$

Work out the value of $p$.

**18**   The quadratic equation $y^2 + qy - 12 = 0$ has a solution $y = 3$

Work out the value of $q$.

**⚠ 19**   The length of the rectangle PQRS is $x$ cm and its width is $(x - 5)$ cm.

A triangle $PTU$, where $PT = 6$ cm and $PU = 4$ cm, is removed from one corner of the rectangle as shown.

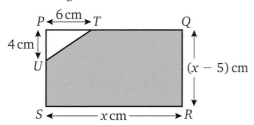

**a**   Show that the shaded area is $(x^2 - 5x - 12)$ cm.

**b**   The shaded area is 164 cm².

Form a quadratic equation and solve it to find the length of the rectangle.

**20**   **a**   The quadratic equation $x^2 - 14x + 49 = 0$ has only one solution. Why?

  **b**   Write down another quadratic equation that has only one solution.

**21**   Anna thinks of a number, squares it and then adds twice the original number. The result is 99.

Write down a quadratic equation and solve it to find the two possible numbers that Anna started with.

**22**   A rectangular garden is $y$ metres long.
The width of the garden is 5 metres less than the length.
The area of the garden is 234 square metres.

Form a quadratic equation in $y$ and solve it to find the length of the garden.

**Learn...** 9.5 Solving equations with fractions

To solve an equation that has fractions:

- first put in any 'hidden brackets'

- give the fractions a common denominator then combine fractions and simplify

- then multiply both sides of the equation by the common denominator

- finally rearrange the terms and simplify/factorise.

*Example:*    Solve the equation $\dfrac{4}{x+2} - \dfrac{3}{x-2} = 5$

*Solution:*

$\dfrac{4}{(x+2)} - \dfrac{3}{(x-2)} = 5$          First put in the 'invisible' brackets.

$\dfrac{4(x-2) - 3(x+2)}{(x+2)(x-2)} = 5$          Combine the fractions, giving them a common denominator: $(x+2)(x-2)$.

$\dfrac{4x - 8 - 3x - 6}{(x+2)(x-2)} = 5$          Multiply out the brackets in numerator.

$\dfrac{x - 14}{(x+2)(x-2)} = 5$          Collect like terms.

$x - 14 = 5(x+2)(x-2)$          Multiply both sides of the equation by the denominator.

$x - 14 = 5(x^2 - 4)$          Simplify.

$x - 14 = 5x^2 - 20$          Multiply out brackets.

$5x^2 - x - 6 = 0$          Rearrange the quadratic with 0 on right-hand side.

$(5x - 6)(x + 1) = 0$          Factorise.

Either $(5x - 6) = 0$ or $(x + 1) = 0$  Solve.

$x = \frac{6}{5} = 1.2$ or $x = -1$

**Practise...** 9.5 Solving equations with fractions  D C B A A*

**A**

**1**    Solve the equation $x = \dfrac{6}{x+1}$

**2**    Solve the equation $\dfrac{x}{x-2} - \dfrac{3}{x} = 1$

**3**    Solve the equation $\dfrac{3}{x} - \dfrac{2}{x+2} = 1$

**A***

**4**    Solve the equation $\dfrac{6}{x-2} - \dfrac{4}{x+2} = 1$

**5**    Solve the equation $\dfrac{1}{x-3} - \dfrac{3}{x+2} = \dfrac{1}{2}$

**6**  A car is travelling at $x$ km/h. It travels 60 km to its destination. On the way back, its speed is 20 km/h more, so the journey takes less time. If the times taken for each part of the journey are added together, the total journey time is $2\frac{1}{2}$ hours.

   **a**  By writing down expressions for the time taken for each part of the journey, form an equation for the total time taken.

   **b**  Solve this equation to find the speed for each part of the journey.

> **Hint**
>
> Remember that speed $= \dfrac{\text{distance}}{\text{time}}$

> **Study tip**
>
> Remember to check that your answer makes sense in the context of the question.

**7**  Shaun and Ben both play cricket. During the season they each score a total of 45 runs.

Shaun plays $x$ games and Ben plays $x + 4$ games.

   **a**  Write down an expression for the batting average for each of them.

   **b**  There is a difference of 4 runs between their batting averages.
       Using your answers to part **a**, write down an equation in $x$.

   **c**  Solve your equation to find out how many games Shaun played.

## Learn... 9.6 Solving quadratic equations by completing the square

Some quadratics are perfect squares. Perfect squares are where both factors are the same.

$$x^2 + 6x + 9 = (x + 3)^2 \qquad\qquad y^2 - 2y + 1 = (y - 1)^2$$

half of $+6 = +3$ \qquad\qquad half of $-2 = -1$

The number before the $x$ (the $x$ coefficient) is twice the number in the perfect square.

The number before the $y$ (the $y$ coefficient) is twice the number in the perfect square.

> **Study tip**
>
> Your first step is to halve the coefficient of $x$.

Quadratics can be rearranged to include a perfect square.
This is called 'completing the square'.

For $x^2 + 6x + 7$, the perfect square is $(x + 3)^2$
       and $(x + 3)^2 = x^2 + 6x + 9$

So $x^2 + 6x + 7$ is the same as $x^2 + 6x + 9 - 2$ or $(x + 3)^2 - 2$

$+7 = +9 - 2$

For $y^2 - 2y - 5$, the perfect square is $(y - 1)^2$
       and $(y - 1)^2 = y^2 - 2y + 1$

So $y^2 - 2y - 5$ is the same as $y^2 - 2y + 1 - 6$ or $(y - 1)^2 - 6$

$-5 = +1 - 6$

You can use this method to solve any **quadratic equation**, giving the answer in **surd** form.

**Example:**     Solve the equation $x^2 + 6x + 7 = 0$ by completing the square.

**Solution:**     Complete the square as shown above     $(x + 3)^2 - 2 = 0$

           Add 2 to both sides                          $(x + 3)^2 = 2$

           Take the square root of both sides          $x + 3 = \pm\sqrt{2}$

           Write the answer in the form '$x = \ldots$'        $x = 3 \pm\sqrt{2}$

> **Study tip**
>
> If the number on the right of the equation is negative, the equation cannot be solved, so check you have not made a mistake.

**Example:**     Solve the equation $y^2 - 2y - 5 = 0$ by completing the square.

**Solution:**     Complete the square as shown above     $(y - 1)^2 - 6 = 0$

           Add 6 to both sides                          $(y - 1)^2 = 6$

           Take the square root of both sides          $y - 1 = \pm\sqrt{6}$

           Write the answer in the form '$y = \ldots$'        $y = 1 \pm\sqrt{6}$

## 9.6 Solving quadratic equations by completing the square

**Practise...**                                            

**A\***

**1**     $x^2 + 4x + 1 \equiv (x + 2)^2 - a$

Work out the value of $a$.

**2**     $y^2 - 14y + 8 \equiv (y - 7)^2 + b$

Work out the value of $b$.

Solve these equations by completing the square.

Give your answers in surd form.

> **Hint**
>
> Start by looking for a common factor.

**3**     $x^2 + 2x - 1 = 0$

**8**     $q^2 + 4q + 2 = 0$

**4**     $y^2 - 6y + 1 = 0$

**9**     $u^2 + 3 = 8u$

**5**     $z^2 + 8z - 2 = 0$

**10**     $v^2 + 22 = 20v$

**6**     $t^2 - 4t - 8 = 0$

**11**     $2a^2 - 4a - 8 = 0$

**7**     $p^2 + 12p + 30 = 0$

**12**     $3c^2 - 18c + 3 = 0$

**13**     You are given the identity $x^2 + mx + 25 \equiv (x + n)^2$

Work out the values of $m$ and $n$.

**14**     You are given the identity $x^2 - px + 121 \equiv (x + q)^2$

Work out the values of $p$ and $q$.

**15**     You are given the identity $4x^2 + 12x + 3 \equiv (2x + a)^2 + b$

Work out the values of $a$ and $b$.

**16**     Explain why you cannot solve the equation $y^2 + 3y + 5 = 0$

## 9.7 Solving quadratic equations by using the quadratic formula

Quadratic equations may be solved by using the **quadratic formula**:

$$x = \frac{-b \pm \sqrt{b^2 - 4ac}}{2a}$$

where $a$, $b$ and $c$ are the **coefficients** of the terms in the quadratic equation $ax^2 + bx + c = 0$.

This formula is obtained from completing the square with the general quadratic $ax^2 + bx + c = 0$.

The proof is shown overleaf. However, you will only be expected to use the formula, not to prove it.

**Proof of the quadratic formula**

$ax^2 + bx + c = 0$

| | |
|---|---|
| $x^2 + \dfrac{bx}{a} + \dfrac{c}{a} = 0$ | Divide by $a$. |
| $\left(x^2 + \dfrac{b}{2a}\right)^2 = -\dfrac{c}{a} + \dfrac{b^2}{4a^2}$ | Complete the square. |
| $\left(x + \dfrac{b}{2a}\right)^2 = \dfrac{-4ac + b^2}{4a^2}$ | Combine the fractions on the right-hand side. |
| $x + \dfrac{b}{2a} = \pm\sqrt{\dfrac{-4ac + b^2}{4a^2}}$ | Square root both sides. |
| $x + \dfrac{b}{2a} = \pm\dfrac{\sqrt{b^2 - 4ac}}{2a}$ | Square root $4a^2$ and rearrange. |
| $x = -\dfrac{b}{2a} \pm \dfrac{\sqrt{b^2 - 4ac}}{2a}$ | Subtract $\left(\dfrac{b}{2a}\right)$ from both sides. |
| $x = \dfrac{-b \pm \sqrt{b^2 - 4ac}}{2a}$ | Combine the fractions on the right-hand side. |

*Example:*    Solve the quadratic equation $2x^2 - x - 9 = 0$.

Give your answers correct to two decimal places.

*Solution:*    $2x^2 - x - 9 = 0$

First write down the values of $a$, $b$ and $c$    $a = 2$, $b = -1$ and $c = -9$

Using the formula $x = \dfrac{-b \pm \sqrt{b^2 - 4ac}}{2a}$

| | |
|---|---|
| $x = \dfrac{-(-1) \pm \sqrt{(-1)^2 - 4(2)(-9)}}{2(2)}$ | Substitute the values for $a$, $b$ and $c$. |
| $x = \dfrac{+1 \pm \sqrt{1 + 72}}{4}$ | Take care with the signs as you simplify this. |
| $x = \dfrac{+1 \pm \sqrt{73}}{4}$ | Work out the values under the square root before splitting into two parts. |
| $x = \dfrac{+1 + \sqrt{73}}{4}$ or $= \dfrac{+1 - \sqrt{73}}{4}$ | |

**Study tip**

If the number underneath the square root is negative, there are no solutions.
If it is negative, check your working as it is likely you have made a mistake.

Store the value of the square root in the memory of your calculator so that you can use it in each part.

$$x = \frac{1 + 8.5440...}{4} \text{ or } \frac{1 - 8.5440...}{4}$$

$$x = \frac{9.5440...}{4} \text{ or } \frac{-7.5440}{4}$$

$$x = 2.3860... \text{ or } -1.886...$$

$$x - 2.39 \text{ or } x = -1.89 \text{ (to 2 d.p.)}$$

You will have to use the formula when you are asked to give an answer correct to a number of significant figures or decimal places. You would only be asked to leave your answer in **surd** form in Unit 2.

### Study tip

The quadratic formula can be used to find the solution of a quadratic which has whole number answers but it is easier to factorise these quadratics without the formula.

So, before you use the quadratic formula, look at the quadratic you have been given to check whether it has whole number factors, e.g. $2x^2 + x - 3 = (2x + 3)(x - 1)$

---

**Example:** A window is 15 cm longer than it is wide. The area of the window is 225 cm².

  **a**   Form a quadratic equation in $x$ for the area of the window.

  **b**   Solve the equation to find the value of $x$.

  **c**   What are the dimensions of the window? Give the answers correct to 2 d.p.

**Solution:**  **a**   Let the width of the window be $x$ cm so the length of the window is $(x + 15)$ cm.

        Area $= x(x + 15)$

        So $x(x + 15) = 225$

        $x^2 + 15x - 225 = 0$

$x$ cm

$(x + 15)$ cm

  **b**   In $x^2 + 15x - 225 = 0$, $a = 1$, $b = 15$ and $c = -225$

        Using the formula $x = \dfrac{-b \pm \sqrt{b^2 - 4ac}}{2a}$

        Substituting the values for $a$, $b$ and $c$:

$$x = \frac{-15 \pm \sqrt{(15^2) - 4 \times 1 \times (-225)}}{2 \times 1}$$

$$= \frac{-15 \pm \sqrt{225 + 900}}{2}$$

$$= \frac{-15 \pm \sqrt{1125}}{2}$$

$$x = \frac{-15 + \sqrt{1125}}{2} \text{ or } \frac{-15 - \sqrt{1125}}{2}$$

Reject the negative value because $x$ is a length.

$$x = \frac{-15 + 33.5410...}{2}$$

$$x = 9.27 \text{ (to 2 d.p.)}$$

### Study tip

Watch out for solutions that do not fit the context of the question.

They are usually negative solutions but not always.

  **c**   Width $= x = 9.27$ cm (to 2 d.p.)

        Length $= x + 15 = 24.27$ cm (to 2 d.p.)

        The dimensions of the window are 24.27 cm by 9.27 cm (to 2 d.p.).

## 9.7 Solving quadratic equations by using the quadratic formula

**Practise...**

D C B A A*

**1** Solve these equations, giving your solutions correct to two decimal places.

   **a** $x^2 + 8x + 9 = 0$

   **b** $3z + z^2 - 5 = 0$

   **c** $2x^2 - 7x + 4 = 0$

   **d** $5y^2 - 15y + 2 = 10$

   **e** $3x^2 + 6x - 2 = 0$

   **f** $4p^2 - 6p = p - 2$

   **g** $1.2x^2 + 0.8x - 14 = 0$

   **h** $2 - 3x - x^2 = 0$

   **i** $5x^2 = 4x + 2$

**Hint**

For part **g** either work with decimal values or multiply throughout by 10.

**2** Solve the equation $\dfrac{2}{(x + 1)} - \dfrac{3}{(2x + 3)} = \dfrac{1}{2}$

**Hint**

Rearrange the equation so that both fractions are on the same side.

**3** Solve the equation $\dfrac{2}{(x + 2)} = 4 - \dfrac{1}{(x + 3)}$

**4** The surface area of an open cylinder is given by the formula $S = 2\pi r h$
The radius of the cylinder is $x$ cm and its height is 9 cm more than the radius.

   **a** If the surface area of the cylinder is $16\pi$ cm², find the value of $x$.

   **b** What is the height of the cylinder?

**5** A ball is thrown vertically upwards with a speed of 22 m/s.
After $t$ seconds, its height above the ground, $h$ metres, is given by the formula:

   $h = 22t - 4.9t^2$

   **a** Find the time taken for the ball to reach a height of 8 metres.
      Give your answer to two decimal places.

   **b** Explain why there are two valid answers to this problem.

**6** A courtyard consists of a patio area with four **quadrant-**shaped flowerbeds at each corner.
They are all of radius $x$ m. The patio has an area of 20 m².

   **a** Form an equation in $x$, to find the radius of the flower beds.

   **b** Calculate the dimensions of the courtyard.

   **c** Use your answers to parts **a** and **b** to check your working.

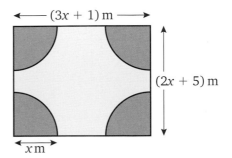

**7** Explain why you cannot solve the equation $x^2 + 3x + 7 = 0$

**8** Sam is using the quadratic formula to solve a quadratic equation. He writes his solution as:

   $\dfrac{(-3 + \sqrt{17})}{2}$

Write down the quadratic equation Sam is trying to solve.

## Learn... 9.8 Solving quadratic equations graphically

### How to draw the graph of a quadratic

1. **Complete or construct a table of values.**

   This is the table for the quadratic equation $y = x^2$

   | $x$ | $-3$ | $-2$ | $-1$ | $0$ | $1$ | $2$ | $3$ |
   |---|---|---|---|---|---|---|---|
   | $y$ | $9$ | $4$ | $1$ | $0$ | $1$ | $4$ | $9$ |

   When drawing the graphs of straight lines (linear graphs), you were taught to plot three points.

   The graphs of quadratics are all curves, so you need more than three values in the table.

   The $y$-values are found by substituting the $x$-values into the equation of the quadratic,
   e.g. for $y = x^2$

   when $x = 2$        $y = 2^2 = 4$

   when $x = -3$        $y = (-3)^2 = 9$

   Sometimes you are asked to construct the table for yourself.

   Make sure that you construct this table for the range of values given in the question.

2. **By looking at your table, find the smallest and largest $y$-values that you will need on the $y$-axis.**

3. **Draw a pair of axes for your graph and label them $x$ and $y$.**

4. **From your table of values, plot the points on the graph as small crosses.**

   The points from this table would be $(-3, 9)$, $(-2, 4)$, $(-1, 1)$, $(0, 0)$, $(1, 1)$, $(2, 4)$, $(3, 9)$.

5. **Join the points with a smooth curve.**

   It should be smooth at the bottom, not 'pointy'.

   Always draw your line with a sharp pencil, making sure that it passes clearly through the centre of the points plotted.

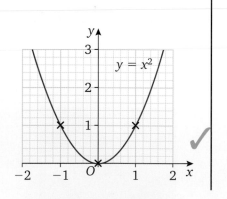

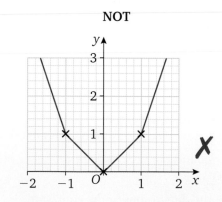

NOT

### Study tip

Make sure that the curve passes through the middle of all the plotted points.
- Join the points with one continuous curved line.
- If you join the points with straight lines, you will lose marks.
- If you are right handed, you will find it easier to join the points by turning your page upside down.

The graph obtained is a curve. A curve of this shape is called a **parabola**.

$y = x^2$ is a U-shaped graph and has a minimum (lowest) point at $(0, 0)$.

All quadratics are parabolas. They are also symmetrical about a line.
Notice that this graph is symmetrical about the line $x = 0$, the $y$-axis.

You can sometimes see the pattern in the table. If you look back at the table for this graph, you will see that the values for $x = -1$ and 1 give the same $y$-values. (The points are equally spaced about $x = 0$.)

**Graph of $y = x^2$**

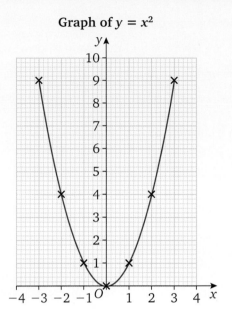

With more complicated quadratics, it is useful to construct a more detailed table.

**Graph of $y = x^2 + 2x$**

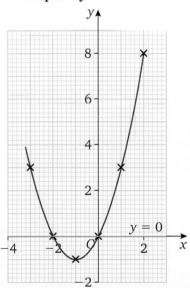

When drawing the graph of $y = x^2 + 2x$, you would construct a table that shows a row for each term in the expression.

Add these two rows to get the $y$-values

| $x$ | $-3$ | $-2$ | $-1$ | 0 | 1 | 2 |
|-----|------|------|------|---|---|---|
| $x^2$ | 9 | 4 | 1 | 0 | 1 | 4 |
| $+2x$ | $-6$ | $-4$ | $-2$ | 0 | 2 | 4 |
| $y$ | 3 | 0 | $-1$ | 0 | 3 | 8 |

The points to be plotted are the $x$ and $y$ rows.

For example, $(-3, 3)$, $(-2, 0)$ and $(-1, -1)$.

**Study tip**

All quadratic graphs should be smooth curves.

They are either U-shaped (the $x^2$ term is positive)  or  hill-shaped (the $x^2$ term is negative)
and have a minimum (lowest) point  and have a maximum (highest) point.

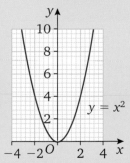

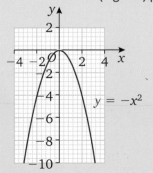

If your graph does not look like one of these, check your working in the table.

You can use these graphs to find the solution of quadratic equations.

If you were asked to find the solution to the equation $x^2 + 2x = 0$, you would do this by adding a straight line to your graph.

To get from $y = x^2 + 2x$ to $x^2 + 2x = 0$ ($0 = x^2 + 2x$), the $y$ has been replaced by 0.

The $y$-coordinate equals zero.

In solving the equation, you are trying to find the $x$-values for which $y = 0$.

To find these, draw the straight line $y = 0$ (the $x$-axis) on your graph.

The solutions are the $x$-values where this line crosses the curve, that is, $x = 0$ and $x = -2$

If the equation given equals a constant as in $x^2 + 2x = 4$, you would solve this by drawing the straight line $y = 4$ on your graph.

The solutions are still the $x$-values where the straight line crosses the curve.

Sometimes you have to rearrange the equation before you can decide which straight line to draw.

Given the equation $x^2 + 2x - 6 = 0$, you must rearrange the equation so that the left-hand side is the same as for the quadratic that you have drawn.

This means that $x^2 + 2x - 6 = 0$, would be rearranged by adding 6 to both sides which gives $x^2 + 2x = 6$.

To find the solutions you need to draw the straight line $y = 6$.

**Example:**   **a**   Draw the graph of $y = 3 + 2x - x^2$ for values of $x$ from $-2 \leqslant x \leqslant 4$

  **b**   Write down the coordinates of its maximum point.

  **c**   Use your graph to find the solutions of the equation $3 + 2x - x^2 = 0$

  **d**   Use the graph of $y = 3 + 2x - x^2$ to solve the following equations.

  **i**   $4 + 2x - x^2 = 0$      **ii**   $2x - x^2 = -1$

**Solution:**   **a**

| $x$ | −2 | −1 | 0 | 1 | 2 | 3 | 4 |
|---|---|---|---|---|---|---|---|
| **3** | 3 | 3 | 3 | 3 | 3 | 3 | 3 |
| $+2x$ | −4 | −2 | 0 | 2 | 4 | 6 | 8 |
| $-x^2$ | −4 | −1 | 0 | −1 | −4 | −9 | −16 |
| $y$ | −5 | 0 | 3 | 4 | 3 | 0 | −5 |

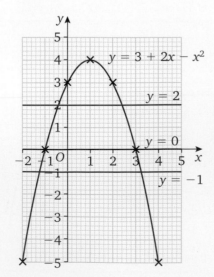

> **Study tip**
>
> In the exam you may be asked to work with the shortened table. Sometimes you may be able to choose which you use.
>
> Whenever you use the shortened form, make sure that you show how you obtained each $y$-value.

**b**   Maximum point $= (1, 4)$

**c**   The solutions of the equation $3 + 2x - x^2 = 0$ are found where the line $y = 0$ ($x$-axis) crosses the curve.

Reading from the graph, these are $x = -1$ and $3$.

**d**   **i**   To solve:   $4 + 2x - x^2 = 0$

$4 - 1 + 2x - x^2 = -1$   Subtract 1 from both sides.

$3 + 2x - x^2 = -1$   The left-hand side of the equation now matches the equation of the line drawn.

Solutions are found where the line $y = -1$ crosses the curve.

Reading from the graph, these are $x = -1.2$ and $3.2$ (to 1 d.p.).

**ii**   To solve:   $2x - x^2 = -1$

$1 + 2x - x^2 = 0$   Rearrange the equation into the same format as the original.

$1 + 2 + 2x - x^2 = 0 + 2$   Add 2 to both sides.

$3 + 2x - x^2 = 2$   The left-hand side of the equation now matches the equation of the line drawn.

Solutions are found where the line $y = 2$ crosses the curve.

Reading from the graph, these are $x = -0.4$ and $2.4$ (to 1 d.p.).

# Practise...

## 9.8  Solving quadratic equations graphically

D  C  B  A  A*

**1**   **a**   Copy and complete this table for $y = x^2 - 2x - 8$.

| $x$ | $-2$ | $-1$ | $0$ | $1$ | $2$ | $3$ | $4$ | $5$ |
|---|---|---|---|---|---|---|---|---|
| $x^2$ | 4 | 1 | 0 | | 4 | | 16 | 25 |
| $-2x$ | 4 | | 0 | $-2$ | $-4$ | $-6$ | $-8$ | $-10$ |
| $-8$ | $-8$ | | $-8$ | | $-8$ | | | $-8$ |
| $y$ | 0 | | $-8$ | | $-8$ | | | 7 |

**b**   Draw the graph of $y = x^2 - 2x - 8$ for values of $x$ from $-2$ to 5.

**c**   When $x = 3$, what is the value of $y$?

**d**   Use your graph to find the solutions of the equation $x^2 - 2x - 8 = 0$.

**2**   **a**   Construct a table for the quadratic $y = x^2 + 1$ for $-3 \leqslant x \leqslant 3$.

**b**   Draw the graph of $y = x^2 + 1$ for these values.

**c**   Write down the coordinates of the minimum point.

**d**   Look at the graph.

**i**   What is different about this graph compared to all the other graphs you have drawn so far?

**ii**   Explain what relevance this has to solving the equation $x^2 + 1 = 0$.

C

**B**

**3**

**a** Copy and complete this table for $y = 2x^2 - 7x + 5$

| $x$ | 0 | 0.5 | 1 | 1.5 | 2 | 2.5 | 3 |
|---|---|---|---|---|---|---|---|
| $2x^2$ | 0 | 0.5 | | 4.5 | | | 18 |
| $-7x$ | | −3.5 | −7 | | −14 | | −21 |
| $+5$ | +5 | +5 | +5 | +5 | +5 | +5 | +5 |
| $y$ | | 2 | | | | | 2 |

**b** Draw the graph of $y = 2x^2 - 7x + 5$ for values of $x$ between 0 and 3.

**c** Find the coordinates of the minimum point.

**d** What are the values of $x$ when $y = 4$?

**A**

**4**

**a** Draw the graph of $y = 2x^2 - 7x + 3$ for values of $x$ from $0 \leqslant x \leqslant 3$ at intervals of 0.5

**b** It has a minimum when $x = 1.75$
Find the $y$-coordinate of this point.

**c** Use your graph to find the solutions of these equations.

**i** $2x^2 - 7x + 5 = 0$       **ii** $2x^2 - 7x + 3 = 0$

**d** Use your graph to explain why you cannot solve the equation $2x^2 - 7x + 7 = 0$.

**⚠ 5**

**a** Draw the graph of $y = 1 + 4x - \frac{1}{2}x^2$ for values of $x$ from $-1 \leqslant x \leqslant 9$

**b** Write down the coordinates of its maximum point.

**c** Use your graph to find the solutions of the equation $1 + 4x - \frac{1}{2}x^2 = 9$

**d** Find solutions to these equations.

**i** $1 + 4x - \frac{1}{2}x^2 = 7$       **ii** $1 + 4x - \frac{1}{2}x^2 = 0$

**e** What is the significance of the answers in part **d**?

**⚙ 6**

A square of side $x$ cm is removed from a triangle of card as shown. The remaining area of card (shaded in the diagram) is 5 cm².

**a** Form an equation for the area of the shaded part.

**b** Simplify this equation into the form $ax^2 + bx + c = 0$.

**c** Construct a table for the quadratic, taking values of $x$ from 0 to 3, at intervals of 0.5

**d** Draw the graph of the quadratic.

**e** Use your graph to find the $x$-value that satisfies the equation in part **b**.

**f** What are the dimensions of the triangle and the square?

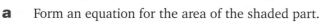

**⚙ 7**

A flower bed is in the shape of a semicircle as shown.
The quadratic $A = \frac{1}{2}\pi r^2$ gives the area for the flower bed in square metres.

**a** Copy and complete the following table, giving values of $A$ to one decimal place.

| $r$ | 1 | 2 | 3 | 4 | 5 |
|---|---|---|---|---|---|
| $A = \frac{1}{2}\pi r^2$ | | 6.3 | | 25.1 | 39.3 |

**b** Draw the graph of $A = \frac{1}{2}\pi r^2$ using 2 cm to represent 1 m on the $r$-axis and 2 cm to represent 10 m² on the $A$-axis.

**c** Use your graph to estimate the area of the flower bed when the radius is:

**i** 1.5 m       **ii** 3.8 m

**d** Use your graph to estimate the radius $r$, of the flower bed when the area is:

**i** 30 m²       **ii** 16 m²

## Learn...    9.9 Algebraic proof

A proof is a series of logical mathematical steps that confirms the truth of a mathematical statement.

You must use correct notation and symbols in your proof. Algebra can be used to solve many mathematical proofs.

Proof questions might require you to offer some explanation.

---

**Example:** Show that if $n$ is a positive even number then $n^2 - n$ is even.

**Solution:** $n^2 = n \times n$ and even $\times$ even = even.

Also even $-$ even = even.

**Alternative solution**

$n^2 - n = n(n - 1)$

$n$ is even, and so $n - 1$ is odd.

Even $\times$ odd = even.

---

**Example:** Prove that $2(9x - 14) - 3(x - 1) \equiv 5(3x - 5)$

**Solution:** Work from the left hand side (LHS) of the identity only.

Multiply out, simplify and factorise the expression on the left to reach the expression on the right.

LHS    $2(9x - 14) - 3(x - 1) = 18x - 28 - 3x + 3$

$= 15x - 25$

$= 5(3x - 5)$

$=$ RHS

> **Study tip**
>
> Remember the symbol $\equiv$ means 'identical to'.

> **Study tip**
>
> Never work with both sides of the identity together.

> **Study tip**
>
> If your solution is incorrect, check your signs when multiplying.

---

**Example:** If $5(2x + 1) - 3(x - 3) \equiv a(x + b)$

Work out the values of $a$ and $b$.

**Solution:** LHS    $5(2x + 1) - 3(x - 3) = 10x + 5 - 3x + 9$

$= 7x + 14$

$= 7(x + 2)$

From RHS $a = 7$ and $b = 2$

---

**Example:** If $(2x + 9)^2 \equiv 4(x - 1)^2 + a(4x + b)$

Work out the values of $a$ and $b$.

**Solution:** LHS $(2x + 9)^2 = (2x + 9)(2x + 9)$

$= 4x^2 + 36x + 81$

RHS $4(x - 1)^2 + a(4x + b) = 4(x^2 - 2x + 1) + 4ax + ab$

$= 4x^2 - 8x + 4 + 4ax + ab$

Compare the coefficients of $x$ on each side

$36 = -8 + 4a$

$4a = 44$

$a = 11$

Compare the number terms on each side.

$81 = 4 + 11b$

$b = 7$

**Example:** Prove that the difference between two **consecutive** square numbers is always an odd number.

**Solution:** Let the first number be $x$ and the square of this number is $x^2$.

The next consecutive number is $x + 1$ and the square of this number is $(x + 1)^2$.

You need to prove that the difference between $x^2$ and $(x + 1)^2$ is an odd number.

The difference can be written as $(x + 1)^2 - x^2$

$$= (x^2 + 2x + 1) - x^2$$
$$= 2x + 1$$

Since the number $2x$ is always an even number then the number $2x + 1$ must be an odd number.

So the difference between two consecutive square numbers is always an odd number.

**Study tip**

It is a good idea to take the smaller number from the larger number when finding the difference, so you don't get a negative answer.

## Practise... 9.9 Algebraic proof

**D**

**1** Prove that $5(2x + 5) + 11(x - 2) \equiv 3(7x + 1)$

**2** Prove that $11(x - 1) + 4(x + 14) \equiv 15(x + 3)$

**3** If $4(x - 3) + a(3x + 11) \equiv 10(x + b)$

Work out the values of $a$ and $b$.

**4** Prove that the sum of two consecutive odd numbers is always an even number.

**5** Prove that the sum of three consecutive numbers is equal to three times the middle number.

**6** Tasha says that $(a + b)^2 = a^2 + b^2$

Show that Tasha is incorrect.

**7** Part of a number grid is shown.

The shaded shape is called $B_{11}$ because it has 11 in the top left-hand corner.

| 1 | 2 | 3 | 4 | 5 | 6 | 7 | 8 |
|---|---|---|---|---|---|---|---|
| 9 | 10 | 11 | 12 | 13 | 14 | 15 | 16 |
| 17 | 18 | 19 | 20 | 21 | 22 | 23 | 24 |
| 25 | 26 | 27 | 28 | 29 | 30 | 31 | 32 |
| 33 | 34 | 35 | 36 | 37 | 38 | 39 | 40 |
| 41 | 42 | 43 | 44 | 45 | 46 | 47 | 48 |
| 49 | 50 | 51 | 52 | 53 | 54 | 55 | 56 |
| 57 | 58 | 59 | 60 | 61 | 62 | 63 | 64 |

**a** This is $B_n$.

| $n$ | |
|---|---|
| | |

Copy and fill in the empty boxes on $B_n$.

**b** Farakh notices that $11 \times 20 = 220$

and that $19 \times 12 = 228$

Show, using algebra, that the difference of the products of the diagonals is always 8.

**8** Prove that the product of three consecutive even numbers is a multiple of 8.

**9** Prove that if you add the squares of three consecutive numbers and then subtract two, the answer is a multiple of 3.

**10**   Prove that $\dfrac{n+1}{n} - \dfrac{n}{n+1} = \dfrac{2n+1}{n(n+1)}$

**11**   The $n$th triangle number is given by the formula $\frac{1}{2}n\,(n+1)$.

**a**   Write down the first three triangle numbers.

**b**   Prove that the sum of any two consecutive triangle numbers is always a square number.

**⚠ 12**   Take a 3-digit number such that the three digits are different.
Reverse the number.
Subtract the smaller number from the bigger one.
If the difference is a 2-digit number add a zero before it.
Reverse the new 3-digit number and add the reversed number to the difference.
Explain why the answer is always 1089.

# 9   Assess

**1**   Prove that $5(x-4) + 2(4x-3) \equiv 13(x-2)$.

**2**   Prove that the product of two odd numbers is always an odd number.

**3**   If $\dfrac{4x-2}{3} - \dfrac{x-a}{4} \equiv \dfrac{13(x+1)}{12}$

Work out the value of $a$.

**4**   Factorise:

**a**   $a^2 + 3a + 2$

**b**   $c^2 - 4c + 3$

**c**   $f^2 - f - 12$

**d**   $h^2 + 8h - 20$

**e**   $m^2 - 9$

**f**   $n^2 - 5n - 24$

**g**   $p^2 + 12p + 11$

**h**   $q^2 + 21q + 20$

**i**   $r^2 - 2r - 35$

**j**   $t^2 + t - 2$

**k**   $3x^2 - 7x + 2$

**l**   $5y^2 + 14y - 3$

**m**   $5z^2 - 27z + 10$

**n**   $2w^2 + 5w - 3$

**o**   $6u^2 + 11u + 3$

**p**   $4v^2 - 13v + 10$

**5**   Factorise completely:

**a**   $18x^2 - 2$

**b**   $3y^2 - 24y + 21$

**c**   $2t^2 - 18t - 20$

**d**   $8x^2 + 20x - 12$

**6**   Simplify:

**a**   $\dfrac{x^2 + 5x + 4}{x^2 + x - 12}$

**b**   $\dfrac{y^2 - 2y - 35}{y^2 - 25}$

**c**   $\dfrac{z^2 + 5z - 24}{z^2 - 5z + 6}$

**d**   $\dfrac{25 - x^2}{x^2 + 7x + 10}$

**A**

**7** Solve the following equations.

  **a** $\dfrac{x}{(x+1)} - \dfrac{4}{(x-1)} = 1$    **b** $\dfrac{12}{(x+3)} + \dfrac{x}{(x+5)} = 2$

**8** Solve these equations.

  **a** $(a-2)(a+6) = 0$        **f** $f^2 = 3f + 40$

  **b** $b^2 + 8b + 7 = 0$        **g** $k^2 = 1$

  **c** $c^2 - 9c + 8 = 0$        **h** $m^2 - 14m - 32 = 0$

  **d** $d^2 + d = 6$          **i** $2n^2 - 7n + 5 = 0$

  **e** $e^2 - 5e = 0$          **j** $3p^2 - p - 14 = 0$

**9** One solution of the equation $x^2 - 5x + p = 0$ is $x = 3$
  Work out the value of $p$.

**10** One solution of the equation $y^2 - qy - 25 = 0$ is $y = -1$
  Work out the value of $q$.

**A\***

**11** Solve these equations by using the quadratic formula.

  Give your answers as decimals to two decimal places.

  **a** $x^2 + 8x + 6 = 0$        **d** $5x^2 + 10x + 4 = 0$

  **b** $4x^2 - 3x - 2 = 0$        **e** $3x^2 - 4x - 7 = 0$

  **c** $x^2 - 5x - 3 = 0$

**12** If $\dfrac{x^2 - 9}{x^2 + 4x - a} \equiv \dfrac{x+3}{x+7}$

  Work out the value of $a$.

**13** The $n$th term of a sequence is given by the formula $\frac{1}{2}n(n-1)$

  **a** Write down the first three terms of the sequence.

  **b** Prove that the sum of any two consecutive terms of the sequence is always a square number.

**14** Solve these equations by completing the square.
  Give your answers in surd form.

  **a** $x^2 + 10x + 4 = 0$        **c** $z^2 - 16z + 12 = 0$

  **b** $y^2 - 4y + 1 = 0$        **d** $5c^2 + 30c - 40 = 0$

**15** You are given the identity $x^2 - ax + 49 \equiv (x-b)^2$
  Work out the values of $a$ and $b$.

**16** Solve $\dfrac{x}{x+1} + \dfrac{2}{1-x} = 1$

**17** Solve $\dfrac{3}{2x+1} - \dfrac{1}{x-5} = \frac{4}{3}$

**18** The area of this rectangle is 56 cm².
  Form a quadratic equation in $y$ and solve it to find the length of the rectangle.

$(y+7)$ cm

$(y-3)$ cm

**? 19**    The dimensions of this cuboid are all in cm.

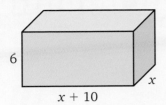

6

$x$

$x + 10$

The volume of the cuboid is $450\,\text{cm}^3$.

Form a quadratic equation in $x$ and solve it to find the width of the cuboid.

# Practice questions Ⓚ

**1**    **a**    Copy and complete the table of values for $y = x^2 - x - 5$.

| $x$ | $-2$ | $-1$ | 0 | 1 | 2 | 3 | 4 |
|-----|------|------|---|---|---|---|---|
| $y$ | 1 | | $-5$ | $-5$ | $-3$ | 1 | |

*(2 marks)*

**b**    On graph paper draw the graph of $y = x^2 - x - 5$ for values of $x$ from $-2$ to 4.    *(2 marks)*

**c**    An approximate solution of the equation $x^2 - x - 5 = 0$ is $x = 2.8$
Explain how you can find this from the graph.

*(1 mark)*

AQA 2008

**2**    The diagram shows a garden in the shape of a rectangle measuring 10 m by 8 m.
On two sides of the garden there is a path $x$ metres wide.
The remaining area is covered by grass.

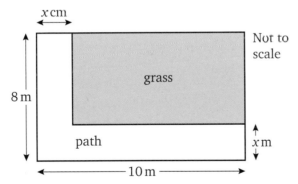

$x$ cm

Not to scale

grass

8 m

path

$x$ m

10 m

**a**    The area covered by grass is $\frac{3}{5}$ of the area of the garden.
Show that $x$ satisfies the equation $x^2 - 18x + 32 = 0$    *(3 marks)*

**b**    Hence, or otherwise, find the width of the path.    *(2 marks)*

AQA 2008

**3**    Solve the equation $2x^2 + 3x - 7 = 0$.
Give your answers correct to two decimal places.
You **must** show your working.    *(3 marks)*

AQA 2008

**4**    **a**    $n$ is a positive integer.

    **i**    Explain why $n(n + 1)$ must be an even number.    *(1 mark)*

    **ii**    Explain why $2n + 1$ must be an odd number.    *(1 mark)*

**b**    Expand and simplify $(2n + 1)^2$.    *(2 marks)*

**c**    Prove that the square of any odd number is always 1 more than a multiple of 8.    *(3 marks)*

AQA 2004

## Objectives

Examiners would normally expect students who get these grades to be able to:

### B

solve a pair of simultaneous equations such as $x + 3y = 9$ and $3x - 2y = 5$

solve a pair of linear equations graphically; identifying the point of intersection as the solution

### A

solve a pair of simultaneous equations such as $y = 4x + 5$ and $y = x^2$

find the point of intersection of a linear and a quadratic equation; recognising that the solution could be found from the points of intersection of the graphs.

### Key terms

simultaneous equations
coefficient
variable
eliminate
substitution

### Did you know?

## Supply and demand

The financial world uses simultaneous equations to model the balance between the supply and demand for a product or service.

When a product/service is in demand, the price will increase. However, if the price increases too much, the demand for the product/service will decrease as fewer people buy it.

The use of simultaneous equations can help foresee any problems and can try to determine where the balance between supply and demand might lie.

## You should already know:

✔ how to simplify algebraic terms

✔ how to solve a linear equation

✔ how to draw linear and quadratic graphs

✔ how to multiply out brackets

✔ how to rearrange an equation to make $y$ or $x$ the subject

✔ how to solve a quadratic equation by factorisation, completing the square or by use of the quadratic formula

✔ the theorems associated with circles.

## 10.1 Solving simultaneous equations by elimination

$$4x + 3y = 12$$

The coefficient of $x$ is 4.
The coefficient of $y$ is 3.

$x$ and $y$ are the variables

**Simultaneous equations** can be solved by making the **coefficients** of one of the **variables** the same in both equations.

In these simultaneous equations, the coefficients of $y$ are the same value. This means that you do not have to make them the same value to start with:

$$4x + 3y = 12 \qquad \text{The coefficient of } x \text{ is 4 and the coefficient of } y \text{ is 3.}$$
$$3x - 3y = 2 \qquad \text{The coefficient of } x \text{ is 3 and the coefficient of } y \text{ is } -3.$$

The coefficients of $y$ have the same value.
Because they have different signs, the equations are ready to be **added**: $+3y$ added to $-3y$ equals zero.

In these simultaneous equations, the coefficients of $y$ do not have the same value:

$$7x - 5y = 2 \qquad \text{The coefficient of } x \text{ is 7 and the coefficient of } y \text{ is } -5.$$
$$2x - 10y = 8 \qquad \text{The coefficient of } x \text{ is 2 and the coefficient of } y \text{ is } -10.$$

To make the coefficient of $y$ the same value, you have to multiply the first equation by 2 throughout:

$$14x - 10y = 4$$
$$2x - 10y = 8$$

The coefficients of $y$ now have the same value.
Because the coefficients have the same signs, the equations are ready to be **subtracted**: $-10y$ subtracted from $-10y$ equals zero.

After making the coefficients of one variable the same, you can **eliminate** that variable by adding or subtracting.

If their <u>s</u>igns are the <u>s</u>ame, <u>s</u>ubtract the equations (remember this by s s s).

If their signs are different, add the equations.

---

**Example:** Solve these simultaneous equations.
$$2x + 3y = 15$$
$$3x - 2y = 3$$

**Solution:** Step 1: Multiply the first equation by 2 and the second equation by 3.
This makes the coefficients of $y$ the same value.
Because the signs are different, you add the equations.
$$4x + 6y = 30$$
$$9x - 6y = 9$$

> **Study tip**
> Don't forget to multiply **both sides** of each equation.

Step 2: Add the equations.
$$4x + 6y = 30$$
$$\underline{9x - 6y = 9}$$
$$13x = 39$$
$$x = 3$$

The coefficients of $y$ are matching numbers with different signs, so add the equations to eliminate $y$.

Step 3: To find the value of $y$, substitute $x = 3$ in the first equation.
$$2 \times 3 + 3y = 15$$
$$6 + 3y = 15$$
$$3y = 9$$
$$y = 3$$

> **Study tip**
> Always substitute back into the more straightforward of the two original equations. This is usually the one with positive numbers and/or smaller numbers in it.

Step 4: Use the second equation to check your answers.

$$3 \times 3 - 2 \times 3 = 9 - 6$$
$$= 3 \checkmark$$

**Study tip**

Make sure you do a check. Use the equation not used in Step 3. You will then know whether you have made a mistake.

**Remember**

- You must have a pair of terms with matching coefficients.
- If their signs are the same, subtract the equations (remember this by s s s).
- If their signs are different, add the equations.

## Practise...

## 10.1 Solving simultaneous equations by elimination

**B**

**1** Solve these simultaneous equations by elimination.

**a** $4x + y = 10$
$5x - y = 8$

**c** $a - 3b = 2$
$3b + a = 8$

**e** $3p + 2r = 3$
$8r + 3p = 21$

**b** $3x + 2y = 20$
$x + 2y = 9$

**d** $e + 2f = 6$
$e - f = 3$

**f** $x + 2y = 8$
$x + y = 6$

**2** Solve these simultaneous equations by elimination.

**a** $s + t = 7$
$2s + 5t = 26$

**c** $a + 2b = 4$
$3a + 5b = 9$

**e** $2p - r = 2$
$7p - 5r = 4$

**b** $x + 3y = 2$
$3x - y = 26$

**d** $e + 2f = 1.2$
$2e - f = 6.5$

**f** $4x - 3y = 2$
$x - y = 1$

**3** Solve these simultaneous equations by elimination.

**a** $3e - 8f = 11$
$2e - 5f = 6$

**c** $2x + 3y = 13$
$7x - 5y = -1$

**e** $2.5g - h = 4.5$
$g - 2.5h = 6$

**b** $2v - 7w = 57$
$3w - 11v = 6$

**d** $4i + 7j = 6$
$3i - 2j = 19$

**f** $5x + 4y = 5$
$6y + 2x = 13$

**4**

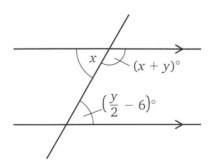

**a** Using the diagram above, form two equations in $x$ and $y$.

**b** Solve these equations simultaneously to find the values for $x$ and $y$.

**5** Julie is thinking of a fraction $\dfrac{x}{y}$

If she adds 5 to the numerator and to the denominator, her fraction equals $\dfrac{8}{9}$
If she subtracts $\dfrac{1}{2}$ from the numerator and the denominator, her fraction equals $\dfrac{5}{7}$

What is Julie's fraction?

**6**  A taxi firm charges a set amount of £*x* per journey plus £*y* for every mile travelled.
A three-mile journey costs £5.70 and a four-mile journey costs £7.20.

Find the set amount of pounds per journey and the charge per mile.

 **7**  In a training camp, the members of staff take five flashlights with them on night
expeditions.
Two different brands of batteries are available.

- Brand *A* has an average life of *x* hours.
- Brand *B* has an average life of *y* hours.

Assuming that the batteries run at the average rate:

- three brand *A* batteries and two brand *B* batteries would run for 48 hours and
  45 minutes in total
- four brand *A* batteries and one brand *B* battery would run for 40 hours in total.

Form a pair of simultaneous equations and solve them to find the average battery
running time for each brand.

 **8**  Martin works in a café. At the end of each day he counts the money in the till.

- On Monday he has *x* £10 notes and *y* £5 notes. The total amount of money
  equals £125.
- On Tuesday he has half the number of £10 notes and five times the number
  of £5 notes that he had on Monday. After he counts the money, he pays the
  milkman £25 out of the total amount and then has £150 left.

Form a pair of simultaneous equations in *x* and *y* and solve them to find how many
of the different notes he had at the end of each day.

 **9**  Two ice lollies and three ice-cream cones cost £3.50.
Three ice lollies and two ice-cream cones cost £3.25.
The cost of an ice lolly is £*c* and the cost of an ice-cream cone is £*d*.

Write down a pair of simultaneous equations and solve them to find *c* and *d*.

 **10.2 Solving simultaneous equations by substitution**

Simultaneous equations can also be solved by **substituting** one equation into the other.

This method is used when one of the variables is already the subject of one of the equations.

If this is not the case, you will have to rearrange one of the equations to make *x* or *y* the subject.

*Example:*

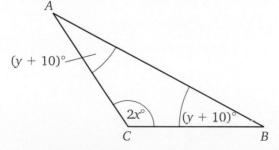

Triangle *ABC* is isosceles.
*x* is 20° more than *y*.

**a**  By forming two simultaneous equations in *x* and *y*, find the values of *x* and *y*.

**b**  Write down the value of each of the three angles in the triangle and use these to check
your answers.

**Solution:**

**a** The angles in a triangle add up to 180°.

So $2x + y + 10 + y + 10 = 180$

$\quad\quad\quad 2x + 2y + 20 = 180$      Collect like terms.

$\quad\quad\quad\quad\quad 2x + 2y = 180 - 20$     Subtract 20 from both sides.

$\quad\quad\quad\quad\quad 2x + 2y = 160$      Divide both sides by 2.

$\quad\quad\quad\quad\quad\quad x + y = 80$

As $x$ is 20° more than $y$, if you add 20 to $y$ it will equal $x$.

So $x = y + 20$

The two equations to be solved are:

$\quad\quad x + y = 80$

and $\quad\quad x = y + 20$

In the second equation, $x$ is already the subject, i.e. it is in the form $x = \dots$

Substituting for $x$ in the first equation gives:

$\quad\quad\quad y + 20 + y = 80$     Replace $x$ with $y + 20$.

$\quad\quad\quad\quad 2y + 20 = 80$     Collect the $y$ terms.

$\quad\quad\quad\quad\quad\quad 2y = 80 - 20$     Subtract 20 from both sides.

$\quad\quad\quad\quad\quad\quad 2y = 60$     Divide both sides by 2.

$\quad\quad\quad\quad\quad\quad y = 30$

Now substitute $y = 30$ into the first equation.

$\quad\quad\quad x + 30 = 80$

$\quad\quad\quad\quad x = 80 - 30$

$\quad\quad\quad\quad x = 50$

> **Study tip**
>
> Make sure you do a check. You will then know whether you have made a mistake.

Finally use the second equation to check your answers.

$50 = 30 + 20$ ✓

**b** The angles in the triangle are:

$\quad\quad 2x = 2 \times 50° = 100°$

$\quad\quad y + 10° = 30° + 10° = 40°$ for the other two angles

Check that these angles add up to 180° because the angles in a triangle add up to 180°.

$100° + 40° + 40° = 180°$ ✓

**Example:** On a particular internet site, it costs £$x$ to download a film and £$y$ to download a track of music.
Ragini downloaded two films and nine tracks of music. It cost her £12.48.
Jamie downloaded five films and two tracks of music. It cost him £20.95.

Write down two simultaneous linear equations in $x$ and $y$.

Solve these by substitution to find $x$, the cost of downloading a film and $y$, the cost of downloading a track of music.

**Solution:** For Ragini, £$2x$ + £$9y$ = £12.48

For Jamie, £$5x$ + £$2y$ = £20.95

The simultaneous equations are:

$\quad\quad 2x + 9y = 12.48$

$\quad\quad 5x + 2y = 20.95$

Rearrange the first equation to make $x$ the subject.
$$2x = 12.48 - 9y$$
$$x = 6.24 - 4.5y$$

Substitute this expression for $x$ into the second equation.
$$5x + 2y = 20.95$$
$$5(6.24 - 4.5y) + 2y = 20.95$$
$$31.2 - 22.5y + 2y = 20.95$$
$$31.2 - 20.5y = 20.95$$
$$10.25 = 20.5y$$
$$20.5y = 10.25$$
$$y = 0.5 \qquad £0.5 = £0.50 = 50p$$

Substitute this value for $y$ into the formula $x = 6.24 - 4.5y$
$$x = 6.24 - 4.5(0.5)$$
$$x = 3.99 \qquad £3.99$$

Now check the answers. Substitute both the $x$- and $y$-values back into the equations to see whether the values are correct.
$$2(3.99) + 9(0.5) = 7.98 + 4.50 = 12.48 \checkmark$$
$$5(3.99) + 2(0.5) = 19.95 + 1.00 = 20.95 \checkmark$$

# 10.2 Solving simultaneous equations by substitution 🄺

**Practise...**

**1** Solve these simultaneous linear equations by substitution.

**a**  $x + y = 8$
    $y = x + 2$

**b**  $c - d = 1$
    $c = 2d - 3$

**c**  $r = 2p - 5$
    $p + 2r = 0$

**d**  $v = 2w - 0.5$
    $4v - 5w = 1$

**2** Solve these simultaneous linear equations by substitution.

**a**  $m + n = 7$
    $m = 3 + n$

**b**  $2x + 3y = 28$
    $3x + 4y = 37$

**c**  $7x - 2y = 4$
    $6x + y = 17$

**d**  $2e - f = 22$
    $3e + 2f = 40$

**3** The diagram shows a circle with centre $X$.
The angle formed by the triangle at the circumference of the circle is $x + 3y$.
$x$ is 30° more than $y$.

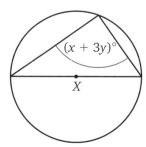

**a** From this, and your knowledge of circles, write down two equations in $x$ and $y$.

**b** Solve these simultaneous equations to find the values of $x$ and $y$.

A

**4**    Angle $x$ is 24° larger than angle $y$.
The bearing of $A$ from $B$ is 256°.

Not drawn accurately

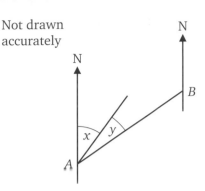

**a**    Find the values of $x$ and $y$ by forming two linear equations in $x$ and $y$ and solving them by substitution.

**b**    Write down the bearing of $B$ from $A$.

**5**    In the diagram, the ratio of $x:y$ is $4:5$

$O$ is the centre of the circle, and $AB$ is a tangent to the circle.

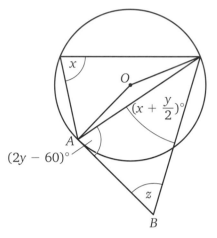

**a**    Set up and solve two simultaneous equations in $x$ and $y$.

**b**    Use these answers to find the value of $y$.

**6**    These are the rules for a quiz.

- You score $x$ points for a correct answer.
- $y$ points are taken away for an incorrect answer.
- If you correctly answer a bonus question, you score $z$ points.
- If you do not answer, you score no points.

Three friends' results were as follows.

Adrian:    6 correct
           1 incorrect
           1 bonus          Total = 54 points

Beth:      5 correct
           2 incorrect
           2 bonus          Total = 38 points

Charlie:   7 correct
           0 incorrect
           4 bonus          Total = 86 points

Find the values of $x$, $y$ and $z$.

**7**    John went to buy some of his favourite aftershave. It is manufactured in two sizes.

- The small size contains $x$ millilitres.
- The large size contains $y$ millilitres.

If he bought two small ones, he would have 30 ml less than the amount in the large size. The small size and the large size together contain a total of 135 ml.

How much aftershave is in each sized container?

**8**    Poppy and her three friends were going to a nightclub.
It costs less to go in before 9pm than it does to go in after 9pm.
Unfortunately, one of her friends can't get there before 9pm.
If three of them go in early and one later, it will cost £15.
Her friend does not really want to go in on her own.
If two go in early and two later, it will cost £16.

If £$x$ is the cost of early entry and £$y$ is the cost of the later entry, find the two different entry costs.

**9**   Susie is $x$ years old and her brother is $y$ years old.
Susie is 5 years older than her brother.
They both have an aunt who is 45 years old.
The aunt is three times her brother's age plus Susie's age.

How old are Susie and her brother?

**10**   Two teenagers have heights of $x$ metres and $y$ metres.
If you add their heights together, they measure 2.53 metres in total.
The difference between their heights is 11 cm.

   **a**   Write down two simultaneous equations in $x$ and $y$.

   **b**   Solve them by substitution to find each of their heights.

 **Learn...**

## 10.3 Solving simultaneous linear equations graphically

Simultaneous linear equations can also be solved graphically.

Begin by finding the coordinates of some points on each straight line.

The minimum number of points needed to draw a straight line is three; two to draw it and one as a check.

This is true for linear equations but to draw quadratics, you would need more $x$-values.

The point of intersection of two straight lines represents the solution to the simultaneous equations.

Drawing the lines will also confirm whether or not there is
a solution to the pair of simultaneous equations.

- If they are parallel, there would be no solution because the lines do not cross.
- If they are the same line, there would be an infinite number of solutions.

**Example:**   Solve these simultaneous equations graphically by plotting both lines on the same set of axes.

$$x + y = 3$$
$$x - y = 1$$

To help you, you can copy and complete these tables of values for the two equations.

$x + y = 3$

| $x$ | 0 | 1 | 3 |
|---|---|---|---|
| $y$ | 3 | | |

$x - y = 1$

| $x$ | 0 | 1 | 2 |
|---|---|---|---|
| $y$ | −1 | | |

**Solution:**   In this question the tables have already been given to you to complete.

$x + y = 3$

| $x$ | 0 | 1 | 3 |
|---|---|---|---|
| $y$ | 3 | 2 | 0 |

$$x - y = 1$$

| $x$ | 0 | 1 | 2 |
|---|---|---|---|
| $y$ | −1 | 0 | 1 |

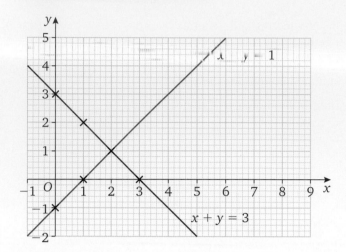

The straight lines cross at the point (2, 1).

This point represents the solution to the simultaneous equations.

$$x = 2, y = 1$$

Now check your solutions in both of the equations.

$$2 + 1 = 3 ✓$$

$$2 - 1 = 1 ✓$$

---

*Example:*   Solve the following simultaneous equations graphically.

$$y = 4 - x$$

$$2x - y = 2$$

*Solution:*   If you are not given the *x*-values that you have to use, or tables to complete, you will have to choose your own values.

One way is to begin by finding the points at which the graphs cross the *x*-axis and the *y*-axis.

This will give you a hint as to what other values to choose for each equation.

Starting with $y = 4 - x$

When $x = 0, y = 4$                   (0, 4)

When $y = 0, x = 4$                   (4, 0)

Choose one more value for *x*.

When $x = 1, y = 3$                   (1, 3)

Now work out three points on the other line.

$$2x - y = 2$$

When $x = 0, -y = 2$ so $y = -2$   (0, −2)

When $y = 0, x = 1$                   (1, 0)

Choose one more value for *x*.

When $x = 3, 6 - y = 2$ so $y = 4$   (3, 4)

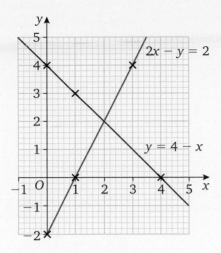

The two graphs cross at the point (2, 2). This point represents the solution to the simultaneous equations.

$$x = 2, y = 2$$

Now check your solutions in both equations.

$$2 = 4 - 2 \checkmark$$
$$4 - 2 = 2 \checkmark$$

**Example:**   Cinema tickets cost £$x$ for adults and £$y$ for children.
Three adult tickets and one child's ticket cost £18.
Four adult tickets and two children's tickets cost £26.

Solve these equations graphically to find the prices of each type of ticket.

**Solution:**   If 3 adult tickets and 1 child's ticket cost £18, the equation is $3x + y = 18$

If 4 adult tickets and 2 children's tickets cost £26, the equation is $4x + 2y = 26$
This can be simplified to $2x + y = 13$

So, the equations are:

$$3x + y = 18$$
$$2x + y = 13$$

Neither $x$ nor $y$ can be negative because they represent amounts of money.

Starting with $3x + y = 18$

When $x = 0, y = 18$                  (0, 18)

When $y = 0, 3x = 18$ so $x = 6$      (6, 0)

Choose one more value for $x$.

When $x = 3, 9 + y = 18$ so $y = 9$     (3, 9)

Now work out three points on the other line.

$$2x + y = 13$$

When $x = 0, y = 13$                  (0, 13)

When $y = 0, 2x = 13$ so $x = 6\frac{1}{2}$     $(6\frac{1}{2}, 0)$

Choose one more value for $x$.

When $x = 3, 6 + y = 13$ so $y = 7$     (3, 7)

The point of intersection is (5, 3).

An adult's ticket costs £5 and a child's costs £3.

Now check your solutions in your original equations.

$3 \times 5 + 3 = 15 + 3 = 18$ ✓

$2 \times 5 + 3 = 13$ ✓

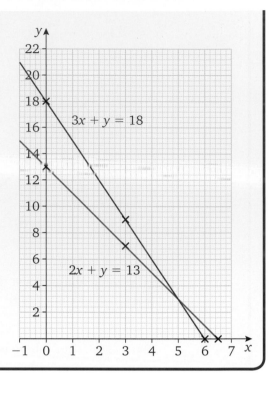

# 10.3 Solving simultaneous linear equations graphically

D C B A A*

**Practise...**

**B**

**1** Solve the following simultaneous equations graphically.

For each question part, consider $x$-values from 0 to 5.

**a** $x + y = 6$
$x + 2y = 8$

**c** $x + 2y = 5$
$3x - y = 8$

**e** $7x + 3y = 5$
$15x - 3y - 6$

**b** $y = x + 2$
$y = 3x - 3$

**d** $3x + 2y = 10$
$2x - 2y = 5$

**f** $5y + 2x = 15.5$
$3x - 5y = 4.5$

**2** For each question, consider $x$-values from $-5$ to 5.

**a** $x + y = -1$
$2x + 5y = 1$

**c** $2x + y = -8$
$x - 2y = 6$

**e** $5x - 2y = 12$
$2x + y = 3$

**b** $y = x - 4$
$x - 2y = 7$

**d** $2x + y = 0$
$x + 3y = 2\frac{1}{2}$

**f** $x + y = -1$
$2x - y = -\frac{1}{2}$

**3** A Chinese buffet costs £$x$ for an adult and £$y$ for a child.
A family of two adults and a child paid £30.
Another family of one adult and two children paid £24.

How much did the buffet cost for each adult and each child?

Solve this using a graphical method.

**Hint**

Consider $x$-values from 0 to 14.

**4** A coffee and a hot chocolate cost £$x$ and £$y$ respectively.
Two coffees and a hot chocolate cost £9.50.
One coffee and three hot chocolates cost £13.50.

How much do you pay for each type of drink?

Solve this using a graphical method.

## 10.4 Solving simultaneous equations algebraically, where one is linear and one is quadratic

The substitution method is especially useful when there is one linear equation and one quadratic equation. The substitution leads to a quadratic with one unknown.

When solving these, you are finding the coordinates of any points where the straight line intersects with the curve. There are three possibilities.

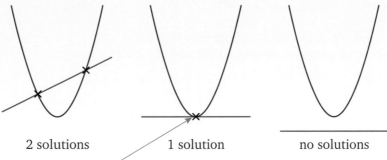

|   2 solutions   |   1 solution   |   no solutions   |

The line here is a tangent to the graph.

To solve these types of problem:

- Make sure that the linear equation expresses $y$ in terms of $x$ or $x$ in terms of $y$. If the equation is not in either format, rearrange the equation so that it is.
- Substitute this expression into the quadratic equation.
- Rearrange the new equation into the quadratic form: $ax^2 + bx + c = 0$
- Solve the equation.
- Substitute each value of $x$ into the linear equation to find the corresponding value of $y$.
- Check your solutions by substituting them back into the quadratic equation.

*Example:*    Solve the simultaneous equations.

$y = 1 - 4x$        linear equation

$y = x^2 - 4$        quadratic equation

*Solution:*    As the linear equation expresses $y$ in terms of $x$, substitute this expression into the quadratic equation.

$1 - 4x = x^2 - 4$

$1 = x^2 + 4x - 4$        Collect all the $x$ terms on one side.

$0 = x^2 + 4x - 5$        Rearrange the equation into the quadratic form $ax^2 + bx + c = 0$

$(x + 5)(x - 1) = 0$        Factorise the quadratic.

Now solve the equation.

Either     $x + 5 = 0$ so $x = -5$

or          $x - 1 = 0$ so $x = 1$

Substitute each value of $x$ in the linear equation to find the corresponding value of $y$.

$y = 1 - 4x$

When $x = -5$     $y = 1 - 4 \times (-5) = 1 + 20 = 21$        First pair of values is $(-5, 21)$.

When $x = 1$     $y = 1 - 4 \times 1 = 1 - 4 = -3$        Second pair of values is $(1, -3)$.

To check, substitute both pairs of values into the quadratic equation, $y = x^2 - 4$

$(-5)^2 - 4 = 25 - 4 = 21$ ✓

$1^2 - 4 = 1 - 4 = -3$ ✓

# 10.4 Solving simultaneous equations algebraically, where one is linear and one is quadratic $k$

**Practise...**

D | C | B | A | A*

**A**

**1**    Solve these simultaneous equations by substitution.

    **a**    $y = 3x + 10$      **b**    $3.5c + d = -1$      **c**    $g = h^2$        **d**    $v = 4w^2$

        $y = 4x^2$             $d = 2c^2 - 2$          $g = 9h - 14$      $v = 9w - 5$

**2**    Solve these simultaneous equations by substitution.
      Where necessary, give your answers correct to two decimal places.

    **a**    $m = n^2 + 2$      **b**    $f = e^2 + 3e + 1$      **c**    $y = 2x^2 - 1$      **d**    $b = 7a^2 - 4a + 3$

        $n + m = 3$          $f = 7e - 1$          $y = 3x + 2$         $b = 4a + 1$

**A***

**3**    Solve the following two equations simultaneously.

$$(x - 2)^2 + y^2 = 4 \qquad y = x - 1$$

Give your answers correct to two decimal places.

**?**   **4**    Susie thinks of two whole numbers, $x$ and $y$.

If she squares the first number and then subtracts the square of the second number, it gives the same answer as when the two numbers are added together.

The second number is also twice the first number minus 8.

What are the numbers?

**?**   **5**    The total area of the square and the rectangle is 64 cm².
The width of the rectangle ($y$) is five times the side length of the square ($x$) minus 14.

Find the dimensions of the square and the rectangle.

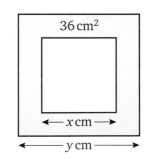

Not drawn accurately

**?**   **6**    The diagram shows two squares, one inside the other.
The area of the shaded part is 36 cm².
The difference between the side lengths of the squares is 2 cm.

Find the side length of each square.

# 10.5 Solving simultaneous equations graphically, where one is linear and one is quadratic

**Learn...**

In Learn 20.4, linear and quadratic equations were solved algebraically, using substitution.

For the higher grades, you also need to be able to solve them graphically.

The linear equations can be plotted in the same way as in Learn 20.3, by finding three points on the line.

As quadratic equations are curves, you will need more than three points to plot them. This usually involves the construction of a table for between six and ten points as shown in the examples.

When solving a linear and a quadratic equation, remember that you could obtain one or two solutions, or sometimes, no solutions at all.

Sometimes straight lines are used to solve quadratic equations. In these questions, the straight line used is embedded in the equation itself and the first step is to identify the straight line to be used.

In Chapter 17, Learn 17.5, equations such as $x^2 + 2x = 0$ were solved by considering where the graph $y = x^2 + 2x$ intersected with the $y = 0$ line.

For $x^2 + 2x = 4$, the solutions were where the graph $y = x^2 + 2x$ intersected with the $y = 4$ line.

The second worked example shows you how to solve several different quadratic equations from one graph.

*Example:*  Solve these simultaneous equations graphically by plotting both graphs on the same set of axes.

$$y = -x^2 + 4x - 3 \qquad \text{Take values of } x \text{ from 0 to 5.}$$

$$2 - 2x = y$$

*Solution:*  For the quadratic $y = -x^2 + 4x - 3$

| $x$ | 0 | 1 | 2 | 3 | 4 | 5 |
|---|---|---|---|---|---|---|
| $-x^2$ | 0 | $-1$ | $-4$ | $-9$ | $-16$ | $-25$ |
| $+4x$ | 0 | 4 | 8 | 12 | 16 | 20 |
| $-3$ | $-3$ | $-3$ | $-3$ | $-3$ | $-3$ | $-3$ |
| $y$ | $-3$ | 0 | 1 | 0 | $-3$ | $-8$ |

$$2 - 2x = y \qquad \text{Rearrange the linear equation.}$$

$$y = 2 - 2x$$

To draw the straight line, you will need three points.

When $x = 0, y = 2$      (0, 2)

When $y = 0, x = 1$      (1, 0)

When $x = 2, y = -2$      (2, −2)

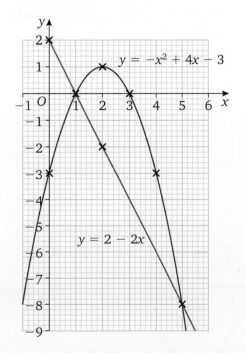

The straight line crosses the graph at (1, 0) and (5, −8).

The solutions are $x = 1$ and $x = 5$

Now check your solutions.

When $x = 1$ and $y = 0$

$$y = -x^2 + 4x - 3 \qquad -1^2 + 4 - 3 = -1 + 4 - 3 = 0 ✓$$

$$2 - 2x = y \qquad 2 - 2 - 0 ✓$$

When $x = 5$ and $y = -8$

$$y = -x^2 + 4x - 3 \qquad -5^2 + 4 \times 5 - 3 = -25 + 20 - 3 = -8 ✓$$

$$2 - 2x = y \qquad 2 - 2 \times 5 = 2 - 10 = -8 ✓$$

*Example:*   **a**   Draw the graph of $y = x^2 - 6x + 8$ for values of $x$ from $0 \leqslant x \leqslant 6$

**b**   Use your graph and suitable straight lines to solve these equations.

   **i**   $x^2 - 6x + 5 = 0$

   **ii**   $x^2 - 7x + 6 = 0$

   **iii**   $x^2 - 4x + 4 = 0$

*Solution:*   For the quadratic $y = x^2 - 6x + 8$

| $x$ | 0 | 1 | 2 | 3 | 4 | 5 | 6 |
|-----|---|---|---|---|---|---|---|
| $x^2$ | 0 | 1 | 4 | 9 | 16 | 25 | 36 |
| $- 6x$ | 0 | −6 | −12 | −18 | −24 | −30 | −36 |
| $+ 8$ | +8 | +8 | +8 | +8 | +8 | +8 | +8 |
| $y$ | 8 | 3 | 0 | −1 | 0 | 3 | 8 |

You can use the shortened table if you prefer but it is easier to make mistakes.

**b**   **i**   $x^2 - 6x + 5 = 0$        Write down the equation you wish to solve.

        $x^2 - 6x + 5 + 3 = 0 + 3$   Add 3 to both sides.

        $x^2 - 6x + 8 = 3$         The left-hand side is now the quadratic function for $y$.

Solutions are found where the line $y = 3$ crosses the curve.

$x = 1$ and $x = 5$

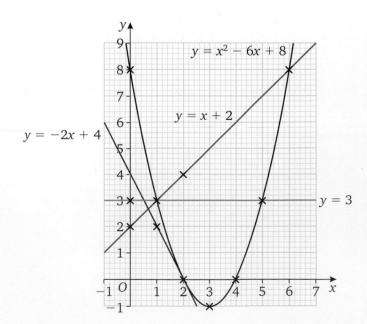

**ii** $x^2 - 7x + 6 = 0$         Write down the equation you wish to solve.

$x^2 - 7x + x + 6 = x$      Add $x$ to both sides to make the term in $x$ become $-6x$.

$x^2 - 6x + 6 + 2 = x + 2$    Add 2 to both sides to make the constant term $+8$.

$x^2 - 6x + 8 = x + 2$    The left-hand side is now the quadratic function for $y$.

Solutions are found where the line $y = x + 2$ crosses the curve.

To plot this straight line you need three points.

When $x = 0$, $y = 2$        (0, 2)

When $y = 0$, $x = -2$    (−2, 0)      (not in the range plotted for the quadratic)

When $x = 1$, $y = 3$        (1, 3)

When $x = 2$, $y = 4$        (2, 4)

Reading from the graph, the solutions are $x = 1$ and $x = 6$

**iii** $x^2 - 4x + 4 = 0$        Write down the equation you wish to solve.

$x^2 - 4x - 2x + 4 = -2x$      Subtract $2x$ from both sides to make the term in $x$ become $-6x$.

$x^2 - 6x + 4 + 4 = -2x + 4$    Add 4 to both sides to make the constant term $+4$.

$x^2 - 6x + 8 = -2x + 4$    The left-hand side is now the quadratic function for $y$.

Solutions are found where the line $y = -2x + 4$ crosses the curve.

To plot this you need three points.

When $x = 0$, $y = 4$              (0, 4)

When $y = 0$, $2x = 4$ so $x = 2$    (2, 0)

When $x = 1$, $y - -2 + 4 = 2$      (1, 2)

This line touches the curve at (2, 0). The line is a tangent to the curve so there is only one distinct solution, $x = 2$

> **Study tip**
>
> Remember that there are three possible cases when solving a linear and a quadratic equation: you could obtain 1, 2 or 0 solutions. If the straight line and the quadratic do not intersect, there will be no solution.

## 10.5 Solving simultaneous equations graphically, where one is linear and one is quadratic 🅚

**Practise...**      D C B A A*

**1**   Solve these simultaneous equations graphically by plotting both graphs on the same set of axes.      **A**

    **a**   $y = x^2 + 3$        Take values of $x$ from 0 to 5.
        $y = 4x$

    **b**   $x + y = 4$        Take values of $x$ from −5 to 5.
        $y = x^2 - 8$

    **c**   $y = x^2 - 3x - 4$        Take values of $x$ from −2 to 5.
        $y = 1 + x$

    **d**   $y = 2x^2 - 9x + 9$        Take values of $x$ from 0 to 5.
        $x + y = 9$

    **e**   $y = 3 + 2x - x^2$        Take values of $x$ from −2 to 4.
        $2y = x + 4$

**A**
**A\***

**2** **a** Draw the graph of $y = x^2 - 5x + 4$ for $0 \leqslant x \leqslant 5$

**b** Use your graph and suitable straight lines to solve these equations.

   **i** $x^2 - 5x + 4 = 0$     **ii** $x^2 - 5x + 6 = 0$     **iii** $x^2 - 6x + 5 = 0$

**3** **a** Draw the graph of $y = x^2 - 4x - 5$ for $-2 \leqslant x \leqslant 6$

**b** Use your graph and suitable straight lines to solve these equations.

   **i** $x^2 - 4x - 5 = 0$     **ii** $x^2 - 4x + 1 = 0$     **iii** $x^2 - x - 6 = 0$

**4** **a** Draw the graph of $y = 6x - x^2$ for $-1 \leqslant x \leqslant 7$

**b** Use your graph and suitable straight lines to solve these equations.

   **i** $6x - x^2 = 0$     **ii** $6x - x^2 - 4 = 0$

**c** Use the graph to explain why you cannot solve the equation $6x - x^2 - 10 = 0$.

**5** Here are the equations of a curve and a line.

$y = 3x^2 - 5x + 2$     $y = x - 1$

Show that the line is a tangent to the curve at the point $(1, 0)$.

**⚠ 6** The graph shows a sketch of the curve $y = 2x^2 - 5x + 3$ and the line $y = x + 11$
They cross at the points $A$ and $B$.

Show that the points $A$ and $B$ can be found
using the quadratic equation:

$x^2 - 3x - 4 = 0$

Hence find the coordinates of $A$ and $B$.

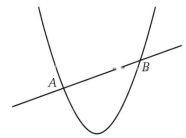

---

# 10 Assess 🄚

**B**

**1** Solve these simultaneous equations.

   **a** $3x + 2y = 11$            **c** $3x + 5y = 5$
      $4x - 2y = 10$                  $4x - 3y = 26$

   **b** $2x + y = 7$             **d** $4x + 2y = 0$
      $2x - y = 9$                  $3x + y = \frac{1}{2}$

**2** A vanilla smoothie costs £$x$ and a strawberry smoothie costs £$y$.
Two vanilla and one strawberry smoothies cost £5.75.
One vanilla and two strawberry smoothies cost £6.25.

How much do they cost each?

**3** A mother is $x$ years old and her son is $y$ years old.
The difference between their ages is 20 years.
Five years ago the mother was five times her son's age.

How old are they both now?

Solve this using a graphical method.

**4**  Solve these simultaneous equations.
Where necessary, give your answers to 2 decimal places

a  $y = 2x^2$
$y = 7x - 3$

b  $y = x^2$
$y = 4x + 5$

c  $y = x^2 + 4x + 7$
$y = 3 - x$

d  $y = x^2 - 2x + 5$
$2y - x = 20$

**5**  The diagram shows a square with an isosceles triangle removed from the corner.
The area of the shaded region is 8.5 cm².
The difference between $x$ and $y$ is 2 cm.

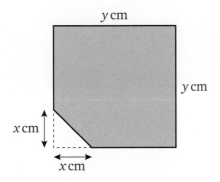

Find the values of $x$ and $y$.

**6**  A couple are carpeting two rooms in their house with carpet tiles.
The tiles are sold in packs of four 50 cm × 50 cm square.
They have picked out two types of carpet that they like.

One is £$x$ per pack and the other is £$y$ per pack.
They decide to buy both carpets, using the more expensive in one room and
the cheaper one in the other.
They are not sure which carpet to put in which room.

If they put the expensive carpet in the dining room and the cheaper one in the
living room it will cost them £425. If they change these over, it will cost
them £475.

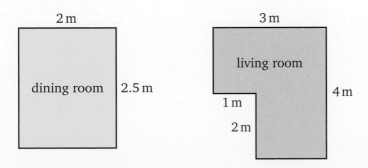

What is the cost per pack of each of the carpets?

# Practice questions 🄺

1   Solve these simultaneous equations.

$$5x + 6y = 28$$
$$x + 3y = 2$$

You **must** show your working.
**Do not** use trial and improvement.

*(3 marks)*

AQA 2007

  a   The line $x + y = 5$ has been drawn on the grid.
      Copy the graph and draw the line of $y = 2x - 5$ for values of $x$ from $-1$ to $+5$.

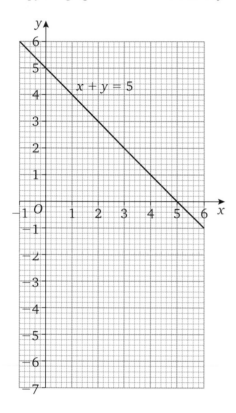

*(2 marks)*

  b   Use the graphs to find the solution to the simultaneous equations.

$$x + y = 5$$
$$y = 2x - 5$$

*(3 marks)*

AQA 2008

2   Solve the simultaneous equations.

$$y = 5x - 1$$
$$y = 2x^2 + 1$$

**Do not** use trial and improvement.
You **must** show your working.

*(6 marks)*

AQA 2007

# 11 Construction

## Objectives

Examiners would normally expect students who get these grades to be able to:

### D

draw a quadrilateral such as a kite, parallelogram or rhombus with given measurements

understand that giving the lengths of two sides and a non-included angle may not produce a unique triangle

### C

construct perpendicular bisectors and angle bisectors

match one angle and one side of congruent triangles given some dimensions

### B

construct perpendicular lines from a point to a line, perpendicular at a point on a line and an angle of 60°

match sides and angles of similar triangles

### A

prove two triangles are congruent

prove construction theorems.

**Key terms**

| | |
|---|---|
| construction | similar |
| equilateral | corresponding |
| perpendicular | scale factor |
| bisector | congruent |

*Did you know?*

## This type of mathematics is part of geometry and is very old

The ancient Greek mathematician Euclid is the inventor of geometry. He did this over 2000 years ago, and his book *Elements* is still the ultimate geometry reference. He used construction techniques extensively. They give us a method of drawing things when simple measurement is not appropriate.

## You should already know:

✔ how to use scales and scale diagrams

✔ how to recognise enlargements

✔ how to find scale factors

✔ facts about angles in circles

✔ facts about angles in parallel lines

✔ angle properties of polygons

✔ how to use compasses

✔ how to measure an acute and an obtuse angle with a protractor.

# Learn... 11.1 Drawing triangles accurately

There are different ways to draw a triangle accurately. The method you use depends on what you know about the triangle.

**Drawing a triangle when all three sides are known**

The following example shows how to draw a triangle when all three sides are known.

*Example:* Draw a triangle with sides 4.2 cm, 5.3 cm and 6 cm.

*Solution:* First draw a sketch to see what the triangle looks like.

Now, draw your **construction**. Draw and measure the longest side using a ruler and pencil. You should clearly mark end points on the line.

Open your compasses to the same length as one of your other sides. It does not matter which one you draw first. Put the point of the compasses on one end of the line and draw an arc.

Do the same from the other end of the line, with the compasses open to the length of the other side. Make sure that your arcs cross each other.

The arcs cross at the position of the third vertex. Join this point to the ends of the lines and label the diagram with the side lengths.

**Sketch**

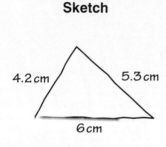

**Construction**

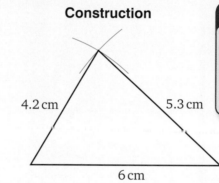

> **Study tip**
>
> Do not rub out your construction arcs as they are your working out. The arcs show your method and will score you marks in an exam.

**Drawing a triangle when one side and two angles are known**

The following example shows how to draw a triangle when one side and two angles are known.

*Example:* Construct a triangle with base 8 cm and two angles at the base of 50° and 40°.

*Solution:* Start by drawing the base, then measure one of the given angles carefully. It does not matter which one you measure first.

Mark a point on the protractor's scale at the value of the first angle and draw in the line. Extend it beyond the point you have marked. It is much better to have a line that is too long than too short.

Repeat for the other angle.

Extend this line to meet the line you have already drawn. Label the triangle with two known angles and one known side.

**Sketch**

**Construction**

> **Study tip**
>
> It is best to draw the two angles from either end of the given side. If one of these angles is the angle not given, then you can work out its size using the fact that angles of a triangle add up to 180°.

**Drawing a triangle when one angle and two sides are known**

The following example shows how to draw a triangle when one included angle and two sides are known.

**Example:**   Construct a triangle with two sides 6 cm and 7 cm, and an included angle of 60°.

**Solution:**   Start with the longest side, then measure the angle given, using a protractor.

Draw in the side. Make it long enough as before; it is better too long than too short.

Now measure this side carefully. Mark on the line the point where it should end.

Join from this point to the end of the starting line.

Label the triangle.

**Sketch**

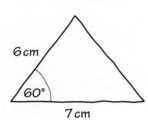

**Construction**

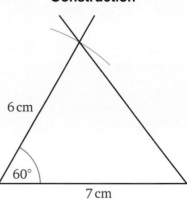

## Practise...   11.1 Drawing triangles accurately (k) (D)(C)(B)(A)(A*)

The shapes in these exercises have not been drawn accurately.

**1**   Draw these triangles accurately.

**a**

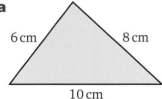

**b**

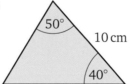

**c**

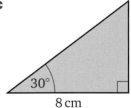

**2**   Draw this shape accurately.

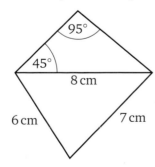

**3**   Bill and Ben have been asked to draw a triangle accurately.
The triangle has sides of 8 cm, 5 cm and a non-included angle 30°.
They both draw it correctly, but their diagrams look different.
Can you draw both Bill's and Ben's diagrams?

**D**

**4** Draw a rhombus accurately, which has all sides equal to 6 cm and a shorter diagonal of 7 cm.

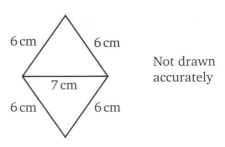

Not drawn accurately

**5** John is making a triangular prism from card.

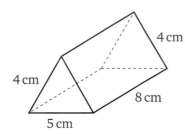

Not drawn accurately

Draw an accurate net for his prism.

**6** Make an accurate drawing of a rectangle that has longer sides of 8 cm and diagonals of length 10 cm.

What is the length of the shorter sides?

**7** A piece of material is cut to make a skirt.
The material is shown in this sketch and is in the shape of an isosceles trapezium.

Using a scale of 2 cm to 50 cm, make an accurate scale drawing of this piece of material.

Not drawn accurately

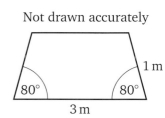

**8** A field is in the shape of a pentagon as shown.

**a** Make a scale drawing of the field.

**b** Use your scale drawing to find the perimeter of the field.

Not drawn accurately

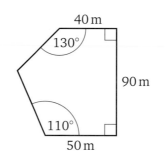

**9** On a map, two hotels (Sleep Inn and Stay Well Inn) are 8.8 cm apart. Sleep Inn is due north of Stay Well Inn. A third hotel (Lie Inn) is due east of Stay Well Inn and on a bearing of 143° from Sleep Inn.

**a** Draw the positions of the hotels accurately.

**b** If the map is drawn using a scale of 1 : 50 000, what are the actual distances between the hotels?

 **10** This is a sketch of Hilary's bedroom.

She plans to reorganise her room, using a scale drawing to help decide where to put her furniture. She uses an A4 sheet of graph paper.

Draw an accurate plan of her bedroom using an appropriate scale.

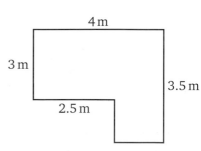

Not drawn accurately

**11**    The diagram shows the front elevation of Patrick's garage.

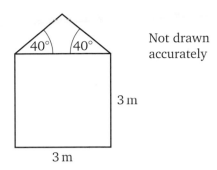

Not drawn accurately

3 m

3 m

Patrick has a boat on a trailer, which he wants to keep in the garage.
The top of the mast is 4.4 metres above the ground.
Can Patrick keep the boat in the garage? Explain your answer.

 **Learn...**    **11.2 Constructions**

Constructions are drawn using only a straight edge and a pair of compasses. You need to be able to construct **equilateral** triangles, the **perpendicular** bisectors of a line, and angle bisectors; perpendiculars from a point to a line, and perpendiculars at a point on a line.

A **bisector** is a line that cuts something into two equal parts. A line bisector cuts a line into two equal parts. An angle bisector cuts an angle into two equal parts.

**Equilateral triangles**

The following example shows how to construct an equilateral triangle.

*Example:*    Construct an equilateral triangle.

*Solution:*    Start with a line that will become one of the sides in your triangle, with a point $P$, where one vertex will be.

Open your compasses to the length of one side. With the point of your compasses on $P$ draw a large arc that intersects the line at $Q$.

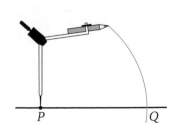

Keep the radius of your compasses the same. Put the point of the compasses on $Q$ and draw an arc that passes through $P$ and cuts the first arc at $R$.

Join $P$ to $R$, and $Q$ to $R$. You have now finished your construction.

You can use this technique to construct an angle of 60°. Follow the first two steps above, and then just join $P$ to $R$ (or $R$ to $Q$).

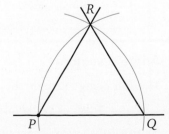

**Study tip**

Remember to leave your arcs. They show your method and will score you marks.

## Line bisectors

The following example shows how to construct the bisector of a line.

*Example:*   Construct the bisector of line *AB*.

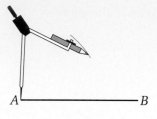

*Solution:*   Open your compasses to more than half of *AB*. Put the point on *A* and draw arcs above and below *AB*.

Keep the radius of your compasses the same. Put the point of your compasses on *B* and draw two new arcs to cut the first two at *C* and *D*.

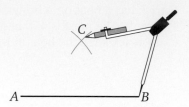

Join *CD*.

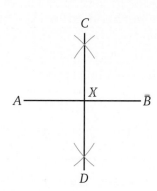

*X* is the midpoint of *AB*. *CD* not only bisects *AB*, it is called the perpendicular bisector of *AB*. This is because it meets *AB* at 90°.

### Study tip

You have constructed a rhombus whose diagonals bisect each other at 90°.

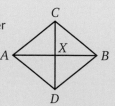

## Angle bisectors

The following example shows how to construct the bisector of an angle.

*Example:*   Construct the bisector of angle *BAC*.

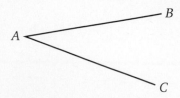

***Solution:***   Open your compasses to less than the length of the shorter line. Put the point on *A* and draw arcs to cut *AB* at *X* and *AC* at *Y*.

Keep the radius of your compasses the same. Put the point of your compasses on *X* and *Y* in turn and draw arcs that intersect at *Z*.

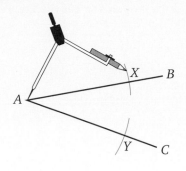

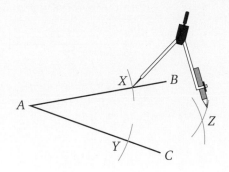

Join *AZ*.

*AZ* is the angle bisector of angle *BAC*.

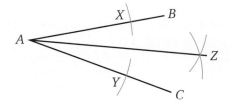

To construct an angle of 30° you first construct an angle of 60° (as part of an equilateral triangle), then bisect it. To construct an angle of 45° you construct an angle of 90°, and then bisect it. There are lots of other possible angles that can be constructed in a similar way.

## Perpendiculars

The following examples show how to construct a perpendicular from a point to a line, and at a point on a line.

***Example:***   Construct a perpendicular from a point to a line.

***Solution:***   With the point of your compasses on *P*, draw two arcs that intersect the line at *A* and *B*.

Put the point on *A* and *B* in turn and draw arcs that intersect at *C*.

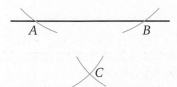

Join *PC*. This is the perpendicular to the original line from the point *P*.

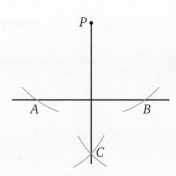

*Example:* Construct a perpendicular at a point $P$ on a line $l$.

*Solution:*

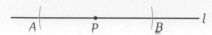

With the point of the compasses on $P$, draw two arcs to cut the line either side of $P$.

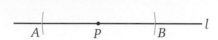

Make the radius of your compasses larger.
Put the point on $A$ and $B$ in turn drawing arcs that intersect.

Where the arcs intersect, label this new point $C$.

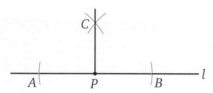

Join the point of intersection to $P$.

This method simply 'made' a line segment with $P$ as the midpoint, and constructed the perpendicular bisector of it.

## Practise... 11.2 Constructions k

D C B A A*

**1** Construct the perpendicular bisector of a line 8 cm long.

**2** Draw this rectangle accurately.

Using only a ruler and compasses, construct the perpendicular bisector of the diagonal $BD$.

Not drawn accurately

**3** Construct an equilateral triangle of side 6 cm.

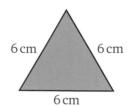

Not drawn accurately

**4** Construct an angle of 60°. Bisect your angle to show an angle of 30°.

**5**    Draw a line segment 10 cm long.

   **a**    Construct the perpendicular bisector of your line segment.

   **b**    Your diagram shows four right angles. Bisect one of them to show an angle of 45°.

**6**    Draw a triangle with sides 8 cm, 9 cm and 10 cm accurately.
Construct the perpendicular bisector of each of the sides.

   What do you notice?

**7**    **a**    Use only a ruler and compasses to construct this net accurately.

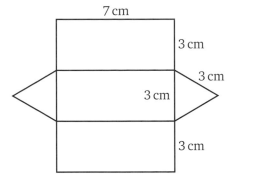

Not drawn accurately

   **b**    Put tabs on your net, cut it out and make the shape. What is the name of the shape you have made?

**8**    Accurately draw a triangle with sides 8 cm, 9 cm and 10 cm. Construct the angle bisector for each of the angles. What do you notice?

**9**    **a**    Construct this rectangle.

   **b**    Label your diagram carefully and draw in the diagonal *AC*.

   **c**    Construct the perpendicular from vertex *B* to the diagonal *AC*.

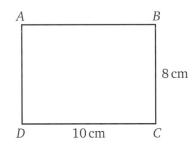

Not drawn accurately

**10**    Construct a right-angled triangle that has a hypotenuse 10 cm long and a shorter side 8 cm long.

   Measure the third side. You may find it helpful to draw a sketch of the triangle first.

**11**    The diagram shows the roof truss design for a house.

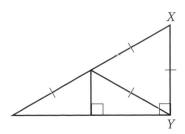

   Construct the diagram starting with *XY* = 5 cm. Measure the width of the base of the roof truss to the nearest millimetre.

**12** This diagram shows the space under the stairs in a house.

Jack wants to put a cupboard under the stairs.
The cupboard is 1.8 metres high, 40 centimetres deep and
1.2 metres wide. It has two doors on the front, each is
60 centimetres wide.

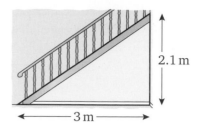

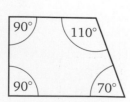

Not drawn
accurately

1.8 m

1.2 m

40 cm

Does this cupboard fit under the stairs? If so, can the doors open?
Show your working to justify your answers.

## Learn... 11.3 Similar shapes

Two shapes are mathematically **similar** if they have the same shape but different sizes. That is, one shape
is an enlargement of the other.

**Shapes that are similar have the same angles**

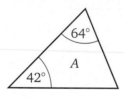

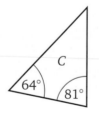

Not drawn
accurately

These triangles are not all similar.

In triangle $A$ the third angle $= 180° - (42° + 64°) = 74°$  So the angles are 42°, 64° and 74°.

In triangle $B$ the third angle $= 180° - (74° + 64°) = 42°$  So the angles are 42°, 64° and 74°.

In triangle $C$ the third angle $= 180° - (81° + 64°) = 35°$  So the angles are 35°, 64° and 81°.

So, triangles $A$ and $B$ are similar as they have the same angles.

Note: for shapes with more than three sides, the angles need to be the same and in the same order.

Consider the following two diagrams.

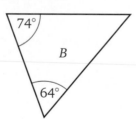

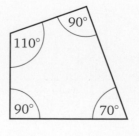

Not drawn
accurately

These quadrilaterals have the same angles, but the angles are not in the same order.
They are therefore not similar.

## Corresponding sides

To solve problems using similar triangles, you need to first identify **corresponding** sides.

In the two triangles, *CA* and *EF* are corresponding sides. This means they are in the same position in each triangle. They are both between the angles 42° and 64°.

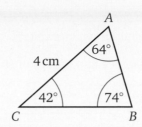
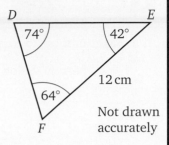

Not drawn accurately

## Scale factor

To find a **scale factor**, you divide one side by the corresponding side from the other triangle.

For the two triangles above, the scale factor from triangle *ABC* to triangle *FDE* is $\frac{12}{4} = 3$

You can use this to find the lengths of other sides, for example $ED = 3 \times CB$

*Example:*   In the diagram *DE* and *BC* are parallel, *BC* is 12 cm, *AE* is 10 cm and *EC* is 5 cm.

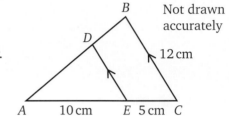

Not drawn accurately

  **a**   Explain why triangles *ADE* and *ABC* are similar.

  **b**   Find *DE*.

  **c**   If *DB* is 4 cm, find *AD*.

*Solution:*   **a**   Angle *A* is common to both triangles.

Angle *ABC* = angle *ADE* as they are corresponding angles (*BC* and *DE* are parallel).

Angle *ACB* = angle *AED* as they are corresponding angles (*BC* and *DE* are parallel).

As both triangles have the same angles, they are similar.

  **b**   *DE* and *BC* are corresponding sides as they are in the same position in the similar triangles. (Angle *ABC* = angle *ADE*, and angle *ACB* = angle *AED* as has just been shown in part **a**.)

*AE* and *AC* are corresponding sides.   Note *AC* = 15 cm (10 + 5 = 15)

Scale factor $= \dfrac{AC}{AE} = \dfrac{15}{10} = 1.5$

$BC = 1.5 \times DE$

$12 = 1.5 \times DE$

$DE = \dfrac{12}{1.5} = 8 \text{ cm}$

  **c**   $AB = 1.5 \times AD$

We know $AB = AD + DB$, and $DB = 4$

So, $1.5 \times AD = AD + 4$

$0.5 \times AD = 4$        Subtract *AD* from each side, as you did with equations.

$AD = \dfrac{4}{0.5} = 8$

$AD = 8 \text{ cm}$

### Study tip

Finding *AD* in the example above is as hard as these questions will get.

Learning to solve these problems, showing your working out, can really boost your marks.

## Practise... 11.3 Similar shapes ⓚ

**B**

The shapes in these exercises are not drawn accurately.

**1** Sort the following triangles into groups of similar triangles.

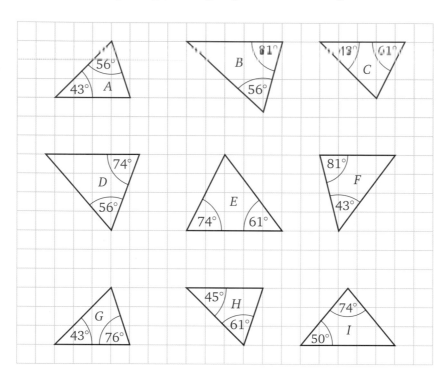

Not drawn accurately

**2** Name three pairs of corresponding sides in these triangles.

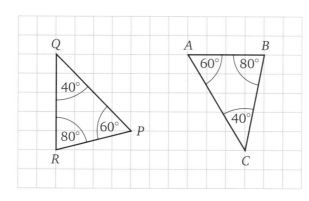

Not drawn accurately

**3**

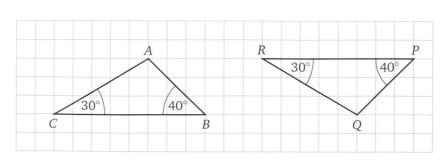

Not drawn accurately

**a** Show that these triangles are similar triangles.

**b** Name all the pairs of corresponding sides.

**4**   These pairs of shapes are all similar, but are not drawn accurately. Find the missing angles and sides.

**a**

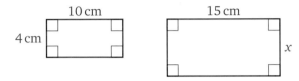

Not drawn accurately

**b**

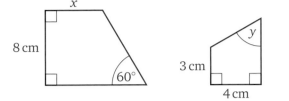

**c**

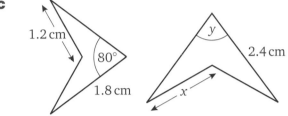

**d**

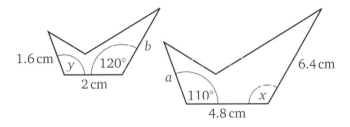

**5**   Each pair of triangles is similar.

Find the missing sides and angles.

**a**

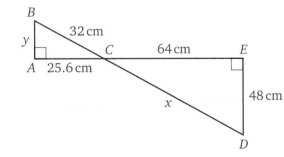

Not drawn accurately

**b**

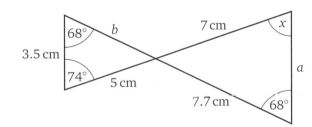

**B**

**6** Find the sides marked with the letters in these diagrams.

**a**

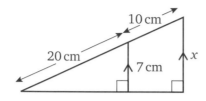

**c** Not drawn accurately

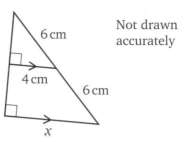

**b**

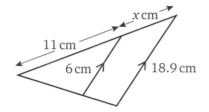

**d**

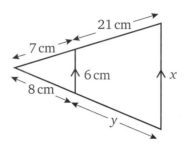

**7** In this triangle *BC* and *DE* are parallel.

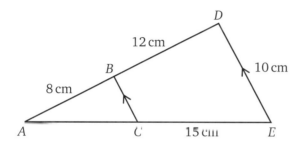

Not drawn accurately

**a** Explain how you can tell that triangle *ABC* and triangle *ADE* are similar.

**b** Work out: **i** *BC* **ii** *AC*

**8** *ABCD* is a trapezium with *AD* parallel to *BC*.

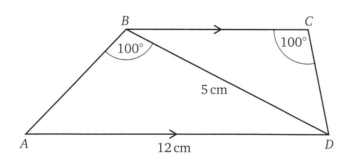

Not drawn accurately

**a** Explain why triangle *ABD* is similar to triangle *DCB*.

**b** Find the length of *BC*.

**9** In the diagram *CB* is parallel to *ED*.
Find the lengths *AB* and *AC*.

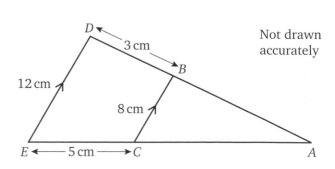

Not drawn accurately

**10**   **a**   Explain a method that can be used to find an estimate of the height of the tree in the diagram.

Your method should include any measuring equipment you need.

**b**   Using your method, find a tree, flagpole or tall building near you and calculate an estimate of its height.

## Learn... 11.4 Congruent shapes

Two shapes are **congruent** if they have both the same shape and the same size. That is, the two shapes are identical.

When two triangles *ABC* and *DEF* are congruent you write △*ABC* ≡ △*DEF*. The '≡' sign means 'is congruent to'. The order of the letters is important, in this case it tells you that ∠*A* = ∠*D*, ∠*B* = ∠*E*, and ∠*C* = ∠*F*

You need to be able to prove that two triangles are congruent.

To do this, you need to show that one of these sets of conditions applies:

- Both triangles have three corresponding sides equal (SSS).
- Both triangles have two angles and one corresponding side equal (ASA).
- Both triangles have two corresponding sides and the angle between them equal (SAS).
- Both triangles have a right angle, hypotenuse and another side equal (RHS).

You need to give reasons for every fact you state.

Congruent triangles can be used to prove the constructions from Learn 15.2 in this chapter.

*Example:*   **a**   Prove that triangles *ABC* and *BCD* are congruent.

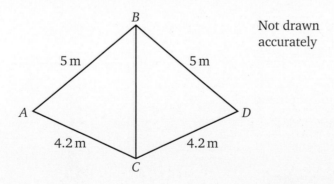

Not drawn accurately

**b**   Prove that triangles *ABC* and *CDE* are congruent.

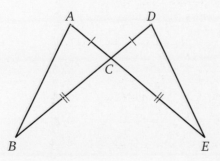

**Solution:**   **a**   In triangle $ABC$ and triangle $BCD$:

$AB = DB$   (given)

$AC = DC$   (given)

$BC = BC$   (same line)

So triangle $ABC \equiv$ triangle $DBC$   (SSS)

**b**   In triangle $ABC$ and triangle $CDE$:

$AC = DC$   (given)

$BC = EC$   (given)

angle $ACB =$ angle $DCE$   (opposite angles)

So triangle $ACB \equiv$ triangle $DCE$   (SAS)

**Example:**   Prove that the method for bisecting an angle does actually give the angle bisector.

**Solution:**

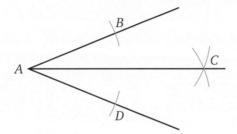

Think of this diagram as showing two triangles.

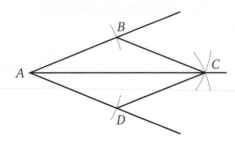

$AB = AD$   (given in method)

$BC = DC$   (given in method)

$AC$ is common to both triangles.

So $\triangle ABC \equiv \triangle ADC$ (SSS)

and $\angle BAC = \angle DAC$

**Study tip**

When writing a proof, always give reasons clearly.
Remember that the angles in a triangle **add up** to 180°.
Do not say that they equal 180° because this implies
that they are all 180°, which is incorrect.

# Practise... 11.4 Congruent shapes

D C B A A*

B

**1** State whether each of the following pairs of triangles is congruent.
For each pair that is congruent, give the condition that is being met.
The shapes are not drawn accurately.

**a**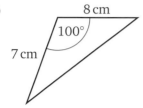

**f**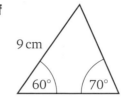

**b**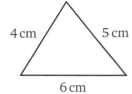

**g**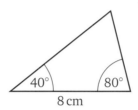

**c**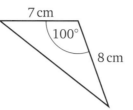

**h**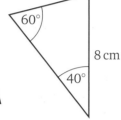

**d**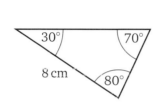

**i**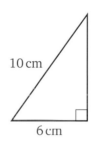

**e**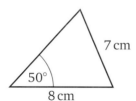

**j**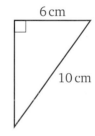

**2** The triangles *ABC* and *DEF* are congruent.

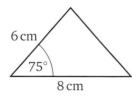

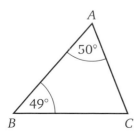

Not drawn
accurately

**a** Find angles at  **i** *C*  **ii** *D*  **iii** *E*  **iv** *F*

**b** Which side in △*ABC* is equal to 8 cm?

B
A

**3**

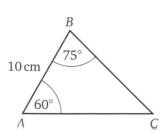

Not drawn accurately

Jen says that $AB = DF$, $\angle A = \angle D = 60°$, $\angle B = \angle F = 75°$, so $\triangle ABC$ is congruent to $\triangle DFE$ (ASA).

Malachie says Jen has made a mistake.

Who is correct? Explain your answer.

**4**    In this diagram $AB = DE$, $CD = 4$ cm and $CE = 9$ cm.

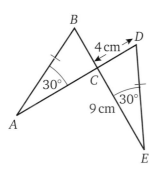

Not drawn accurately

Find the length of $BC$ and $AC$.

A

**5**    Prove that each of the following diagrams contains a pair of congruent triangles.

**a**

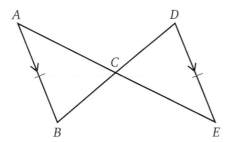

**b**

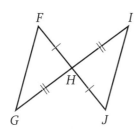

Not drawn accurately

**c**

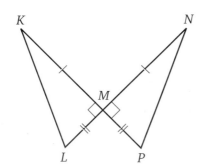

**6**     *ABCD* is a rectangle

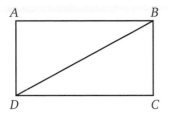

Prove triangles *ABD* and *CDB* are congruent.

**7**     *ABCDEF* is a regular hexagon.

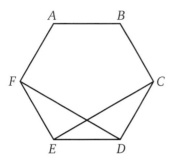

Prove triangles *DEF* and *CDE* are congruent.

**8**     Prove that the method of constructing a perpendicular at a point **on** a line does actually construct a perpendicular to the line.

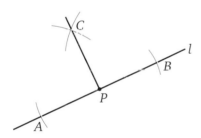

**Hint**

A completed diagram is shown to help you. Start by proving that triangle *APC* is congruent to triangle *BPC*, then use this to explain why *PC* is perpendicular to line *l*.

**9**     Prove that the method of constructing a perpendicular from a point **to** a line does actually construct a perpendicular to the line.

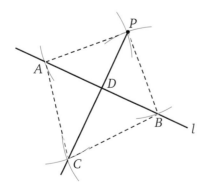

**Hint**

A completed diagram is shown to help you. Start by proving that triangle *APC* is congruent to triangle *BPC*. What does this tell you about the angles at *P*?

Then prove that triangle *APD* is congruent to triangle *BPD*. How does this tell you that *PD* is perpendicular to line *l*?

**⚠ 10**     This is the standard construction of the perpendicular bisector of line *AB*. Draw and label the construction yourself.
Prove that the construction does in fact give the perpendicular bisector. You will need two steps, as in Question 9.

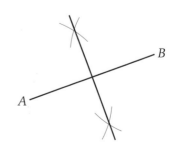

# 11   Assess *k*

**D**

**1**   Draw this shape accurately.

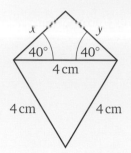

Not drawn accurately

**2**   Jamie was asked to draw this triangle accurately:

- a triangle of sides 6 cm and 8 cm and a non-included angle of 39°.

Nancy drew the same triangle but got a different diagram.
Both were correct.

   **a**   Explain how they can both have different but correct answers.

   **b**   Draw both their triangles.

**D**
**C**

**3**   Draw this parallelogram accurately.

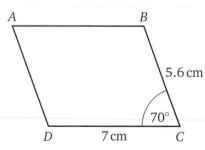

Not drawn accurately

Construct the angle bisector of angle *D*.

**B**

**4**   Find *x* in the following diagram.

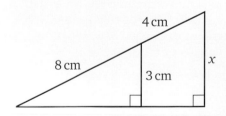

Not drawn accurately

**5**   In this diagram *AB* and *CD* are parallel.

   **a**   Prove that the two triangles are similar.

   **b**   Calculate the lengths *x* and *y*.

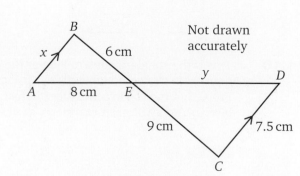

Not drawn accurately

**6**    In this diagram there are two parallel lines.

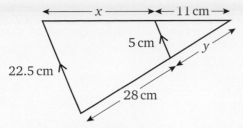

Not drawn accurately

Find the values of *x* and *y*.

**7**    In this diagram *TA* and *TB* are tangents to the circle with centre *O*.

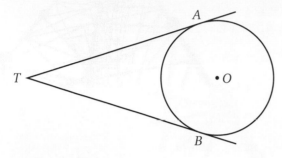

Not drawn accurately

Use your knowledge of angles to show that triangles *TAO* and *TBO* are congruent.

**8**    *AXB* and *PXQ* are two straight lines that bisect each other.

Prove that triangle $AXQ \equiv$ triangle $BXP$

**9**    *PQR* is any triangle.
Equilateral triangles *PAQ* and *PBR* are drawn outside triangle *PQR*.

Prove that triangle $APR \equiv$ triangle $QPB$.

A

A*

# Practice questions   (k)

1    In the diagram *ABCD* and *PQRC* are squares.

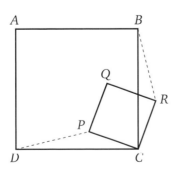

Use congruent triangles to prove that $DP = BR$

*(4 marks)*

AQA 2007

# 12 Loci

## Objectives

Examiners would normally expect students who get these grades to be able to:

### D

understand the idea of a locus

### C

construct the locus of points equidistant from two fixed points

construct the locus of points equidistant from two fixed lines

Solve loci problems, for example find the points less than 3 cm from a point $P$.

## Did you know?

### Mobile phone masts

Some mobile phone masts have a range of 40 km.

Hills, trees and buildings all reduce this distance to as little as 5 km.

In some places, mobile phone masts are only 1 or 2 km apart. This is because they could not cope with the number of calls being made in the area on their own.

### Key terms

locus, loci
perpendicular
bisect, bisector
equidistant

## You should already know:

✓ how to construct the perpendicular bisector of a line

✓ how to bisect an angle

✓ how to construct and interpret a scale drawing.

**Learn...**   **12.1  Constructing loci**

A **locus** can be thought of in two different ways.

It is the path that a moving point follows, or a set of points that follow a rule.

For example, a circle with a radius of 10 cm, centre C, can be thought of as all the points 10 cm from C, or as the path of a moving point which is always 10 cm from a fixed point, C.

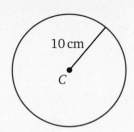

You need to remember the work on constructions from Chapter 15.

A **perpendicular bisector** of the line AB joins all the points **equidistant** (the same distance) from A and B.

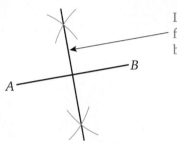

Locus of points equidistant from A and B: perpendicular bisector

Draw four arcs of the same radius, two with centre at A, two with centre at B. Join the points of intersection.

An angle bisector joins all points equidistant from two lines.

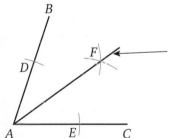

Locus of points equidistant from AB and AC: angle bisector

Draw two arcs of equal radius, centre A, to cut AB and AC at D and E.

Draw equal arcs from D and E to intersect at F.

Join AF and extend.

The perpendicular from a point to a line is the shortest distance from the point to the line.

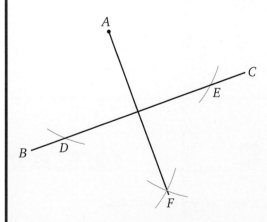

To draw the perpendicular from A to BC:

Draw two arcs of the same radius, centre A, to cross BC at D and E.

With D and E as centres, draw two more arcs of equal radius to meet at F.

AF is perpendicular to BC.

**Example:** An electricity pylon has to be placed so that it is equidistant from *AB* and *AC*, and no more than 200 m from *D*. It must be within the boundary.

Mark the points where the pylon could be placed.

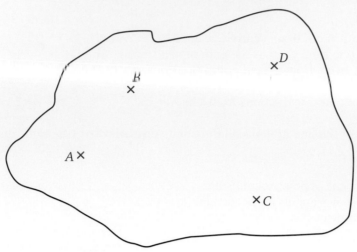

Scale: 1 cm = 100 m

**Solution:** Draw *AB* and *AC*.

Construct the angle bisector of *BAC*, as this marks the locus of points equidistant (the same distance) from *AB* and *AC*.

The points less than 200 m from *D* form a circle, radius 200 m.

With a scale of 1 cm to 100 m, this circle needs to have a radius of 2 cm.

The possible positions for the pylon are on the angle bisector and inside the circle.

This is shown in green.

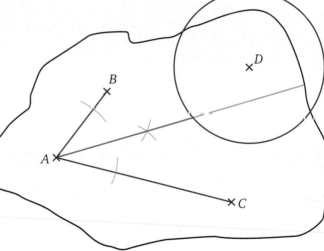

Scale: 1 cm = 100 m

> **Study tip**
>
> To get full marks, make sure that you leave your construction lines showing.

# Practise... 12.1 Constructing loci Ⓚ

D C B A A*

**1** Most cars have one of the three arrangements of windscreen wipers shown below.

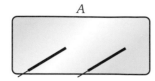
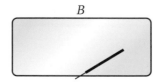
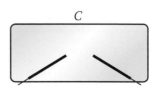

For each arrangement, sketch the area of windscreen that the wipers will clear.

Which is the best arrangement? Give a reason for your answer.

**D**

**2**   Bill throws a ball from his window.
Harry, Hope and Oli try to sketch the locus of the ball.

Harry draws this:

Hope draws this:

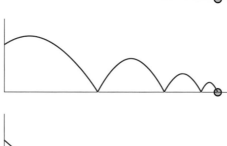

Oli draws this:

Who is correct?
Give a reason for your answer.

**3**   Alice, Kat and Becky tried to draw the locus of points a distance of 1 cm outside a rectangle *ABCD*.

Here are their answers.

Alice

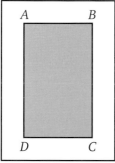

Kat

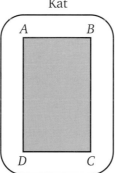

Becky

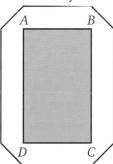

Who is correct: Alice, Kat or Becky?
Give a reason for your answer.

> **Study tip**
>
> You must explain answers when the question asks you to.
> Just choosing the correct answer will not score full marks.
>
> When explaining answers, use mathematical language. Answers do not have to be long, but must explain clearly why you are correct.

**C**

**4**   Draw a line, *AB*, 8 cm long.
Find the locus of points equidistant from *A* and *B*.

**5**   Draw an angle, *ABC*, of 70°.
Find the locus of points equidistant from *AB* and *BC*.

**6**   Draw a line, 8 cm long. Label it *AB*.
   **a**   Find the locus of points that are 6 cm from *A*.
   **b**   Find the locus of points that are 4 cm from *B*.
   **c**   Shade the area containing all the points that are less than 6 cm from *A* and less than 4 cm from *B*.

**C**

**7** Draw a triangle *ABC* with sides at least 10 cm long.

    **a** Draw the locus of points equidistant from *A* and *B*.

    **b** Draw the locus of points equidistant from *A* and *C*.

    **c** Mark the point that is equidistant from *A*, *B* and *C*. Label it *X*.

**8** Three men discover an island.
Each wants to claim it as his own.
Each man plants a flag in part of the island.

    **a** Draw your own sketch of the island.

    **b** Label three points, *A*, *B* and *C*.

    **c** The men agree to divide the island between them, so that they keep the part of the island that is closer to them than to the others.

       Show how the island can be divided up in this way.

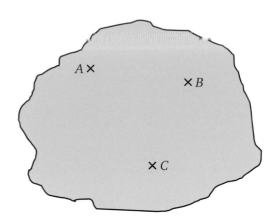

**9** Three telegraph poles, *A*, *B* and *C*, are on the corners of an isosceles triangle.
*AB* = *AC* = 200 m and *BC* = 250 m

    **a** Using a scale of 1 cm to 20 m, make a scale drawing of where the poles are situated.

    **b** A man wants to build a house within the triangle.
The house needs to be at least 90 m from each of the telegraph poles.

       Shade the area on the plan where he can build the house.

    **c** He wants the house to be rectangular, 50 m wide and 70 m long.

       Can he fit a house this size in the shaded area?

**10** Tommy has a rectangular garden, *ABCD*, 12 m by 8 m wide.
He wants to plant a tree in the garden.
He wants the tree to be at least 3 m from the edge *CD* of the garden.
It must be no more than 6 m from *B*.

Using a scale of 1 cm to 1 m, make a drawing of the garden, and shade the region where Tommy can plant the tree.

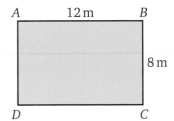

**11** In Suffolk, there are two mobile phone masts, 40 km apart.

    **a** Make a map showing the two masts, using a scale of 1 cm to 4 km. Label them *A* and *B*.

    **b** Each mast has a range of 32 km if you are using a phone outside a building.
If you use a phone inside a building, the range drops to 24 km.

       Find the locus of points where you can get a signal outside but not inside a house.

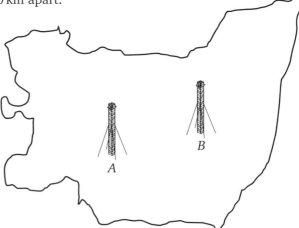

**12** A rectangular lawn is 12 m long and 10 m wide.
A gardener waters the lawn with sprinklers, which spray water in a circle with a radius of 3 m.

Find the smallest number of sprinklers needed to water the entire lawn.

# 12 Assess (k)

**1**   Sketch the locus of:

   **a**   a dog's nose as it chases its tail

   **b**   a snooker ball as it bounces off a cushion into a pocket.

**2**   **a**   Construct a triangle *ABC* with *AC* = 10 cm, *AB* = 8 cm and *BC* = 7 cm

   **b**   Construct the locus of points equidistant from *AB* and *AC*.

**3**   A garden is in the shape of a rectangle, 16 m long and 10 m wide.
There is a tree exactly in the centre of the garden.
There is a border, 2 m wide, all around the garden, and a flower bed that
includes all points up to 3 m from the tree.
The rest of the garden is lawn.

Use a scale of 1 cm to 1 m to make a scale drawing of the garden.

**4**   *ABC* is a triangle.
Angle *ABC* = 90°, *AB* = 8 cm and *BC* = 6 cm

   **a**   Make an accurate drawing of triangle *ABC*.

   **b**   Draw the locus of points equidistant from *A* and *C*.

   **c**   Draw the locus of points 6 cm from *C*.

   **d**   Mark the points that are equidistant from *A* and *C* and that are also less
than 6 cm from *C*.

**5**   Three friends, Alan, Dave and Faye are sitting watching a DVD.
Alan is 4 m from the television, and Faye is 3.5 m from the television.
Alan and Faye are sitting 2.5 m apart.
The distance between Alan and Dave is the same as the distance between Alan
and Faye.
Dave is exactly 3 m from the television.

Use a scale of 2 cm to 1 m to construct a plan of the room.

**6**   Draw a triangle *ABC* with sides at least 10 cm long.

   **a**   Draw the locus of points equidistant from *AB* and *BC*.

   **b**   Draw the locus of points equidistant from *AB* and *AC*.

   **c**   Mark the point that is equidistant from *AB*, *BC* and *AC*. Label it *X*.

D

C

# Practice questions

1      Two radio stations at *A* and *B* pick up a distress call from a boat at sea.
         The station at *A* can tell that the boat is between 50 km and 70 km from *A*.
         The station at *B* can tell that the boat is between a bearing of 060° and 070° from *B*.

         Show clearly, using compasses and a protractor, the region where the boat will be found.

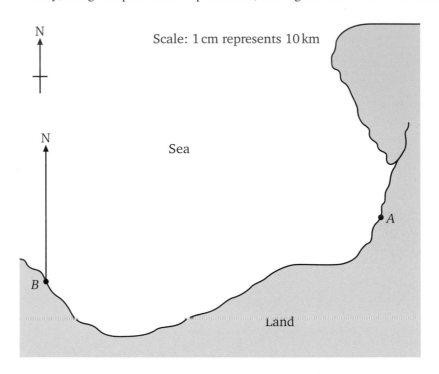

*(3 marks)*

AQA 2008

2      *AB* and *AC* represent two walls.
         A pole must be erected that is

- equidistant from *AB* and *AC*
- between 40 m and 70 m from *A*.

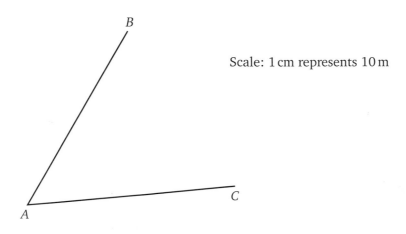

Scale: 1 cm represents 10 m

         Show clearly all the possible positions of the pole.                  *(3 marks)*

AQA 2006

# 13 Cubic, circular and exponential functions

## Objectives

Examiners would normally expect students who get these grades to be able to:

**B**

complete tables for, and draw graphs of, cubic functions and use the graphs to solve equations

**A**

complete tables for, and draw graphs of, reciprocal functions and use the graphs to solve equations

sketch and draw circular graphs such as $\sin x$, and $\cos x$

use the graphs to solve equations

**A\***

sketch and draw graphs of exponential functions and use them to solve equations

understand the graphs of circular functions for angles of any size

use symmetry of circular functions to solve equations

recognise the shapes of graphs of functions including cubic functions, reciprocal functions, circular functions and exponential functions

recognise functions when solving problems.

## Did you know?

### Sound waves

Sound travels in waves.

The shorter the wavelength, the higher the sound pitch.

The maximum displacement of the air molecules is called the amplitude.

The higher the amplitude, the louder the sound.

A pure tone is a tone with the shape of a sine function.

## You should already know:

✔ how to plot and interpret straight line and quadratic graphs

✔ how to use sine, cosine to calculate angles

✔ how to solve simultaneous equations graphically

✔ how to recognise and calculate proportional change.

### Key terms

| | |
|---|---|
| cubic function | circular functions |
| reciprocal | exponential |
| discontinuous | per annum |

## Learn... 13.1 Cubic functions

The general form of a **cubic function** is $f(x) = ax^3 + bx^2 + cx + d$ where $a$, $b$, $c$ and $d$ are constants.

The highest term in a **cubic function** is a term in $x^3$.

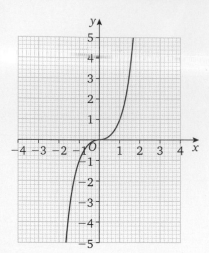

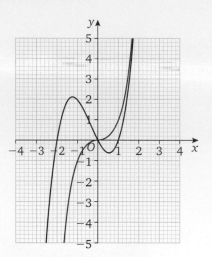

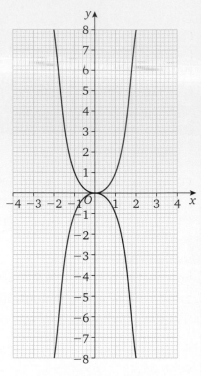

This diagram shows the graph of $y = x^3$, the simplest cubic function.

This diagram shows the graphs of $y = x^3$ in red and $y = x^3 + x^2 - 2x$ in black.

This diagram shows the graph of $y = x^3$ in red and the graph of $y = -x^3$ in black.

To solve a cubic equation graphically such as $x^3 - 2x + 3 = x + 4$, first draw the graph of the cubic equation $y = x^3 - 2x + 3$ (shown in red), then draw the line $y = x + 4$ (shown in black)

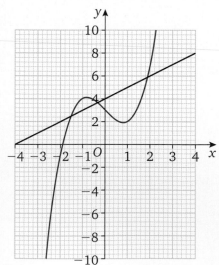

The solutions to the equation are the $x$-values of the points where they meet.

*Example:* **a** Copy and complete the table of values for $y = x^3 - 5$

| $x$ | $-3$ | $-2$ | $-1$ | 0 | 1 | 2 | 3 |
|---|---|---|---|---|---|---|---|
| $x^3$ | $-27$ | | $-1$ | 0 | 1 | | 27 |
| $-5$ | $-5$ | $-5$ | $-5$ | $-5$ | $-5$ | $-5$ | $-5$ |
| $y$ | $-32$ | | $-6$ | $-5$ | $-4$ | | 22 |

**b**   Use your table to draw the graph of $y = x^3 - 5$

**c**   Use your graph to solve these equations.

   **i**    $x^3 - 5 = -10$

   **ii**   $x^3 - 5 = 0$

   **iii**  $x^3 - 5 = 6$

*Solution:*  **a**

| $x$ | $-3$ | $-2$ | $-1$ | $0$ | $1$ | $2$ | $3$ |
|---|---|---|---|---|---|---|---|
| $x^3$ | $-27$ | $-8$ | $-1$ | $0$ | $1$ | $8$ | $27$ |
| $-5$ | $-5$ | $-5$ | $-5$ | $-5$ | $-5$ | $-5$ | $-5$ |
| $y$ | $-32$ | $-13$ | $-6$ | $-5$ | $-4$ | $3$ | $22$ |

These values have been chosen
so the graph fits the axes.

**b**   Draw an $x$-axis labelled from $-3$ to $3$ and a $y$-axis labelled from $-40$ to $30$.

You need a different scale for each axis.

Plot all the points and join them with a smooth curve.

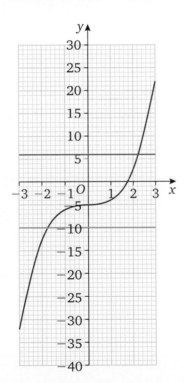

**Study tip**

Sometimes the line crosses the cubic graph more than once.

There may be one, two or three solutions to a cubic equation.

**c**  **i**    Draw the line $y = -10$ across the graph.
Read off the value of $x$ where they cross.
The solution is $x = -1.7$

    **ii**   Read off where the graph crosses the line $y = 0$ (the $x$-axis).
The solution is $x = 1.7$

    **iii**  Draw the line $y = 6$ across the graph.
Read off the value of $x$ where they cross.
The solution is $x = -2.2$

## Practise... 13.1 Cubic functions

**B**

**1** The diagram shows the graph of $y = x^3 - 2x^2 - 8x$

**a** Write down the coordinates of the points where the graph turns.

**b** Use the graph to solve the equation $x^3 - 2x^2 - 8x = 0$

**Hint**

There is more than one solution.

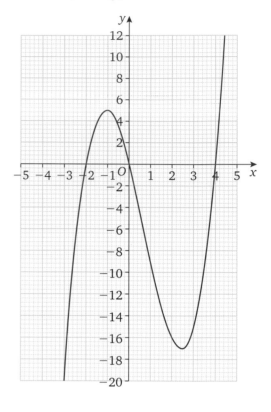

**2** This diagram shows the graph of $y = x^3 - 2x^2 + x - 3$

Use the graph to solve these equations.

**a** $x^3 - 2x^2 + x - 3 = -4$

**Hint**

Read off the $x$-value when $y = -4$

**b** $x^3 - 2x^2 + x - 3 = 0$

**c** $x^3 - 2x^2 + x - 3 = 4$

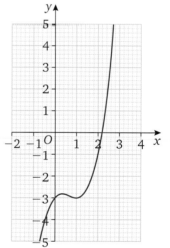

**3** The diagram shows the graph of $y = x^3 + x^2 - 2x$

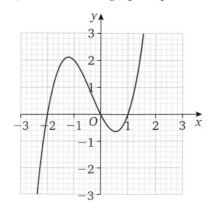

Use the graph to solve each of these equations.

**a** $y = x^3 + x^2 - 2x = 1$

**b** $y = x^3 + x^2 - 2x = 0$

**c** $y = x^3 + x^2 - 2x = -1$

**B**

**4**　**a**　Copy and complete the table of values for $y = x^3 - 3x^2 + 4$ for values of $x$ from $-3$ to $+5$.

| $x$ | $-3$ | $-2$ | $-1$ | 0 | 1 | 2 | 3 | 4 | 5 |
|-----|------|------|------|---|---|---|---|---|---|
| $x^3$ | | $-8$ | | | 1 | | | 64 | |
| $-3x^2$ | | $-12$ | | | $-3$ | | | $-48$ | |
| $+4$ | | $+4$ | | | $+4$ | | | $+4$ | |
| $y$ | | $-16$ | | | 2 | | | 20 | |

**b**　Draw the graph of $y = x^3 - 3x^2 + 4$ for values of $x$ from $-3$ to $+5$.

**c**　Use your graph to solve the following equations.

　　**i**　$x^3 - 3x^2 + 4 = 0$

　　**ii**　$x^3 - 3x^2 + 4 = -10$

　　**iii**　$x^3 - 3x^2 + 4 = 30$

> **Study tip**
>
> You may be able to draw graphs without a table of values. However, if you do, be careful to avoid mistakes when calculating with negative values and powers.

> **Study tip**
>
> The size of the graph paper in an exam is just the right size to fit the graph.

**5**　**a**　Copy and complete the table of values for the cubic function $y = x^3 + 4x^2 - x - 4$ for values of $x$ from $-6$ to $+1$.

| $x$ | $-6$ | $-5$ | $-4$ | $-3$ | $-2$ | $-1$ | 0 | 1 |
|-----|------|------|------|------|------|------|---|---|
| $y$ | | | | 8 | | | | 0 |

**A\***

**b**　Draw the graph of $y = x^3 + 4x^2 - x - 4$

**c**　Use the graph to solve these equations.

　　**I**　$x^3 + 4x^2 - x - 4 = 0$

　　**ii**　$x^3 + 4x^2 - x - 4 = -12$

**⚠ 6**　At a theme park there is a water ride. The horizontal distance travelled from the start, $x$, and the vertical distance above the ground, $y$, are connected by the function:

$$y = \frac{-x^3}{3000} + \frac{3x^2}{40} - 5x + 150$$

where the horizontal distance is $x$ feet and the corresponding height is $y$ feet. The diagram shows part of the graph of this function.

**a**　Use the equation $y = \frac{-x^3}{3000} + \frac{3x^2}{40} - 5x + 150$ to find the value of $y$ when $x = 50$

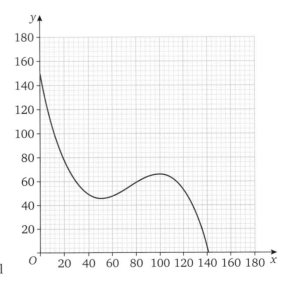

**b**　Use the graph to find:

　　**i**　the height of the ride when the horizontal distance is 50 feet

　　**ii**　the horizontal distances when the height of the ride is 50 feet.

**c**　Use your graph to find the horizontal distance when the ride goes below the water line.

**d**　Malik says that a cubic function is not a good model for the whole of the theme park ride. Give your reasons why Malik is right.

> **Hint**
>
> Your answers to part **a** and part **b i** may not be the same but should be very close. If not, you may have made a mistake when substituting 50 into the equation.

# Learn... 13.2 Reciprocal functions

The **reciprocal** of $x$ is $\frac{1}{x}$ or $x^{-1}$.

$y = \frac{1}{x}$ is the simplest reciprocal function.

For this function, when $x = 0$ the value of $y$ is undefined.

This happens because it is impossible to divide by 0.

So it is impossible to plot a point on the graph for $x = 0$

The value of $y$ when $x$ becomes very large is also undefined.

This happens because it is impossible to find a value of $\frac{1}{x}$ that equals 0.

This causes two breaks in the graph making it **discontinuous**, i.e. it doesn't continue.

There is a horizontal and vertical line that the graph does not cross.

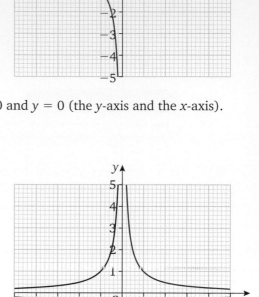

For the graph of $y = \frac{1}{x}$ the equations of these two lines are $x = 0$ and $y = 0$ (the $y$-axis and the $x$-axis).

This gives the reciprocal graph its distinctive shape.

This diagram shows the graph of $y = \frac{1}{x}$ in red and the graph of $y = -\frac{1}{x}$ in black.

Notice the similarities and differences between the shapes of the two graphs.

---

**Example:**  **a**  Copy and complete the table of values for $y = \frac{10}{x}$ for $-6 \leqslant x \leqslant 6$

| x | −6 | −5 | −4 | −3 | −2 | −1 | 0 | 1 | 2 | 3 | 4 | 5 | 6 |
|---|----|----|----|----|----|----|---|---|---|------|---|---|------|
| y | −1.67 |   |   | −3.33 |   |   |   | 10 |   | 3.33 |   |   | 1.67 |

**b**  Draw the graph of the reciprocal function $y = \frac{10}{x}$ for these values.

**c**  From your graph, solve $\frac{10}{x} = 8$

**Solution:**  **a**  Complete the table.

| x | −6 | −5 | −4 | −3 | −2 | −1 | 0 | 1 | 2 | 3 | 4 | 5 | 6 |
|---|-------|----|------|-------|----|-----|---|----|---|------|-----|---|------|
| y | −1.67 | −2 | −2.5 | −3.33 | −5 | −10 | – | 10 | 5 | 3.33 | 2.5 | 2 | 1.67 |

**b** and **c** Draw a pair of axes with values of $x$ from $-6$ to 6 and values of $y$ from $-10$ to 10.
Plot the points and join them with a smooth curve.
Draw the line $y = 8$ and read off the value of $x$ at the point where they cross.
$x = 1.25$

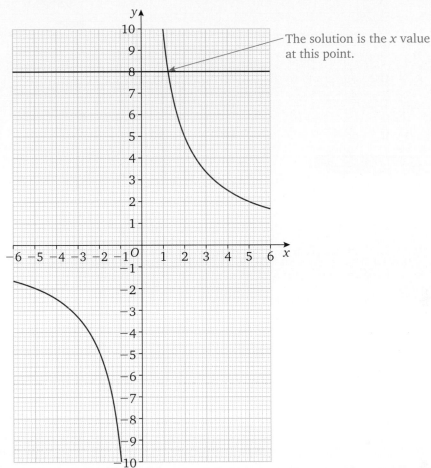

The solution is the $x$ value at this point.

# Practise... 13.2 Reciprocal functions

D C B A A*

**1**   This diagram shows the graph of $y = \dfrac{3}{x}$

**a**   Use the graph to find solutions to these equations.

   **i**   $\dfrac{3}{x} = -2$

   **ii**   $\dfrac{3}{x} = 2$

   **iii**   $\dfrac{3}{x} = 0.5$

**b**   Explain why you cannot find a solution to $\dfrac{3}{x} = 0$

B

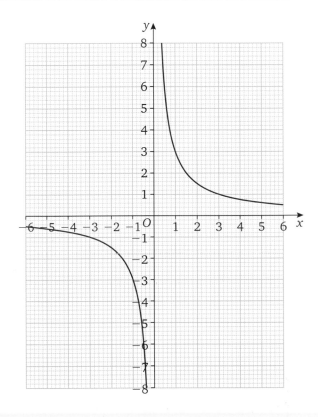

**B**

**2** $y = \dfrac{4}{x}$ is a reciprocal function.

**a** Copy and complete the table of values for $y = \dfrac{4}{x}$

Give values to two decimal places where required.

| $x$ | $-20$ | $-15$ | $-10$ | $-5$ | $-2$ | $-1$ | $-0.5$ | 0 | 0.5 | 1 | 2 | 5 | 10 | 15 | 20 |
|---|---|---|---|---|---|---|---|---|---|---|---|---|---|---|---|
| $y$ | | | | $-0.8$ | | | | | 40 | | | | | | 0.2 |

**b** Draw the graph of $y = \dfrac{4}{x}$ for $-20 \leqslant x \leqslant 20$

**c** Use your graph to solve the following equations.

**i** $\dfrac{4}{x} = 4$  **iii** $20 = \dfrac{4}{x}$

**ii** $\dfrac{4}{x} = -3$  **iv** $\dfrac{4}{x} = -30$

> **Hint**
>
> Rather than draw a line, you can read off numerical values just for $x$.

**3** Dan is investigating a rectangle with an area of $46\,\text{cm}^2$. Its width is $a$ cm and its height is $b$ cm.

**a** Find an equation giving $a$ in terms of $b$.

**b** Explain why $a$ and $b$ cannot be negative in this case.

**c** Draw a graph of $a$ against $b$ for $0 \leqslant a \leqslant 48$

**d** Use your graph to find the width of the rectangle when its height is 9 cm.

**e** Which of these statements is correct?

**i** The product of $a$ and $b$ is a constant.

**ii** The sum of $a$ and $b$ is a constant.

**iii** $a$ is indirectly proportional to $b$.

**iv** $b$ is indirectly proportional to $a$.

**f** Becky is investigating a rectangle with double the area of Dan's rectangle.
Describe the similarities and differences between Dan's and Becky's graphs.

**⚠ 4** **a** On the same axes, sketch the graphs of $y = \dfrac{1}{x}, y = \dfrac{2}{x}$ and $y = \dfrac{3}{x}$

**b** Describe the transformation in the graph of $y = \dfrac{1}{x}$ when the numerator is increased.

## Learn... 13.3 Circular functions

**Circular functions** are also known as trigonometric functions.

They can be used for angles of any size.

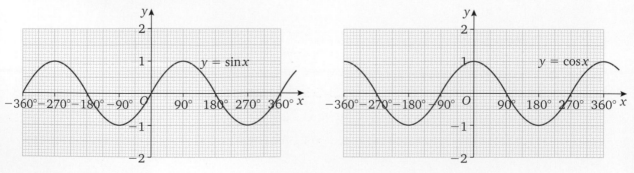

The graphs of $\sin x$ and $\cos x$ can be extended to infinity horizontally in both directions. They are wave curves as the values repeat themselves every $360°$.

You can see from the diagrams that the maximum value of both $\sin x$ and $\cos x$ is $+1$ and the minimum value of both $\sin x$ and $\cos x$ is $-1$.

**Example:**   **a**   Draw the graphs of $y = \sin x$ and $y = \cos x$ for $-270° \leqslant x \leqslant 270°$

**b**   Use your graph to find all the solutions of these equations that lie within this range:

   **i**   $\sin x = 0.6$

   **ii**   $\cos x = -0.2$

**Hint**

You can use symmetry in all the graphs of trigonometric functions to help find solutions.

**Solution:**   **a**

| x | −270° | −225° | −180° | −135° | −90° | −45° | 0° | 45° | 90° | 135° | 180° | 225° | 270° |
|---|---|---|---|---|---|---|---|---|---|---|---|---|---|
| sin x | 1 | 0.71 | 0 | −0.71 | −1 | −0.71 | 0 | 0.71 | 1 | 0.71 | 0 | −0.71 | −1 |

| x | −270° | −225° | −180° | −135° | −90° | −45° | 0° | 45° | 90° | 135° | 180° | 225° | 270° |
|---|---|---|---|---|---|---|---|---|---|---|---|---|---|
| cos x | 0 | −0.71 | −1 | −0.71 | 0 | 0.71 | 1 | 0.71 | 0 | −0.71 | −1 | −0.71 | 0 |

Join the points with a smooth curve.

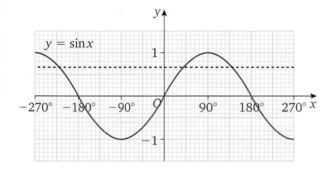

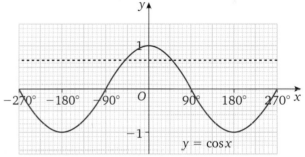

**b**   **i**   $y = 0.6$ at three points when $x = -217°$, 37° and 143°

   **ii**   $y = -0.2$ at four points where $x = 102°$, 258°, −102° and −258°

These are accurate solutions. If you draw a graph carefully you should get readings within a few degrees of these solutions.

# Practise...   13.3 Circular functions    A

**1**   **a**   Copy and complete the table of values for $\sin x$.

| x | −360° | −270° | −180° | −90° | −45° | 0° | 45° | 90° | 180° | 270° | 360° |
|---|---|---|---|---|---|---|---|---|---|---|---|
| sin x | 0 | 1 | | | −0.71 | | | | 0 | −1 | |

**b**   Draw the graph of $\sin x$ for $-360° \leqslant x \leqslant 360°$

**c**   Use your graph to find all the values of $x$ for which $\sin x$ is:

   **i**   0.5   **ii**   0.14   **iii**   0.8   **iv**   0.71   **v**   0.98

**Study tip**

Learn the shapes of the trigonometric functions so you know what they should look like before you draw them.

A

**2**  This diagram shows the graph of $\cos x$ for $-360° \leqslant x \leqslant 360°$

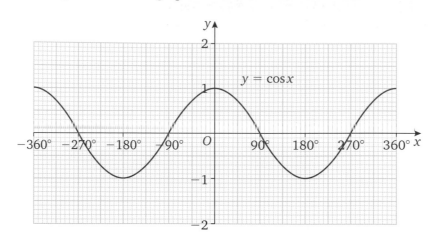

Use the diagram to solve the following equations.

**a**  $\cos x = 0.7$

**b**  $\cos x = -0.5$

**c**  $\cos x = 0$

**d**  $\cos x = 1$

**e**  $\cos x = -1$

**f**  Use your graph to find out which angles between $-360°$ and $360°$ have the same cosine as:

| | | | | | |
|---|---|---|---|---|---|
| **i** | 45° | **iv** | 30° | **vii** | 198° |
| **ii** | 100° | **v** | 14° | **viii** | 286° |
| **iii** | 60° | **vi** | 225° | **ix** | 352° |

**3**  **a**  Draw the graphs of $\cos x$ and $\sin x$ on the same axes for $0° \leqslant x \leqslant 540°$

**b**  Use your graphs to solve the equation $\sin x = \cos x$ for $0° \leqslant x \leqslant 540°$

**c**  Ruth says that $\sin 50° = \cos 40°$ and that $\cos 328° = \sin 58°$. She used her graphs to work it out.
Is she right? Give reasons for your answer.

**d**  Use your graphs to decide which of these statements are true:

| | | | |
|---|---|---|---|
| **i** | $\sin x = \sin (180° - x)$ | **v** | $\sin x = -\cos x$ |
| **ii** | $\cos x = \cos (180° - x)$ | **vi** | $\sin x = \cos (90° + x)$ |
| **iii** | $\sin x = \sin (360° - x)$ | **vii** | $\sin x = \cos (180° - x)$ |
| **iv** | $\cos x = \cos (360° - x)$ | **viii** | $\sin x = -\sin (-x)$ |

In each case, give an example to illustrate your answer.

**4**  **a**  Copy and complete the table of values for $y = \cos 2x$ for $0° \leqslant x \leqslant 360°$

| x | 0° | 30° | 60° | 90° | 120° | 150° | 180° | 210° | 240° | 270° | 300° | 360° |
|---|----|-----|-----|-----|------|------|------|------|------|------|------|------|
| cos 2x | 1 | 0.5 | | −1 | | 0.5 | | | −0.5 | | −0.5 | |

**b**  Draw the graph of $y = \cos 2x$ for $0° \leqslant x \leqslant 360°$

**c**  Compare the graph of $y = \cos 2x$ with what you know about the graph of $\cos x$. How is it different?

## Learn... 13.4 Exponential functions

An **exponential** function is one where the base is a constant and the power is a variable.

The graph of $y = 2^x$ is shown below.

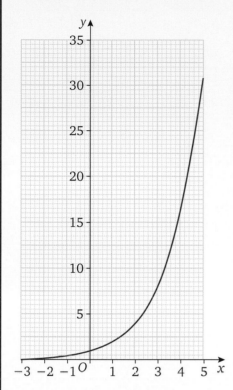

> ### Study tip
>
> If the axes are drawn for you in an examination, your graph should just fit onto them. If points go over the edge of the grid, then you have made an error in your working.

Note that $2^0 = 1$ so the graph goes through (0, 1).

This is true for any number, not just 2.

So the graph of $y = 5x$ also goes through (0, 1).

Exponential functions often occur in real situations. For example, they are used to model the growth of bacteria or to model radioactive decay. They are also relevant to the world of finance, as shown in the next example.

*Example:*    Troy invests £4000 in a fixed interest bank account.

The interest rate is $3\frac{1}{2}\%$ **per annum**.

**a**    Show that the value, $V$, of the investment after $x$ years, can be written as $V = 4000 \times 1.035^x$

**b**    Copy and complete this table of values showing the value of the investment over 20 years.

| x (years) | 0 | 1 | 2 | 3 | 4 | 5 | 10 | 15 | 20 |
|---|---|---|---|---|---|---|---|---|---|
| V (£) | 4000 | | | 4435 | | 4751 | | 6701 | |

**c**    Draw a graph of $V$ against $x$ for $0 \leqslant x \leqslant 20$

**d**    Explain why neither $V$ nor $x$ can be negative.

**e**    Use your graph to:

    **i**    give the value of the investment after 18 years

    **ii**    find out how many years it will take for Troy's investment to grow by 50%

**Solution:**    **a**    After 1 year the value of the investment is £4000 × 1.035

After 2 years the value of the investment is
£(4000 × 1.035) × 1.035 = 4000 × 1.035²

After 3 years the value of the investment is
£((4000 × 1.035) × 1.035) × 1.035 = 4000 × 1.035³

After $y$ years the value of the investment is £4000 × 1.035$^x$

Therefore, $V = 4000 \times 1.035^x$

**b**

| $x$ (years) | 0 | 1 | 2 | 3 | 4 | 5 | 10 | 15 | 20 |
|---|---|---|---|---|---|---|---|---|---|
| $V$ (£) | 4000 | 4140 | 4285 | 4435 | 4590 | 4751 | 5642 | 6701 | 7959 |

**c**

**d**    Time cannot be negative so the value of $x$ must always be positive.

Troy starts with £4000 and his investment increases so the value, $V$, will always be positive.

**e**    **i**    The value of the investment after 18 years is £7400.

**ii**    Read off the value of $x$ when $V = 6000$. It takes 12 years.

## Practise...    13.4 Exponential functions  (k)    D  C  B  A  A*

**A***

**1**    This diagram shows part of the graph of $y = 5^x$

**a**    Use the graph to estimate the value of:

**i**    $5^{0.5}$

**ii**    $5^{1.5}$

> **Hint**
>
> Remember that the powers are the $x$-values.

Use the graph to solve the following equations:

**b**    **i**    $5^x = 1$

**ii**    $5^x = 10$

**iii**    $5^x = 20$

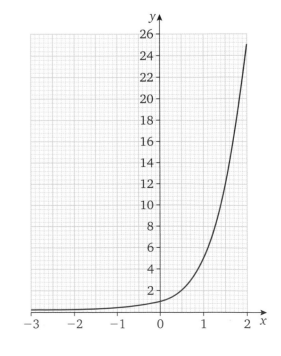

**2**  **a**  Copy and complete this table of values for the exponential function $y = 3^x$ for values of $x$ from $-3$ to $+2$.

| $x$ | $-2$ | $-1$ | 0 | 0.5 | 1 | 1.5 | 2 |
|-----|------|------|---|-----|---|-----|---|
| $y$ | 0.1  |      |   | 1.7 | 3 | 5.2 |   |

**b**  Draw the graph of $y = 3^x$ for values of $x$ from $-2$ to $2$.

**c**  Use your graph to estimate the value of:

  **i**  $3^{1.2}$          **ii**  $3^{0.3}$

**d**  Use your graph to solve the equations:

  **i**  $3^x = 4$          **ii**  $3^x = 2$          **iii**  $3^x = 0.5$

**3**  **a**  On a pair of axes with values of $x$ from $-3$ to 4 and values of $y$ from 0 to 10, sketch the graphs of $y = 2^x$ and the graph of $y = 5^x$

**b**  Write down the coordinates of the point where they cross.

**c**  Write down the solution to the equation $2^x = 5^x$

**d**  Without sketching the graphs of any more functions, give another exponential function that passes through the same point as in **b**.

**4**  Claire invests £5000 in an account paying $2\frac{1}{2}\%$ per annum. The interest is added on at the end of each year.

**a**  Write down an equation for $v$ in terms of $x$ where $v$ is the value of the investment and $x$ is the number of years it is invested.

**b**  Draw a graph of the equation for values of $x$ from 0 to 20.

**c**  Use your graph to estimate the value of the investment after:

  **i**   12 years

  **ii**  17 years

**Learn...**    **13.5  Graph recognition and graphs of loci**

You should be able to recognise the sketch graphs of different functions.
This comes partly from the shape of the graph and partly from its position on the axes.
For example: from its shape you can tell that this is a quadratic graph.

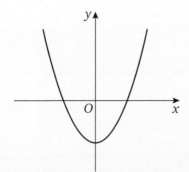

You may be asked to decide which of these could be the equation of this graph.

A $y = x^2$     B $y = 3 - x^2$     C $y = x^2 - 3$     D $y = 3x^2$

A and D both go through $(0, 0)$ so they can be ruled out.

The graph is U-shaped so its equation contains $(+)x^2$ rather than $-x^2$.

This is the graph of C:  $y = x^2 - 3$

Use your knowledge of loci to work out the equation of this graph.

If $P(x, y)$ is a point on the circle, then $x^2 + y^2 = r^2$, where $r$ is the radius of the circle. This graph is the locus of points that are a distance $r$ units from the origin.

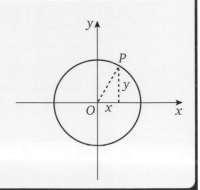

**Study tip**

You will not be tested on the equation of a circle in your exam.

**Example:**    Here are four sketch graphs and six equations.

Match each graph to its equation, giving reasons for your choice.

Graph A

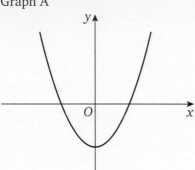

Graph B

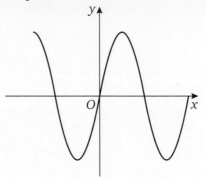

Graph C

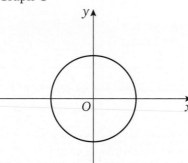

Graph D

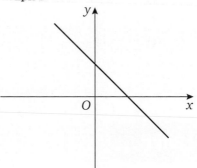

Equation 1: $y = 5 - x$     Equation 2: $y = x^2 - 5$     Equation 3: $x^2 + y^2 = 5$

Equation 4: $y = 5x$         Equation 5: $y = \dfrac{x^3}{5}$     Equation 6: $y = 5 \sin x$

**Solution:**    Graph A is a parabola so its equation must have $x^2$ in it but not any higher powers of $x$. It is U-shaped so the coefficient of $x^2$ must be positive. Check Equation 2: when $x = 0$, $y = -5$ and Graph A crosses the $y$-axis below the origin.

Graph A is $y = x^2 - 5$

Graph B is a repeating wave curve so its equation must contain either $\sin x$ or $\cos x$. It goes through $(0, 0)$ which is true for a sine curve.

Graph B is $y = 5 \sin x$

Graph C is a circle with its centre at the origin. It is therefore of the form $x^2 + y^2 = r^2$

Graph C is $x^2 + y^2 = 5$

Graph D is a straight line. Equation 1 and Equation 4 are linear. Equation 4 goes through $(0, 0)$ and has a positive gradient. Equation 1 has a negative gradient and does not go through $(0, 0)$

Graph D is $y = 5 - x$

# Practise... 13.5 Graph recognition and graphs of loci

**1**   Match each function with its graph.

A: $y = \dfrac{-2}{x}$   B: $y = 2\sin x$   C: $y = x^3 - 2$   D: $y = x^2 - 5x$

**a**

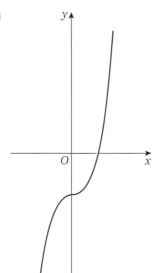

**b**

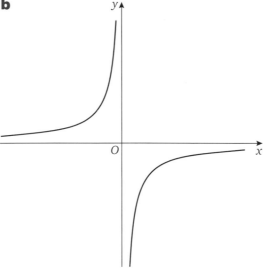

**c**

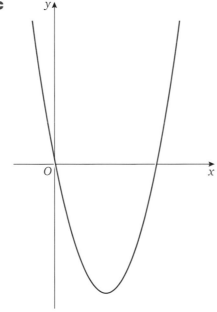

**d**

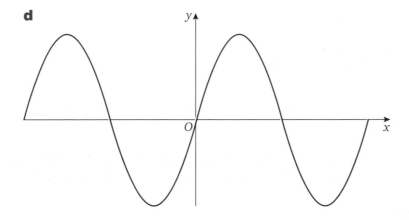

**A***

**2** Match each function with its graph.

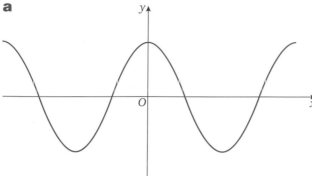

A: $y = 3x^2 - 2x + 1$    B: $y = 3\cos x$    C: $y = \dfrac{3}{x}$    D: $y = 3^x$

**a**

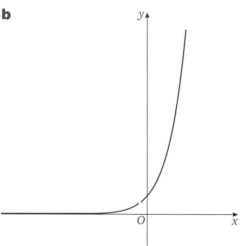

**b**

**c**

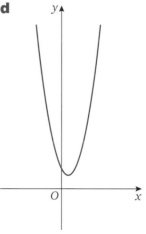

**d**

**3** Anna says this is the graph of $y = 4 - x^3$

Bindia says its is the graph of $y = x^3 - 4x$

Chris says its is the graph of $y = 4x^2 - x^3$

Dave says its is the graph of $y = x^3 + 4$

Who is correct?

Explain why each of the other students is wrong.

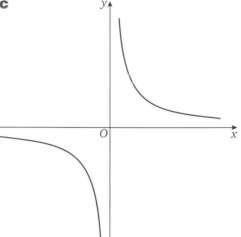

**4** The sketch graph shows four curves, P, Q, R and S.

Match each curve to its equation.

  **a**   $y = (1.5)^x$ is curve …

  **b**   $y = \dfrac{1}{x}$ is curve …

  **c**   $y = 3^x$ is curve …

  **d**   $y = \dfrac{5}{x}$ is curve …

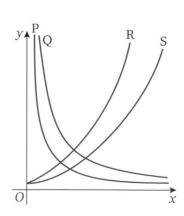

**5** **a** Draw the graph of $x^2 + y^2 = 25$

**b** By drawing a line across your graph, find the points that are 5 units from the origin and satisfy the equation $y = 2x - 3$

A\*

# 13 Assess (k)

**1** **a** Copy and complete this table of values for $y = -x^3 - 5$ for values of $x$ from $-3$ to 3.

B

| $x$ | $-3$ | $-2$ | $-1$ | 0 | 1 | 2 | 3 |
|---|---|---|---|---|---|---|---|
| $-x^3$ | 27 | | 1 | | $-1$ | | $-27$ |
| $-5$ | | $-5$ | $-5$ | | $-5$ | | $-5$ |
| $y$ | | | $-4$ | | $-6$ | | $-32$ |

**b** Use the table to draw the graph of $y = -x^3 - 5$

**c** Use the graph to solve these equations.

**i** $-x^3 - 5 = 0$ **ii** $-x^3 - 5 = -10$ **iii** $-x^3 - 5 = 15$

**2** This diagram shows the graph of $y = \dfrac{6}{x}$

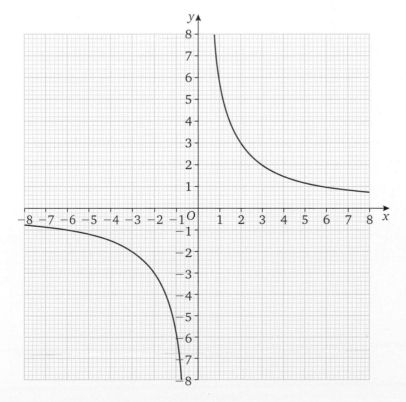

**a** Use the graph to find solutions to these equations:

**i** $\dfrac{6}{x} = -3$ **ii** $\dfrac{6}{x} = 5$ **iii** $\dfrac{6}{x} = 5 - 0.5$

**b** Explain why you cannot find a solution to $\dfrac{3}{x} = 0$

**A**

**3** This diagram shows the graph of $\sin x$ for $-360° \leqslant x \leqslant 360°$

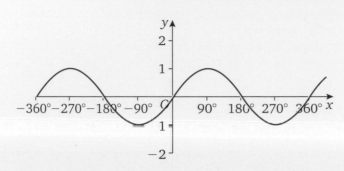

**a** Use the diagram, with your calculator, to find all the solutions of these equations in the range $-360° \leqslant x \leqslant 360°$.

**i** $\sin x = 0.9$   **iv** $\sin x = 1$

**ii** $\sin x = -0.5$   **v** $\sin x = -1$

**iii** $\sin x = 0.2$

**b** Use the graph to find out which angles between $-360°$ and $360°$ have the same sine as:

**i** $45°$   **iii** $20°$   **v** $225°$

**ii** $80°$   **iv** $60°$   **vi** $315°$

**A\***

**4** This diagram shows the graph of $y = x^3 - 3x^2 - 4x + 12$

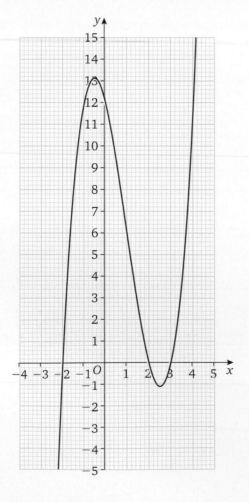

**a** Use the graph to solve $x^3 - 3x^2 - 4x + 12 = 0$

**b** $x^2 - 3x^2 - 4x + 12 = (x - a)(x - b)(x - c)$

Use the graph to find the values of $a$, $b$ and $c$.

**5**   This diagram shows part of the graph of $y = 4^x$

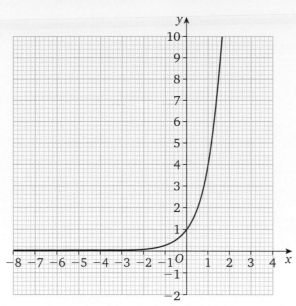

**a**   Use your graph to estimate the value of:

   **i**   $4^{-0.5}$

   **ii**   $4^{1.5}$

   **iii**   $4^{0.75}$

**b**   Use the graph to solve the following equations.

   **i**   $4^x = 0.5$

   **ii**   $4^x = 1$

   **iii**   $4^x = 5$

**6**   **a**   By drawing the graphs of $y = \sin 2x$ and $y = \cos 2x$ for $-180° \leqslant x \leqslant 270°$, solve the equation $\sin 2x = \cos 2x$

   **b**   Without drawing a graph, find the next positive solution for the range of values greater than 270°.

**7**   **a**   Complete the table of values for the cubic function $y = x^3 - 3x - 2$ for values of $x$ from $-4$ to $4$.

| $x$ | $-4$ | $-3$ | $-2$ | $-1$ | 0 | 1 | 2 | 3 | 4 |
|---|---|---|---|---|---|---|---|---|---|
| $y$ | | $-20$ | | 0 | | | | | 50 |

   **b**   Draw the graph of $y = x^3 - 3x - 2$ for values of $x$ from $-4$ to $4$.

   **c**   Use the graph to solve the following equations.

   **i**   $x^3 - 3x - 2 = 0$

   **ii**   $x^3 - 3x - 2 = 20$

   **iii**   $x^3 - 3x - 2 = -30$

**A\***

**8** Match each function with its graph.

A: $y = -2^x$    B: $y = \dfrac{-5}{x}$    C: $y = \cos 3x$    D: $y = 2x^3$

**a**

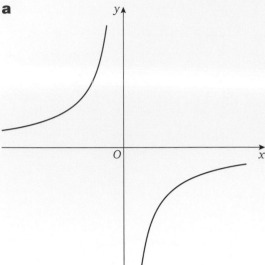

**c**

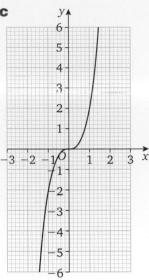

**b**

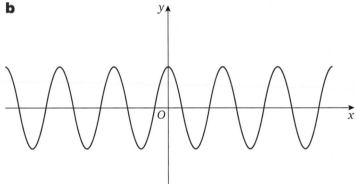

**d**

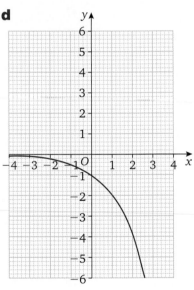

**9** This table shows some of Sumaira's experimental data. Some of the values are missing.

| x | 0 | 1 | 2 | 3 | 4 | 5 | 6 | 7 | 8 | 9 | 10 |
|---|---|---|------|---|------|------|------|------|---|---|------|
| y |   |   | 14.4 |   | 20.7 | 24.9 | 29.9 | 35.8 |   |   | 61.9 |

**a** Plot these points and join them to make a smooth curve.

**b** Use your curve to complete the table of values.

**c** Describe the relationship between $x$ and $y$.

**d** Use your graph to estimate:

   **i** the value of $y$ when $x$ is 0

   **ii** the value of $y$ when $x$ is 9

   **iii** the value of $x$ when $y$ is 40.

# Practice questions

**1**   **a**   Complete the table of values for $y = x^3 - x$

| $x$ | $-2$ | $-1.5$ | $-1$ | $-0.5$ | $0$ | $0.5$ | $1$ | $1.5$ | $2$ |
|---|---|---|---|---|---|---|---|---|---|
| $y$ | | $-1.875$ | $0$ | $0.375$ | $0$ | $0.375$ | | $1.875$ | |

*(2 marks)*

**b**   Copy the grid and draw the graph of $y = x^3 - x$ for values of $x$ from $-2$ to $-2$.    *(3 marks)*

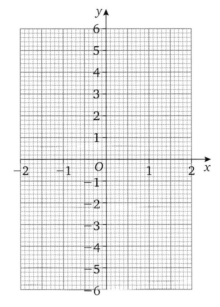

**c**   Use the graph to solve the equation $x^3 - x = 4$    *(2 marks)*

AQA 2008

# 14 Trigonometry 2

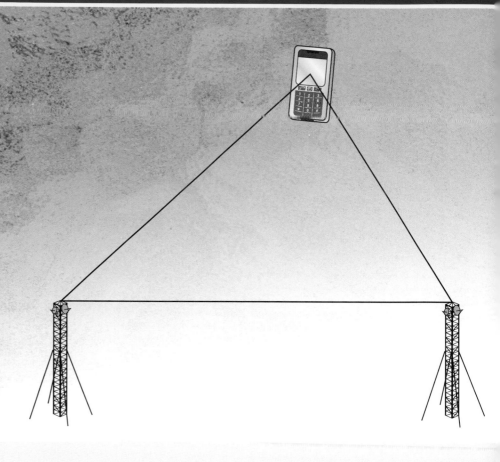

## Objectives

Examiners would normally expect students who get these grades to be able to:

### A

use the sine and cosine rules to solve 2-D problems

calculate the area of a triangle using $\frac{1}{2}ab\sin C$

### A*

use the sine and cosine rules to solve 3-D problems.

## Did you know?

### Finding someone in an emergency using mobile phone signals

An emergency call from a mobile phone can be used to help find the person making the call.

The distance from two masts can be calculated by the time it takes the signal to reach them.

Assuming that you know the distance between the two masts, then the cosine rule covered in this chapter allows you to calculate the angles in the triangle.

This system of triangulation is used in GPS systems as well as astronomy.

## Key terms

sine rule

cosine rule

## You should already know:

✔ how to use trigonometry in right-angled triangles

✔ the formula for the area of a triangle, $A = \frac{1}{2}bh$

✔ how to measure angle bearings.

## Learn... 14.1 The sine rule

It is possible to use trigonometry for triangles without a right angle.

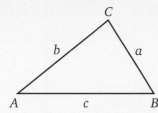

You should use upper case (capital) letters to label the angle at each vertex and lower case letters to label sides.

The sides are named after the angle they are opposite.

The perpendicular height, $CD$, is drawn in to create two right-angled triangles.

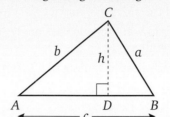

Using triangle $ACD$:

$$\sin A = \frac{\text{opp}}{\text{hyp}}$$

$$\sin A = \frac{h}{b}$$

or    $b \sin A = h$

Using triangle $BCD$:

$$\sin B = \frac{\text{opp}}{\text{hyp}}$$

$$\sin B = \frac{h}{a}$$

or    $a \sin B = h$

So    $a \sin B = b \sin A$

Dividing both sides by $\sin A \times \sin B$,

$$\frac{a \sin B}{\sin A \times \sin B} = \frac{b \sin A}{\sin A \times \sin B}$$

$$\frac{a}{\sin A} = \frac{b}{\sin B}$$

By constructing a different perpendicular, it can be shown that:

$$\frac{a}{\sin A} = \frac{b}{\sin B} = \frac{c}{\sin C}$$

> **Study tip**
>
> This formula is given to you in the formula page of exam papers.
>
> It can be turned upside down, giving:
> $$\frac{\sin A}{a} = \frac{\sin B}{b} = \frac{\sin C}{c}$$
> which is useful for finding angles, but this form is not given in the formula sheet.

This is known as the **sine rule**.

Don't forget that $\sin 40° = \sin 140°$, or, generally, that $\sin a = \sin(180° - a)$

This can lead to two different answers to a question, as shown in the 'Finding an angle' example on the following page.

### Finding a side

**Example:**   A triangle $ABC$ has side $AB = 8$ cm, angle $ACB = 74°$ and $CAB = 59°$

Calculate the length of $BC$ correct to one decimal place.

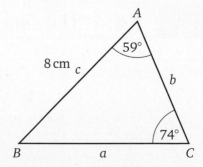

**Solution:**   You know angles $A$ and $C$, and side $c$. You are asked to find side $a$.

So use the parts of the rule containing these measurements.

$$\frac{a}{\sin A} = \frac{c}{\sin C}$$

$$\frac{a}{\sin 59°} = \frac{8}{\sin 74°}$$   Substitute values for $c$, $A$ and $C$.

$$a = \frac{8}{\sin 74°} \times \sin 59°$$   Multiply both sides by $\sin 59°$.

$$= 7.1336...$$   Calculate the answer.

$$a = 7.1 \text{ cm (1 d.p.)}$$   Round off to the required degree of accuracy.

**Finding an angle**

*Example:*    Ship $A$ is 9 km due north of a lighthouse, $L$.

Ship $B$ is 11 km from ship $A$, and is on a bearing of 072° from the lighthouse.

Calculate the bearing of $B$ from $A$.

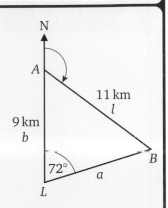

Not drawn accurately

*Solution:*    First, label the sides $a$, $b$ and $l$.

Although you want to calculate angle $A$, you know sides $b$, $l$ and angle $L$, so you have to find angle $B$ first.

Because you want to find an angle, write the rule with the angles as the numerator.

$$\frac{\sin B}{b} = \frac{\sin L}{l}$$

$$\frac{\sin B}{9} = \frac{\sin 72°}{11}$$

$$\sin B = \frac{\sin 72°}{11} \times 9$$

$$= 0.7781\ldots$$

$$B = \sin^{-1} 0.7781\ldots$$

$$B = 51° \text{ (to the nearest degree)}$$

So angle $LAB = 180° - 51° - 72° = 57°$

The bearing of $B$ from $A = 180° - 57° = 123°$.

> **Study tip**
>
> When you use the inverse sine function on a calculator, the angle displayed is an acute angle. To get the obtuse angle which has the same sine, you need to subtract this value from 180°. This is because $\sin x = \sin(180° - x)$.

$\sin B = 0.7781\ldots$ has two possible answers: $B = 51°$ or $129°$ (to the nearest degree).

In this case, 129° is impossible as the angles in the triangle must add to 180°, but you should always check. There is another reason why, in this example, $B$ must be an acute angle. The angle $B$ must be less than 72° because $B$ is opposite the side 9 km and $L$ is opposite the side 11 km.

## Practise...    14.1 The sine rule         D C B A A\*

**A**

**1**    Calculate the lengths of the marked sides in the diagrams below.

**a**

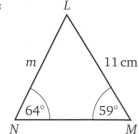

**b**

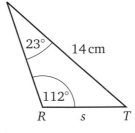

Not drawn accurately

**c**

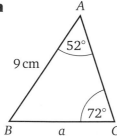

**d**

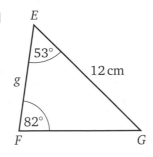

> **Study tip**
>
> If you are given two of the angles in a triangle, you can work out the third by subtraction because the sum of the three angles must be 180°.

**A**

**2**    Calculate the angles marked *x* in these diagrams.

**a**

A

45°

8 cm

*x*

B    6 cm    C

**b**

D

7 cm    9 cm

68°    *x*

F    E

**c**

I

*x*

11 cm

112°

G    7 cm    H

Not drawn
accurately

**3**    Triangle *ABC* has *AB* = 9 cm, *AC* = 7 cm and angle *ACB* = 64°.

Draw a sketch of the triangle and calculate angle *ABC*.

**4**    Triangle *DEF* has *DE* = 7 cm, angle *DFE* = 67° and angle *DEF* = 59°.

Draw a sketch of the triangle and calculate the length of *EF*.

**⚠ 5**    A tent is supported at *A* by two guy ropes, *AB* and *AC*.
*AB* is 1.8 m long, and *AC* is 2.1 m long.
The angle *ABC* is 72°.

Calculate angle *BAC*.

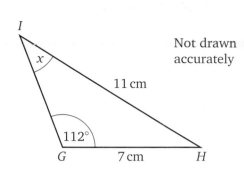

**⚙ 6**    Two coastguards see the same boat.
Coastguard *Y* is 4.2 km due south of coastguard *X*.
The boat is on a bearing of 118° from *X*, and 071° from *Y*.

Calculate the distance of the boat from each coastguard.

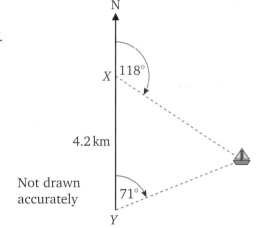

**⚙ 7**    A child's slide has steps that are 1.6 m long.
The horizontal distance from the bottom of the steps to
the end of the slide is 4 m.
The slide makes an angle of 31° with the ground.

Calculate the obtuse angle, *x*, between the slide
and the steps.

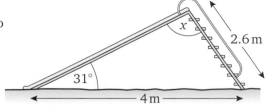

**⚙ 8**    Mike is trying to find the height of a tree on the far side of a river.
He measures the angle of elevation of the tree to be 48°.
He walks a further 15 paces away and the angle of elevation is now 38°.
Mike's pace is about 0.8 metres long.

Use Mike's calculations to find an estimate of the height of the tree.

**Learn...**    **14.2 The cosine rule**

In the triangle $ABC$, $CD$ is perpendicular to $AB$.

$AB = c$, which is split at $D$ into the lengths $AD = x$ and $DB = c - x$

Using Pythagoras' theorem on the two triangles, $h^2 = a^2 - (c - x)^2$, and $h^2 = b^2 - x^2$

So    $a^2 - (c - x)^2 = b^2 - x^2$

      $a^2 = b^2 - x^2 + (c - x)^2$

      $a^2 - b^2 = x^2 + c^2 - 2cx + x^2$

      $a^2 = b^2 + c^2 - 2cx$

But    $\cos A = \dfrac{x}{b}$

So    $x = b \cos A$

So    by substituting for $x$:

      $a^2 = b^2 + c^2 - 2bc \cos A$

This is the **cosine rule**, and can be used when a question involves three sides and an angle.

It has three forms:

      $a^2 = b^2 + c^2 - 2bc \cos A$

      $b^2 = a^2 + c^2 - 2ac \cos B$

      $c^2 = a^2 + b^2 - 2ab \cos C$

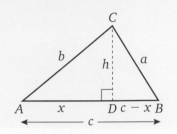

> **Study tip**
>
> The first version is on the formula sheet in exams, but the other two are not.
>
> Make sure that you know how to work out the other two versions from the first.

---

**Finding a side using the cosine rule**

**Example:**    Calculate the length of the side $AB$ in the diagram opposite.

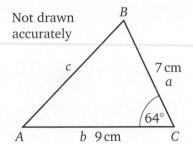

Not drawn accurately

**Solution:**    Copy and label the diagram $a$, $b$ and $c$.

You need $c$, you know $a$, $b$ and $C$.

      $c^2 = a^2 + b^2 - 2ab \cos C$

      $c^2 = 7^2 + 9^2 - 2 \times 7 \times 9 \times \cos 64°$

        $= 74.7652...$

      $c = \sqrt{74.7652...}$

        $= 8.6466...$

      $c = 8.6 \, \text{cm}$ (1 d.p.)

> **Study tip**
>
> Remember to take the square root at the end. Always check that your answer is reasonable.

---

**Calculating an angle using the cosine rule**

**Example:**    Allthorpe is 14 km from Braytown on a bearing of 049°.

Crighton is 20 km from Allthorpe and 11 km from Braytown.

Find the bearing of Crighton from Braytown.

Label the sides $a$, $b$ and $c$.

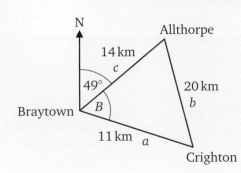

Not drawn accurately

You know $a$, $b$ and $c$ and you need angle $ABC = B$

$$b^2 = a^2 + c^2 - 2ac\cos B$$

$$20^2 = 11^2 + 14^2 - 2 \times 11 \times 14\cos B$$

$$400 = 121 + 196 - 308\cos B$$

$$400 = 317 - 308\cos B$$

$$308\cos B = 317 - 400$$

$$\cos B = \frac{-83}{308}$$

> **Study tip**
>
> To find an angle using the cosine rule, you can rearrange the formula to make $\cos A$ the subject. So:
> $$2bc\cos A = b^2 + c^2 - a^2$$
> $$\cos A = \frac{b^2 + c^2 - a^2}{2bc}$$
> You can learn this formula or practise changing the subject.

$$B = \cos^{-1}\frac{-83}{308}$$

$$= 105.6333...°$$

The bearing is $49° + 105.6333...° = 154.6333...°$

The bearing is **155°** (to the nearest degree).

> **Study tip**
>
> Many candidates round off too soon and lose marks for accuracy. Never round off until the end.

# Practise...   14.2 The cosine rule  (k)                    D  C  B  A  A*

**1**  Calculate the lengths of the marked sides in the diagrams below.

**a**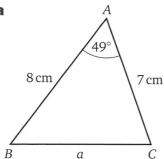

**b**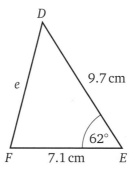

**c** Not drawn accurately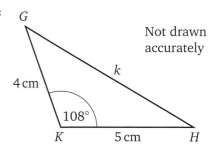

**2**  Calculate the angles marked $x$ in these diagrams.

**a**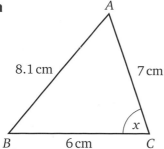

**b**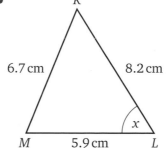

**c** Not drawn accurately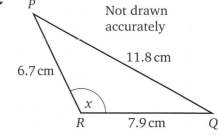

A

**3**    Triangle *ABC* has *BC* = 8 cm, *AC* = 7.2 cm and angle *ACB* = 58°.

Draw a sketch of the triangle and calculate the length of *AB*.

**4**    Triangle *DEF* has *DE* = 8 cm, *DF* = 9.1 cm and *EF* = 6.7 cm.

Draw a sketch of the triangle and calculate the size of angle *DEF*.

**5**    A clock has a minute hand that is 8 cm long and an hour hand that is 6 cm long.

Calculate the distance between the tips of the hands at:

**a**    2 o'clock

**b**    4.30am

**⚠ 6**    A cuboid measures 8 cm × 6 cm × 5 cm as shown.

Calculate angle *BAC*.

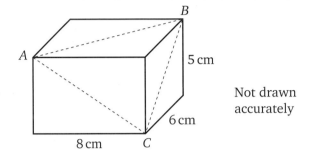

Not drawn
accurately

**⚠ 7**    Bob and Alice are walking along a straight path, *AB*. At point *B*, the path is diverted around a lake.
They can choose path *DEC* or path *DFC*.
*BE* = 80 m, *EC* = 70 m, angle *BEC* = 124°, angle *ABF* = 145° and angle *FCD* = 130°

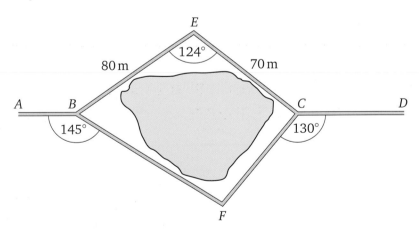

Which is the shorter route, *BEC* or *BFC*?

**⚠ 8**    A house roof has dimensions as shown.
Angle *DCB* = 90° and *BEC* = 21°

Calculate the length of *BD*.

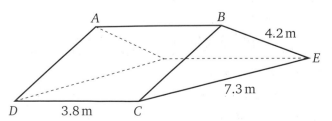

## 14.3 Finding the area of a triangle using trigonometry

**Learn...**

You know that the area of a triangle can be found by the formula:

area $= \frac{1}{2} \times$ base $\times$ height

In the diagram, area $= \frac{1}{2}ch$

But   $\sin A = \dfrac{h}{b}$

or   $h = b \sin A$

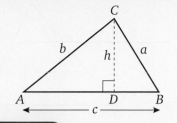

So the area of the triangle is $\frac{1}{2}bc \sin A$

You can also use $\frac{1}{2}ac \sin B$ or $\frac{1}{2}ab \sin C$

Only this last version is given on the formula sheet in examinations.

**Study tip**

You should only use this formula when the triangle has no right angle, and you do not know the height of the triangle, as $A = \frac{1}{2}b \times h$ is easier to use.

---

**Example:**  Find the area of the triangle $ABC$, correct to 1 d.p.

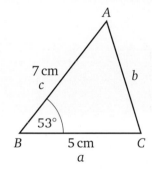

Not drawn accurately

**Solution:**  Label the sides $a$, $b$ and $c$.

You know $a$, $c$ and $B$, so:

area $= \frac{1}{2}ac \sin B$

$= \frac{1}{2} \times 5 \times 7 \times \sin 53°$

$= 14.0 \text{ cm}^2$ (1 d.p.)

---

## 14.3 Finding the area of a triangle using trigonometry

**Practise...**

D  C  B  A  A*

**1**  Find the area of each triangle.

**a**

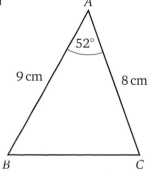

**b**

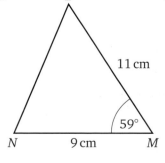

**c**

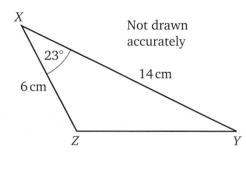

Not drawn accurately

**2**  **a**  $ABC$ is an isosceles triangle, with $AB = BC = 8$ cm and angle $ABC = 68°$.
Draw a sketch of the triangle and find its area.

**b**  $DEF$ is another isosceles triangle, with $DE = EF = 8$ cm and angle $EDF = 68°$.
Draw a sketch of the triangle and find its area.

**A**

**3**

**a** Triangle *ABC* has an area of 24 cm². Find two possible values for angle *B*.

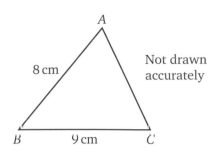

8 cm

9 cm

Not drawn accurately

**b** Triangle *DEF* also has an area of 24 cm². Calculate the length of *DE*.

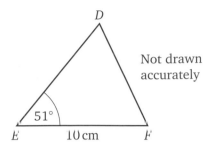

51°

10 cm

Not drawn accurately

**⚠ 4** A farmer has a field between three roads and a hedge as shown.

Calculate the area of the field.

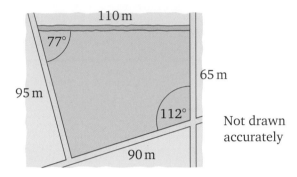

110 m

77°

65 m

95 m

112°

90 m

Not drawn accurately

**? 5** An equilateral triangle and a square have the same area. The square has a perimeter of 20 cm.

Find the perimeter of the triangle.

# 14 Assess ⓚ

**A**

**1** Calculate the sides and angles marked with letters below. The diagrams are not drawn accurately.

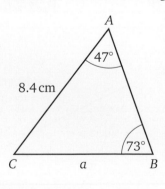

*A*

47°

8.4 cm

73°

*C* *a* *B*

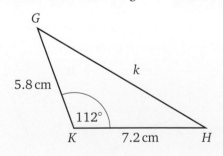

*G*

5.8 cm

*k*

112°

*K* 7.2 cm *H*

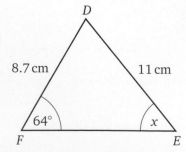

*D*

8.7 cm 11 cm

64° *x*

*F* *E*

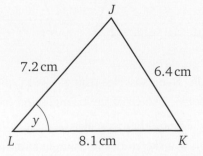

*J*

7.2 cm 6.4 cm

*y*

*L* 8.1 cm *K*

**A**

**2**  A gardener has a triangular flower bed, *ABC*.
He needs to use 7 g of fertiliser per m².

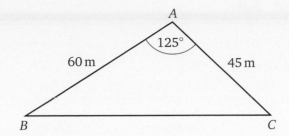

   **a**  Calculate how much fertiliser he needs.

   **b**  Calculate the perimeter of the bed.

**3**  Altown is 5 km from Croy on a bearing of 051°.
Broughton is 8 km from Altown and 7 km from Croy.

Calculate the bearing of Broughton from Croy.

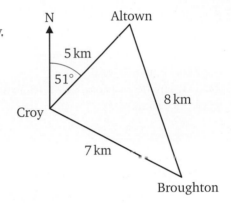

**4**  A parallelogram *ABCD* has *AD* = 5 cm, *AC* = 8 cm
and angle *ADC* = 57°.

Calculate angle *ACD*.

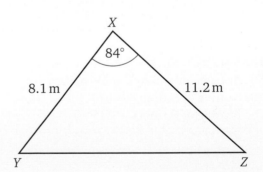

Not drawn accurately

**5**  Calculate the area of the triangle *XYZ*.

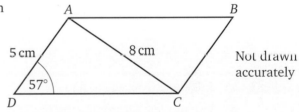

**6**  The cuboid shown has *BC* = 4 cm, *CF* = 5 cm and *EF* = 7 cm.

Calculate angle *BDF*.

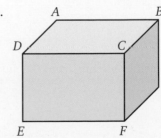

**A\***

# Practice questions  ⓚ

**1**    *PQR* is a triangle.
$PQ = 10\,\text{cm}$, $QR = 12\,\text{cm}$ and angle $PQR = 78°$

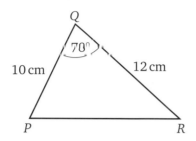

Not drawn accurately

Calculate the length *PR*.      *(3 marks)*

AQA 2007

**2**    *ABCD* is a quadrilateral.
$AB = 12\,\text{cm}$, $BC = 11\,\text{cm}$, $CD = 10\,\text{cm}$ and $DA = 9\,\text{cm}$
$\angle ABC = 74°$ and $\angle DAC = 46°$

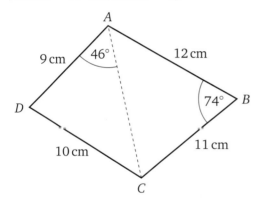

Not drawn accurately

    **a**    Use the cosine rule to find *AC*.      *(3 marks)*

    **b**    Use the sine rule to find the size of angle *ACD*.      *(3 marks)*

AQA 2008

**3**    Jenna is walking due North along a straight path, *ABC*.
There is a hut at *H*.
The distance from *A* to *B* is 140 metres.
The distance from *B* to *C* is 230 metres.
The bearing of *H* from *A* is 040°.
The bearing of *H* from *C* is 115°.

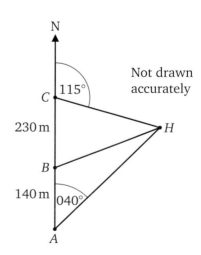

Not drawn accurately

How far is Jenna from the hut when she is at *B*?      *(6 marks)*

AQA 2002

# 15 Vectors

## Objectives

Examiners would normally expect students who get these grades to be able to:

### A

add, subtract and multiply vectors

use addition, subtraction and multiplication of vectors to solve simple geometric problems

understand the relationship between parallel vectors

### A*

solve more difficult geometric problems using vectors.

## Key terms

vector
magnitude
column vector
scalar
vector sum
resultant vector

*Did you know?*

## Wind

Wind can be represented on maps using vectors. This is because wind has direction and speed.

The highest ever, officially recorded wind speed is 372 kph, or 231 mph. It was recorded on 12 April 1934, at New Hampshire's Mount Washington Observatory, USA.

## You should already know:

✔ how to write a column vector

✔ how to translate a shape using column vectors

✔ the meaning of 'parallel'

✔ the relationship between similar triangles

✔ the properties of polygons.

# Learn... 15.1 Vectors

A **vector** is a quantity that has **magnitude** (size) and direction.
A vector can be represented in a number of ways.

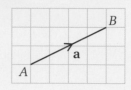

- as a **column vector** $\begin{pmatrix} 4 \\ 2 \end{pmatrix}$ ⟵ horizontal move
  ⟵ vertical move

This is a move of 4 units to the right and 2 units up.

- in type, in a book, as $\overrightarrow{AB}$ or **a**

- handwritten as $\overrightarrow{AB}$ or as $\underset{\sim}{a}$

The arrows on the vectors in the diagram shows the direction.

These vectors are the same size but in opposite
directions so are two different vectors.

Compare the way the two vectors are represented.

One vector is the negative of the other.

$$\begin{pmatrix} 4 \\ 2 \end{pmatrix} \qquad \begin{pmatrix} -4 \\ -2 \end{pmatrix}$$
$$\overrightarrow{AB} \qquad \overrightarrow{BA}$$
$$\mathbf{a} \qquad -\mathbf{a} \qquad \text{If you are handwriting this, it would be } \underset{\sim}{a} \text{ and } -\underset{\sim}{a}$$

In this diagram, the vector on the right is twice
as long as the vector on the left.

Compare the way the two vectors are represented.

The second vector $\overrightarrow{CD}$ can be represented as
$2 \times$ the first vector.

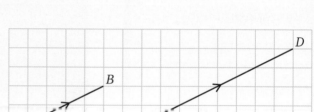

$$\begin{pmatrix} 4 \\ 2 \end{pmatrix} \qquad \begin{pmatrix} 8 \\ 4 \end{pmatrix}$$
$$\overrightarrow{AB} \qquad 2\overrightarrow{AB}$$
$$\mathbf{a} \qquad 2\mathbf{a}$$

When vectors are added, subtracted or multiplied the solution can be found using diagrams or column vectors.

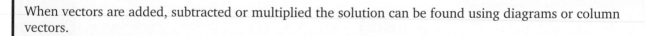

## Parallel vectors

Two vectors are parallel if their column vectors are equal or a multiple
of the same column vector.

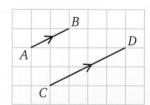

$$\overrightarrow{AB} = \begin{pmatrix} 2 \\ 1 \end{pmatrix} \qquad \overrightarrow{CD} = \begin{pmatrix} 4 \\ 2 \end{pmatrix} = 2 \times \begin{pmatrix} 2 \\ 1 \end{pmatrix} = 2\overrightarrow{AB}$$

$\overrightarrow{AB}$ and $\overrightarrow{CD}$ must be parallel because one is a multiple of the other.

Also, you can see from the diagram that $\overrightarrow{AB}$ is parallel to $\overrightarrow{CD}$.

Now think about the vector from $D$ to $C$.

$$\overrightarrow{AB} = \begin{pmatrix} 2 \\ 1 \end{pmatrix} \qquad \overrightarrow{DC} = \begin{pmatrix} -4 \\ -2 \end{pmatrix} = -2 \times \begin{pmatrix} 2 \\ 1 \end{pmatrix} = -2\overrightarrow{AB}$$

In general, if $\overrightarrow{AB} = \begin{pmatrix} x \\ y \end{pmatrix}$ and $\overrightarrow{CD} = m\begin{pmatrix} x \\ y \end{pmatrix}$ then $\overrightarrow{AB}$ and $\overrightarrow{CD}$ are parallel.

$m$ can be positive or negative.

*Example:*   $\overrightarrow{AB} = \begin{pmatrix} 2 \\ -3 \end{pmatrix}$   $\overrightarrow{BC} = \begin{pmatrix} -4 \\ -2 \end{pmatrix}$

    **a**    Draw a diagram showing $\overrightarrow{AB}$ and $\overrightarrow{BC}$.    **b**    Write $\overrightarrow{AC}$ as a column vector.

*Solution:*    **a**

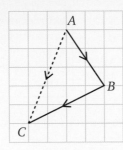

    **b**  $\overrightarrow{AB} + \overrightarrow{BC} = \overrightarrow{AC}$

$$\begin{pmatrix} 2 \\ -3 \end{pmatrix} + \begin{pmatrix} -4 \\ -2 \end{pmatrix} = \begin{pmatrix} -2 \\ -5 \end{pmatrix}$$

$\overrightarrow{AB} + \overrightarrow{BC}$ means $\overrightarrow{AB}$ followed by $\overrightarrow{BC}$

$\overrightarrow{AC} = \begin{pmatrix} -2 \\ -5 \end{pmatrix}$

Make sure that the vector is in the correct direction. You may be tempted to continue drawing clockwise and show the vector $\overrightarrow{CA}$ and not $\overrightarrow{AC}$.

---

*Example:*    $\mathbf{a} = \begin{pmatrix} 2 \\ 3 \end{pmatrix}$    $\mathbf{b} = \begin{pmatrix} -1 \\ 2 \end{pmatrix}$    $\mathbf{c} = \begin{pmatrix} -2 \\ -2 \end{pmatrix}$

Write the following as single column vectors.

    **a**    $\mathbf{a} + \mathbf{b} + \mathbf{c}$

    **b**    $4\mathbf{b} - 3\mathbf{c}$

*Solution:*    **a**  $\mathbf{a} + \mathbf{b} + \mathbf{c} = \begin{pmatrix} 2 \\ 3 \end{pmatrix} + \begin{pmatrix} -1 \\ 2 \end{pmatrix} + \begin{pmatrix} -2 \\ -2 \end{pmatrix} = \begin{pmatrix} -1 \\ 3 \end{pmatrix}$

    **b**  $4\mathbf{b} - 3\mathbf{c} = 4 \times \begin{pmatrix} -1 \\ 2 \end{pmatrix} - 3 \times \begin{pmatrix} -2 \\ -2 \end{pmatrix}$

$= \begin{pmatrix} -4 \\ 8 \end{pmatrix} - \begin{pmatrix} -6 \\ -6 \end{pmatrix}$

$= \begin{pmatrix} 2 \\ 14 \end{pmatrix}$

You can multiply a vector by a number. This number is known as a **scalar**. To multiply a column vector by a scalar, multiply the top number and bottom number by the scalar.

---

*Example:*    Use the information on the diagram to say whether each statement is true or false. If false, give the correct answer.

    **a**    $\mathbf{a} + \mathbf{b} = \mathbf{c} + \mathbf{d}$

    **b**    $\mathbf{b}$ is parallel to $\mathbf{d}$

    **c**    $\mathbf{b} = \mathbf{a} - \mathbf{c} + \mathbf{d}$

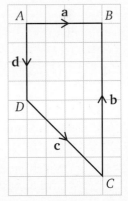

*Solution:*    **a**    False

$\mathbf{a} + \mathbf{b} = \begin{pmatrix} 4 \\ 0 \end{pmatrix} + \begin{pmatrix} 0 \\ 8 \end{pmatrix} = \begin{pmatrix} 4 \\ 8 \end{pmatrix}$

$\mathbf{c} + \mathbf{d} = \begin{pmatrix} 4 \\ -4 \end{pmatrix} + \begin{pmatrix} 0 \\ -4 \end{pmatrix} = \begin{pmatrix} 4 \\ -8 \end{pmatrix}$

    **b**    True

This can be seen on the diagram and also by comparing the column vectors for $\mathbf{b}$ and $\mathbf{d}$.

$\mathbf{b} = \begin{pmatrix} 0 \\ 8 \end{pmatrix}$ and $\mathbf{d} = \begin{pmatrix} 0 \\ -4 \end{pmatrix}$

The scalar value is $-2$ because $\mathbf{b} = -2\mathbf{d}$

This satisfies the general rule for parallel vectors because one vector is a multiple of the other.

    **c**    False

$\mathbf{a} - \mathbf{c} + \mathbf{d} = \begin{pmatrix} 4 \\ 0 \end{pmatrix} - \begin{pmatrix} 4 \\ -4 \end{pmatrix} + \begin{pmatrix} 0 \\ -4 \end{pmatrix} = \begin{pmatrix} 0 \\ 0 \end{pmatrix}$

$\mathbf{b} = \begin{pmatrix} 0 \\ 8 \end{pmatrix}$ so does not equal $\mathbf{a} - \mathbf{c} + \mathbf{d}$.

## Practise... 15.1 Vectors

**A**

**1** In each question part, which four of the five vectors, if drawn together, would create a rectangle?

**a** $\begin{pmatrix} 2 \\ 0 \end{pmatrix}$    $\begin{pmatrix} 0 \\ -2 \end{pmatrix}$    $\begin{pmatrix} 0 \\ -5 \end{pmatrix}$    $\begin{pmatrix} 0 \\ 5 \end{pmatrix}$    $\begin{pmatrix} -2 \\ 0 \end{pmatrix}$

**b** $\begin{pmatrix} 3 \\ 1 \end{pmatrix}$    $\begin{pmatrix} 2 \\ -6 \end{pmatrix}$    $\begin{pmatrix} -2 \\ 6 \end{pmatrix}$    $\begin{pmatrix} -3 \\ 1 \end{pmatrix}$    $\begin{pmatrix} -3 \\ -1 \end{pmatrix}$

> **Study tip**
>
> Draw the vectors to help you answer this question. In an examination you can ask for squared paper to help you draw them.

**2** Which of these vectors are equal? For those that are, give the column vector that represents them.

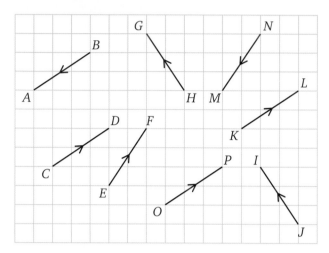

**3** $\overrightarrow{AB} = \begin{pmatrix} 2 \\ -1 \end{pmatrix}$

**a** Which of these column vectors are parallel to $\overrightarrow{AB}$?

**i** $\begin{pmatrix} 4 \\ -2 \end{pmatrix}$    **ii** $\begin{pmatrix} 3 \\ 0 \end{pmatrix}$    **iii** $\begin{pmatrix} -4 \\ 2 \end{pmatrix}$    **iv** $\begin{pmatrix} -10 \\ 5 \end{pmatrix}$    **v** $\begin{pmatrix} 5 \\ 4 \end{pmatrix}$

**b** For those vectors that are parallel, write each as a multiple of $\overrightarrow{AB}$.

**4** $\overrightarrow{AB} = \begin{pmatrix} 3 \\ 2 \end{pmatrix}$    $\overrightarrow{BC} = \begin{pmatrix} 1 \\ -4 \end{pmatrix}$

**a** Draw a diagram showing $\overrightarrow{AB}$ and $\overrightarrow{BC}$.

**b** Write $\overrightarrow{AC}$ as a column vector.

**5** Which of these statements are true and which are false? Give a reason for your answer in each case.

**a** $\begin{pmatrix} 2x \\ -4y \end{pmatrix}$ is parallel to and in the same direction as $\begin{pmatrix} 5x \\ -10y \end{pmatrix}$

**b** $\begin{pmatrix} 0.2x \\ 1.2y \end{pmatrix}$ is parallel to and in the opposite direction to $\begin{pmatrix} -x \\ -6y \end{pmatrix}$

**c** $\begin{pmatrix} -5x \\ 3y \end{pmatrix}$ is parallel to and in the same direction as $\begin{pmatrix} -15y \\ 25x \end{pmatrix}$

**6** $\mathbf{a} = \begin{pmatrix} -1 \\ 2 \end{pmatrix}$    $\mathbf{b} = \begin{pmatrix} 3 \\ -2 \end{pmatrix}$    $\mathbf{c} = \begin{pmatrix} 2 \\ -1 \end{pmatrix}$

**a** Draw a vector diagram for each question part.

**i** $2\mathbf{b} - \mathbf{a}$    **ii** $\mathbf{a} + \mathbf{b} + \mathbf{c}$    **iii** $-\mathbf{a} - \mathbf{b} + \mathbf{a}$

**b** Write each of the solutions to part **a** as a single column vector.

**7** $\mathbf{a} = \begin{pmatrix} 4 \\ 0 \end{pmatrix}$

$\mathbf{b} = \begin{pmatrix} 1 \\ -4 \end{pmatrix}$

$\mathbf{c} = \begin{pmatrix} -1 \\ -4 \end{pmatrix}$

> **Hint**
>
> Draw **a** then **b** then **c** then −**a** and so on, with one vector following on from the one before.

**a**   Draw the **vector sum a** + **b** + **c** − **a** − **b** − **c**.

**b**   Write down the name of the polygon in your diagram.

**8**   $\overrightarrow{AB} = \begin{pmatrix} -2 \\ 4 \end{pmatrix}$      $\overrightarrow{BC} = \begin{pmatrix} -3 \\ 3 \end{pmatrix}$

**a**   Draw a diagram of $\overrightarrow{AB} + 2\overrightarrow{BC}$.

**b**   Find the single vector equal to $\overrightarrow{AB} + 2\overrightarrow{BC}$.

**9**   The diagram shows a section of coastline with the sea and headland marked. There is deep water up to the land making it easy for boats to sail close in.

A small sailing boat is sailing from *A* to *B* and tacking using vectors. The sailor, Roy, plans to sail into the bay, keeping close in to the shore. However, he can only sail at 45° to the wind.

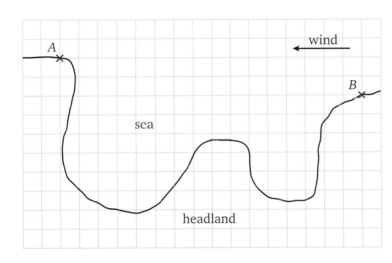

> **Hint**
>
> Sailing boats cannot sail directly towards the wind. They move in a series of zigzag movements, at 45° to the wind direction. This is called tacking.

**a**   Suggest a possible journey Roy could make along the coastline from *A* to *B* using column vectors.

**b**   Roy's friend Gordon is travelling directly from *A* to *B* in a speedboat. Describe Gordon's journey using one column vector.

**c**   Write Roy's journey as a vector sum.

**d**   Gordon says that Roy's vector sum is equal to his single column vector. Is Gordon right?

**10**   **i**   On squared paper, draw each of these polygons.
**ii**   Write vector instructions for each diagram.

**a**   an irregular pentagon

**b**   a right-angled triangle

**c**   a scalene triangle

**d**   an octagon

**11** This diagram shows two sets of vectors jumbled together.
Each set of vectors has a vector sum of zero.

Can you find the two sets of vectors?

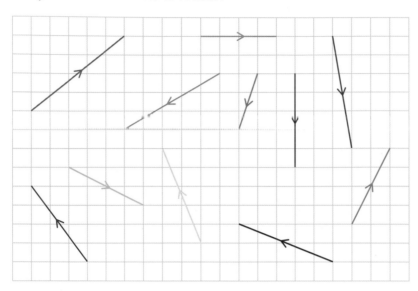

## Learn... 15.2 Vector geometry

Vectors are often used in simple geometric problems.

To solve problems using vector geometry the first step is to form a vector equation.

The shapes below look the same but the directions in two of the vectors are different.

The vector equations for each diagram would be different.

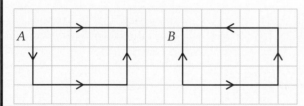

When forming equations, consider the different ways of moving
from one point to another.

In the diagram, there are two ways to get from *A* to *C* using the
vectors shown:

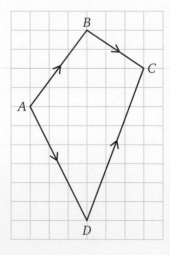

A to B then B to C    $\vec{AC} = \vec{AB} + \vec{BC}$

A to D then D to C    $\vec{AC} = -\vec{AD} + \vec{DC}$

The two routes result in the same thing, $\vec{AC}$, so can be written:

$\vec{AB} + \vec{BC} = \vec{AD} + \vec{DC}$

$\vec{AC}$ is the **resultant vector**.

**Example:**  *ABC* is an isosceles triangle.
*M* is the midpoint of *CB*. $\vec{AB} = \mathbf{a}$
and $\vec{AC} = \mathbf{b}$

Even though the triangle lengths are
the same, the vectors are different
because their directions are different.

**a** Find $\vec{BC}$ in terms of **a** and **b**.

**b** Find $\vec{AM}$ in terms of **a** and **b**.

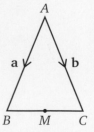

**Solution:**  **a**  $\overrightarrow{BC} = \overrightarrow{BA} + \overrightarrow{AC}$    Form a vector equation.

$\overrightarrow{BC} = -\mathbf{a} + \mathbf{b}$    Note that the direction of **a** is negative because it is going from $B$ to $A$.

**b**  $\overrightarrow{AM} = \overrightarrow{AB} + \overrightarrow{BM}$

$= \overrightarrow{AB} + \frac{1}{2}\overrightarrow{BC}$

$= \mathbf{a} + \frac{1}{2}(-\mathbf{a} + \mathbf{b})$

$= \mathbf{a} - \frac{1}{2}\mathbf{a} + \frac{1}{2}\mathbf{b}$

$= \frac{1}{2}\mathbf{a} + \frac{1}{2}\mathbf{b}$

**Study tip**

When you form vector equations, remember to check the direction of the given vectors. Remember that the opposite of **a** is $-\mathbf{a}$.

# Practise...   15.2 Vector geometry ⓚ          D C B A A*

**1**  This is a kite.

**a**  Write the vector $\overrightarrow{AD}$ in terms of **a** and **b**.

**b**  Write the vector $\overrightarrow{AD}$ in terms of **c** and **d**.

**c**  Write the vector $\overrightarrow{BC}$ in terms of **a** and **d**.

**d**  Write the vector $\overrightarrow{BC}$ in terms of **b** and **c**.

**e**  Use any of your answers to write **a** in terms of **b**, **c** and **d**.

**2**  **a**  If $\overrightarrow{XA} = 2\mathbf{a}$ and $\overrightarrow{XB} = \mathbf{a} + \mathbf{b}$, find $\overrightarrow{AB}$ in terms of **a** and **b**.

**b**  If $\overrightarrow{YC} = \mathbf{c}$ and $\overrightarrow{YD} = \mathbf{d} - \mathbf{c}$, find $\overrightarrow{CD}$ in terms of **c** and **d**.

**c**  IF $\overrightarrow{ZE} = \mathbf{f} - 2\mathbf{e}$ and $\overrightarrow{FZ} = 4\mathbf{f} - \mathbf{e}$, find $\overrightarrow{FE}$ in terms of **e** and **f**.

**3**  $\overrightarrow{OA} = \mathbf{a}$ and $\overrightarrow{AB} = \mathbf{b}$
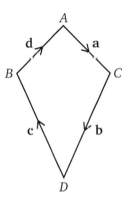

**a**  List all the vectors equal to **a**.

**b**  List all the vectors equal to **b**.

**c**  List all the remaining vectors in terms of **a** and **b**.

**4**  $\overrightarrow{AM} = 2\overrightarrow{MC} = 2\mathbf{b}$
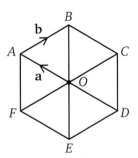

$\overrightarrow{NC} = \dfrac{\overrightarrow{BC}}{3} = \mathbf{c}$

**a**  Find $\overrightarrow{NM}$ in terms of **b** and **c**.

**b**  Find $\overrightarrow{AB}$ in terms of **b** and **c**.

**c**  Danny says that $\overrightarrow{AB}$ and $\overrightarrow{NM}$ are parallel. Is he right?
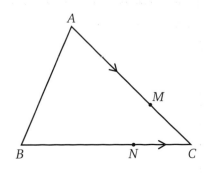

**A\***

**5**   *ABCD* is a trapezium and *ABED* is a parallelogram.
$\overrightarrow{AB} = \mathbf{a}$ and $\overrightarrow{AD} = \mathbf{b}$ and length $CD = 2 \times$ length $AB$

Write each of these vectors in terms of **a** and **b**.

**a**   **i** $\overrightarrow{DC}$      **iii** $\overrightarrow{DB}$      **v** $\overrightarrow{AE}$      **vii** $\overrightarrow{BC}$

   **ii** $\overrightarrow{AC}$      **iv** $\overrightarrow{BE}$      **vi** $\overrightarrow{EC}$

**b**   Prove that *ABCE* is a parallelogram.

**c**   *AC* crosses *BE* at *F*. Write $\overrightarrow{AF}$ in terms of **a** and **b**.

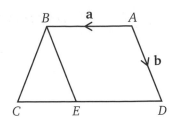

**6**   *ADBO* and *OBEC* are both parallelograms.
$\overrightarrow{OA} = \mathbf{a}$, $\overrightarrow{OB} = \mathbf{b}$ and $\overrightarrow{OC} = \mathbf{c}$

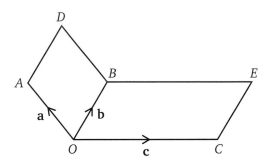

**a**   Write each of these vectors in terms of **a**, **b** and **c**.

   **i** $\overrightarrow{OD}$    **ii** $\overrightarrow{BC}$    **iii** $\overrightarrow{AB}$    **iv** $\overrightarrow{BE}$    **v** $\overrightarrow{DC}$

**b**   *F* is a point such that $\overrightarrow{OF} = \mathbf{a} + \mathbf{b} + \mathbf{c}$
Write $\overrightarrow{CF}$ in terms of **a**, **b** and **c**.

**⚠ 7**   *XYZ* is a triangle. *M* is the midpoint of *YZ* and *S* is the midpoint of *XZ*.

YS crosses *XM* at *R*. The ratio $XR : RM = 2 : 1$
$\overrightarrow{XY} = \mathbf{a}$ and $\overrightarrow{XZ} = \mathbf{b}$

**a**   Write the following vectors in terms of **a** and **b**.

   **i** $\overrightarrow{YS}$        **iii** $\overrightarrow{ZM}$        **v** $\overrightarrow{XR}$        **vii** $\overrightarrow{RS}$

   **ii** $\overrightarrow{ZY}$        **iv** $\overrightarrow{XM}$        **vi** $\overrightarrow{XS}$

**b**   Use your answers to parts **i** and **vii** to calculate the ratio $YS : RS$

# 15   Assess (k)

**A**

**1**   $\mathbf{a} = \begin{pmatrix} 2 \\ -1 \end{pmatrix}$      $\mathbf{b} = \begin{pmatrix} 0 \\ 2 \end{pmatrix}$      $\mathbf{c} = \begin{pmatrix} -1 \\ 0 \end{pmatrix}$

Write each of the following as a single column vector.

**a**   $\mathbf{a} + \mathbf{b} + \mathbf{c}$

**b**   $2\mathbf{a} + \mathbf{b}$

**c**   $2\mathbf{b} - 2\mathbf{a} + \mathbf{c}$

**A**

**2** Which of these vectors are equal? Give reasons for your answers.

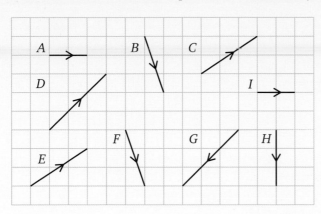

**3** $\overrightarrow{AB} = \begin{pmatrix} 1 \\ 2 \end{pmatrix}$ $\overrightarrow{BC} = \begin{pmatrix} 3 \\ 4 \end{pmatrix}$

**a** Draw a diagram of $3\overrightarrow{AB} + \overrightarrow{BC}$.

**b** Find the single vector equal to $3\overrightarrow{AB} + \overrightarrow{BC}$.

**4** $\overrightarrow{AB} = \begin{pmatrix} 2 \\ -3 \end{pmatrix}$

Which of these column vectors are parallel to $\overrightarrow{AB}$? For those that are, write each as a multiple of $\overrightarrow{AB}$.

**a** $\begin{pmatrix} 4 \\ -2 \end{pmatrix}$ **b** $\begin{pmatrix} 4 \\ -6 \end{pmatrix}$ **c** $\begin{pmatrix} 1 \\ 1.5 \end{pmatrix}$ **d** $\begin{pmatrix} -2 \\ 3 \end{pmatrix}$ **e** $\begin{pmatrix} 20 \\ -30 \end{pmatrix}$

**5** *ABCD* is a parallelogram. $\overrightarrow{CD} = 3\mathbf{b}$ and $\overrightarrow{BD} = 2\mathbf{a}$

**A\***

**a** Write the vector $\overrightarrow{AB}$ in terms of **a** and **b**.

**b** Write the vector $\overrightarrow{AD}$ in terms of **a** and **b**.

**c** Write the vector $\overrightarrow{BC}$ in terms of **a** and **b**.

**d** Write the vector $\overrightarrow{AC}$ in terms of **a** and **b**.

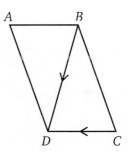

**6** **a** If $\overrightarrow{XA} = \mathbf{a}$ and $\overrightarrow{XB} = \mathbf{a} + 2\mathbf{b}$, find $\overrightarrow{AB}$ in terms of **a** and **b**.

**b** If $\overrightarrow{YC} = 2\mathbf{c}$ and $\overrightarrow{YD} = 2(\mathbf{d} - \mathbf{c})$, find $\overrightarrow{CD}$ in terms of **c** and **d**.

**7** *ABC* is an isosceles triangle.

**a** $\overrightarrow{AM} = \mathbf{a}$ and $\overrightarrow{AN} = \mathbf{b}$

Find **MN** in terms of **a** and **b**.

**b** $\overrightarrow{CB} = 3(\mathbf{b} - \mathbf{a})$

Find $\overrightarrow{MC}$ and $\overrightarrow{NB}$ in terms of **a** and **b**.

**c** Find the ratio of *AM* to *MC*.

**d** Describe the relationship between triangles *ABC* and *ANM*.

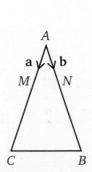

**A\***

**8** *ABCD* is a rectangle. *M* is the midpoint of *AB*. *AN* = 2*ND* and *BO* = 3*OC*

$\overrightarrow{AM} = \mathbf{a}$

$\overrightarrow{AN} = \mathbf{b}$

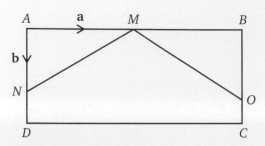

Find the following vectors in terms of **a** and **b**.

**a** $\overrightarrow{MB}$      **b** $\overrightarrow{BO}$      **c** $\overrightarrow{MO}$      **d** $\overrightarrow{NO}$

# Practice questions 🄺

**1** *OAB* is a triangle with *P* the mid point of *OA* and *M* the mid point of *AB*.
$\overrightarrow{OP} = \mathbf{a}$, $\overrightarrow{PA} = \mathbf{a}$ and $\overrightarrow{OB} = 2\mathbf{b}$

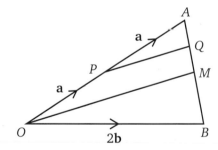

Not drawn accurately

**a** Write down an expression for $\overrightarrow{AB}$ in terms of **a** and **b**. *(1 mark)*

**b** *Q* lies on *AB* such that $\overrightarrow{AQ} = \frac{1}{4}\overrightarrow{AB}$
Show that $\overrightarrow{PQ} = \frac{1}{2}\mathbf{a} + \frac{1}{2}\mathbf{b}$
Explain your answer. *(2 marks)*

**c** Write down, and simplify, an expression for $\overrightarrow{OM}$ in terms of **a** and **b**. *(2 marks)*

**d** Explain why the answers for part **b** and part **c** show that *OPQM* is a trapezium. *(1 mark)*

AQA 2008

*Did you know?*

## The Great Pyramid

The Great Pyramid of Giza is believed to have been built as a tomb for the Egyptian King Khufu. It was completed approximately five and a half thousand years ago and was the world's tallest building for 3800 years. It is the only one of the Seven Wonders of the Ancient World still remaining.

The pyramid has a square base with sides 231 metres long and is approximately 147 metres high, taller than 33 double-decker buses. Its volume is more than a quarter of a million cubic metres, the volume of 50 Olympic swimming pools.

## You should already know:

✔ how to work out the circumference and area of a circle

✔ how to work out the volume and surface area of prisms and cylinders.

## Learn... 16.1 Arcs and sectors

An **arc** is part of the circumference of a circle.

The length of an arc of a circle is proportional to the angle that the arc makes at the centre of the circle.

The whole circumference of a circle, $2\pi r$, makes an angle of 360°.

You can use the unitary method to find the length of any arc.

Length of arc with an angle of 360° is $2\pi r$

Length of arc with an angle of 1° is $\frac{1}{360} \times 2\pi r$.

Length of arc with an angle of $\theta°$ is $\frac{\theta}{360} \times 2\pi r$.

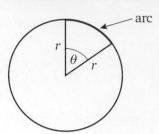

The Greek letter $\theta$, called theta, is often used to represent an angle.

A **sector** of a circle is a wedge-shaped piece of the area of a circle, bounded by two radii and an arc.

The whole area of a circle is $\pi r^2$.

The area of a sector with an angle of $\theta°$ is $\frac{\theta}{360} \times \pi r^2$.

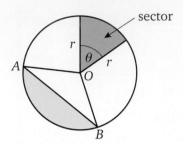

A **segment** of a circle is a region bounded by a chord and an arc.

The area of the shaded segment in the diagram is the area of the sector $OAB$ minus the area of the triangle $OAB$.

---

**Example:** The cross-section of a water trough is the segment of the circle shown shaded in the following diagram. The length of the trough is 3 metres.

Find the volume of the trough.

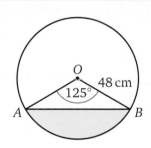

**Solution:** First find the area of the segment.

Area of sector $OAB = \frac{125}{360} \times \pi \times 48^2$ cm²

Area of triangle $OAB = \frac{1}{2}ab \sin C = \frac{1}{2} \times 48^2 \sin 125°$ cm²

So area of segment $= \left(\frac{125}{360} \times \pi \times 48^2 - \frac{1}{2} \times 48^2 \times \sin 125°\right)$ cm²

$= 1569.6109...$ cm²

$= 0.1569...$ m²  The radius of the trough is given in centimetres, but the length is in metres. To find the volume, these must be in the same units, so either convert the length to cm or convert the area to m².

The area of the segment = the area of cross-section of the water trough

Volume of water trough = area of cross-section × length

$= 0.1569...$ m² × 3 m

$= 0.471$ m³ (3 s.f.)

> **Study tip**
>
> When the cross-section of a 3-D shape is uniform, the volume is given by the formula:
>
> $V = A \times h$
>
> where $V$ is volume, $A$ is area of the cross-section and $h$ is the length.

# Practise... 16.1 Arcs and sectors

**A**

**1**  Find the length of the arcs indicated. *O* is the centre of the circle in each case.

**a**     **b**     **c**

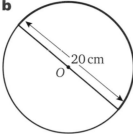

Not drawn
accurately

**2**  Find the areas of the shaded sectors. *O* is the centre of the circle in each case.

**a**     **b**     **c**

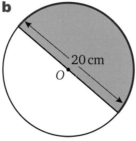 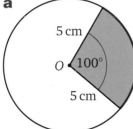 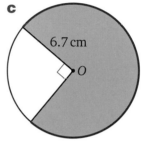

Not drawn
accurately

**3**  Find the length of the arc of a circle that makes:

**a**  an angle of 90° at the centre of a circle with radius 10 cm

**b**  an angle of 150° at the centre of a circle with radius 4 cm

**c**  an angle of 53° at the centre of a circle with radius 12.5 cm.

**4**  An arc makes an angle of 30° in a circle with radius 2 cm.

What angle does an arc of the same length make in a circle with radius 10 cm?

**5**  Find the area of the sector of a circle that makes:

**a**  an angle of 120° at the centre of a circle with radius 5 cm

**b**  an angle of 57° at the centre of a circle with radius 22 cm

**c**  an angle of 210° at the centre of a circle with radius 1 m.

**6**  Find the shaded areas.

**a**  Radius = 12 cm     **b**  Radius = 4.5 cm     **c**  Radius = 62 cm

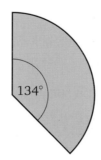 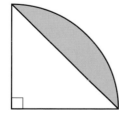 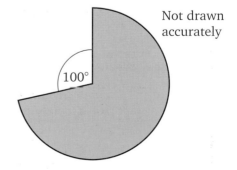 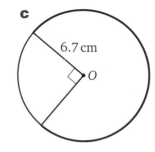

Not drawn
accurately

**A\***

**A\***

**7** Find the shaded areas. The arcs are quarter circles and the squares have sides 10 cm long.

a    b 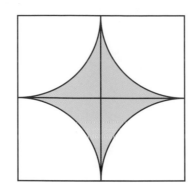   c

**8** Two circles with radius 5 cm overlap so that the centre of one is on the circumference of the other. Find the perimeter and area of the overlap region.

**⚠ 9** A semicircular piece of card of radius $R$ is folded into a cone with height $h$.

Prove that $h = \frac{R}{2}\sqrt{3}$

**⚙ 10** The diagram shows the layout of four flower beds, each in the shape of a quarter circle of radius 6 m.

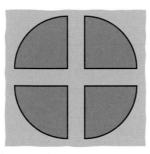

Each bed is to be surrounded with edging strip costing £1.23 per metre. How much will this cost?

**⚙ 11** The diagram shows the pattern for a skirt consisting of three quarters of a circle of radius 55 cm (with a small circle cut out of the centre for the waist). The large circular arc forms the hem of the skirt, to be finished with ribbon.

How long is this circular arc?

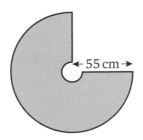

← 55 cm →

 **Learn...**

## 16.2 Volumes and surface areas of pyramids, cones and spheres

### Volume of a pyramid

If a triangle is fitted exactly inside a rectangle with a side in common with the rectangle, then the area of the triangle is half the area of the rectangle.

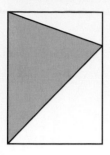 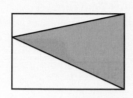

Similarly, a pyramid can be fitted inside a prism sharing the base and height.

The volume of the pyramid is one-third of the volume of the prism.

The volume of a prism is: area of base × height.

So the volume of the pyramid is $\frac{1}{3}$ × area of base × height.

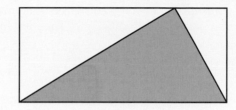

> **Study tip**
>
> A prism has a uniform cross-section, so $V = A \times h$
> For solids that come to a vertex (cone and pyramid),
> $$V = \tfrac{1}{3}A \times h$$

**Example:** A pyramid with height 5 cm and a square base with sides of 4 cm fits inside a cuboid measuring 4 cm by 4 cm by 5 cm.

Calculate the volume of the pyramid.

**Solution:** The volume of the cuboid is $4 \times 4 \times 5$ cm³.

The volume of the pyramid is $\frac{1}{3}$ × area of base × height.

$= \frac{1}{3} \times 4 \times 4 \times 5$ cm³

$= 26.7$ cm³ (3 s.f.)

### Volume of a cone

A cone can be fitted exactly into a cylinder.

The volume of the cone is one third of the volume of the cylinder.

A cone with perpendicular height $h$ cm and base radius $r$ fits into a cylinder with height $h$ and radius $r$.

The volume of the cylinder is $\pi r^2 h$.

So the volume of the cone is $\frac{1}{3}\pi r^2 h$.

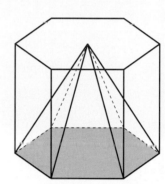

A cone is a pyramid with a circular base.

> **Study tip**
>
> This formula is given on the exam paper.

### Volume of a sphere

The volume of a sphere with radius $r$ is $\frac{4}{3}\pi r^3$.

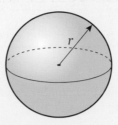

**Example:** A toy consists of a hemisphere of radius 3 cm topped with a cone. The total height of the toy is 8 cm.

Find the volume of the toy.

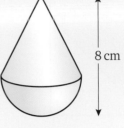

8 cm

Not drawn
accurately

**Solution:** Volume of hemisphere = half volume of sphere

$$= \frac{1}{2} \times \frac{4}{3}\pi \times 3^3 \, \text{cm}^3 = \frac{2}{3}\pi \times 3^3 \, \text{cm}^3$$

$$= 56.5486... \, \text{cm}^3$$

Height of cone $= 8 - 3 = 5$ cm

Volume of cone $= \frac{1}{3}\pi \times 3^2 \times 5 \, \text{cm}^3$

$$= 47.1238... \, \text{cm}^3$$

Total volume of toy = volume of hemisphere + volume of cone

$$= 103.6725... \, \text{cm}^3$$

$$= 104 \, \text{cm}^3 \text{ (3 s.f.)}$$

### Surface areas

The surface area of any solid is the sum of the areas of all the faces.

A **tetrahedron** is a pyramid with a triangular base. A regular tetrahedron is a pyramid whose faces are all equilateral triangles.

The surface area of a regular tetrahedron is the sum of the areas of the four equilateral triangles that form its faces.

If the edges of the tetrahedron have length $x$, the area of each triangle is:

$\frac{1}{2}x^2 \sin 60°$

So the surface area of the tetrahedron $= 4 \times \frac{1}{2}x^2 \sin 60°$

$$= 2x^2 \sin 60°$$

The surface area of a cone is the sum of the area of its circular base and the area of its curved surface.

The area of the curved surface of a cone is $\pi r l$.

So the total surface area of a cone = area of curved surface + area of base

$$= \pi r l + \pi r^2$$

$$= \pi r (l + r)$$

$l$

$r$

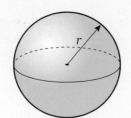

$r$

The surface area of a sphere is $4\pi r^2$.

*Example:*   The **frustum** of a cone has base radius 6 cm and top radius 3 cm. The distance between the top and the base is 3 cm. Find the volume of the frustum.

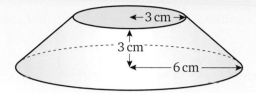

Not drawn accurately

The frustum of a cone is the part remaining when the top of a cone is removed.

*Solution:*   Let the height of the missing part of the cone be $h$ cm.

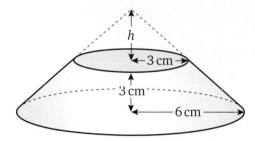

By similar triangles, $\dfrac{h + 3}{h} = \dfrac{6}{3}$

$$h + 3 = 2h$$
$$h = 3$$

(This is obvious from the diagram, but the similar triangle method above applies to any frustum, not just this special case.)

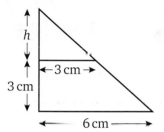

Volume of whole cone $= \frac{1}{3}\pi \times 6^2 \times 6 \text{ cm}^3$
$= 72\pi \text{ cm}^3$

Volume of missing part of cone $= \frac{1}{3}\pi \times 3^2 \times 3 \text{ cm}^3$
$= 9\pi \text{ cm}^3$

So volume of frustum $= 72\pi \text{ cm}^3 - 9\pi \text{ cm}^3$
$= 63\pi \text{ cm}^3$
$= 198 \text{ cm}^3$ (3 s.f.)

## Summary of formulae

Volume of a pyramid $= \frac{1}{3} \times$ area of base $\times$ perpendicular height

Volume of cone $= \frac{1}{3} \times$ area of base $\times$ perpendicular height

$= \frac{1}{3}\pi r^2 h$

Area of curved surface of cone $= \pi r l$

Volume of sphere $= \frac{4}{3}\pi r^3$

Surface area of sphere $= 4\pi r^2$

**Study tip**

All of these formulae are given on the exam paper.

**Practise...**

## 16.2 Volumes and surface areas of pyramids, cones and spheres

A

A*

Give your answers correct to three significant figures unless they work out exactly.

**1** Find the volume of:

   **a** a sphere with radius 5 cm

   **b** a hemisphere with radius 10 cm

   **c** a pyramid with height 12 cm and a hexagonal base with area 36 cm².

**2** Find the total surface area of a square-based pyramid with all edges 5 cm long.

**3** The small cone has base radius 7 cm and height 10 cm.

The large cone has base radius 14 cm and height 20 cm.

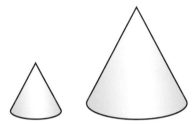

   **a** Find the volume of each cone.

   **b** What fraction of the volume of the large cone is the volume of the small cone?

**4** Two spheres, A and B, have radii 2 cm and 6 cm.

Find the ratio of:

   **a** radius of A : radius of B

   **b** surface area of A : surface area of B

   **c** volume of A : volume of B

**5**  **a** Find the volume of:

      **i** a pyramid with height 15 cm and square base with sides of length 10 cm

      **ii** a cone with base radius 3.5 cm and height 15 cm.

   **b** What is the radius of the base of a cone of height 15 cm that has the same volume as the pyramid in part **a i**?

**6** What is the height of a cone of radius 6 cm that has the same surface area as a hemisphere of radius 6 cm?

**7** A measuring cylinder with radius 3 cm contains water to a depth of 10 cm.
A small metal sphere is dropped into the cylinder and the water level rises by 2 cm.

What is the radius of the sphere?

**8** A semicircular piece of card with radius 10 cm is curved to form a cone.

What is the volume of the cone?

**9** Prove that the area of the curved surface of a cone with radius $r$ and slant height $l$ is $\pi r l$.

**10** The shape of most buckets is an approximation to a frustum of a cone.
One such bucket has top diameter 24 cm, base diameter 18 cm and height
26 cm. These are all internal measurements.

How many litres will the bucket hold?

 **11** A grain hopper is in the form of a cylinder on top of the frustum of a cone. Its
measurements are as shown in the diagram.

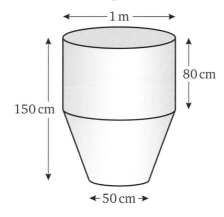

**a** What volume of grain will the hopper hold?

**b** What area of sheet metal is needed to make the hopper?

# 16 Assess ⓚ

Give your answers to three significant figures.

**1** Find the area of each sector.

    **a** Radius 4.9 cm
       Angle 58°

    **b** Radius 15 cm
       Angle 134°

    **c**

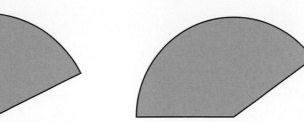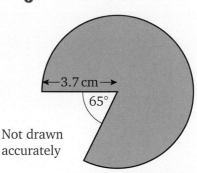

Not drawn
accurately

**2** An arc of a circle of radius 10 cm is $4\pi$ cm long.

What angle does the arc make at the centre of the circle?

**3** Which has the bigger volume, a sphere with diameter 24 cm or a cone with
diameter 24 cm and height 48 cm?

**4** A goat is tethered to the corner of a square field measuring 20 m by 20 m.
The goat can graze half the field.

How long is the goat's tethering rope?

**5** The Pyramid of Menkaure is the smallest of the three main pyramids at Giza.
Its measurements are approximately half those of the Great Pyramid (see start of chapter).

What is its approximate volume?

A*

**6** The diagram shows an equilateral triangle with sides 3 cm long. A sector of a circle with radius 1 cm has been cut from each vertex to make the shaded shape.

Find the area and perimeter of this shaded shape.

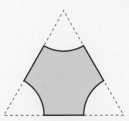

**7** A rectangular block of metal measuring 6 cm by 8 cm by 5 cm is melted down. It is recast as spherical ball bearings of diameter 0.9 cm.

How many ball bearings can be made and how much metal is left over?

**8** From the top of an 8 cm square-based pyramid with height 10 cm, a pyramid of height 6 cm is removed.

   **a** What fraction of the volume of the original pyramid is the volume of the removed pyramid?

   **b** Find the volume of the remaining frustum of the pyramid.

**9** The cross-section of a tunnel is the major segment of a circle with radius 3.2 m. The tunnel is to be 0.75 km long.

How many cubic metres of rock must be removed to make the tunnel?

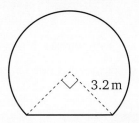

3.2 m

**10** An oil storage tank consists of a cylinder with a hemisphere on each end. The cylinder is 1 m long and its diameter is 75 cm. The metal used to make the tank is 1 cm thick.

How many litres of oil will the tank hold?

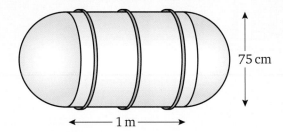

75 cm

1 m

# Practice questions (k)

**1** The sector *AOB* of a circle is shown below.

The length of its arc *AB* is $10\pi$ cm.

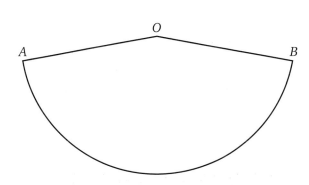

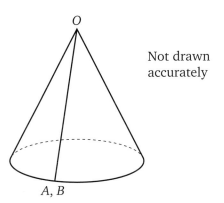

Not drawn accurately

*A, B*

The sector is folded so that the straight edges meet and form a cone as shown.

   **a** Calculate the radius of the base of the cone.    *(3 marks)*

   **b** The volume of the cone is $80\pi$ cm³.
      Work out the perpendicular height of the cone.    *(3 marks)*

AQA 2009

# 17 Transforming functions

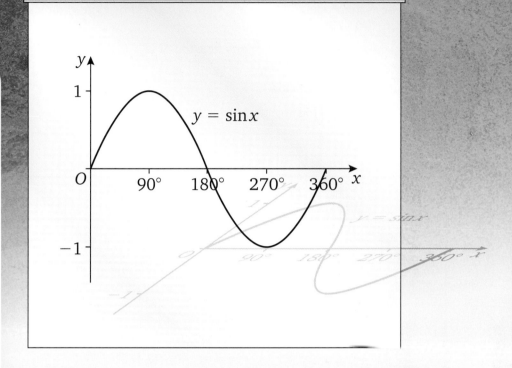

$y = \sin x$

## Objectives

Examiners would normally expect students who get these grades to be able to:

### A/A*

understand and apply function notation

given $y = f(x)$ or a sketch of $y = f(x)$, draw transformations of $f(x)$

understand that $\dfrac{y}{a} = f(x)$ and $y = f\left(\dfrac{x}{a}\right)$ represent a one-way stretch with a scale factor $a$ parallel to the $y$- and $x$-axes respectively of $y = f(x)$

understand that $y = f(x) + a$ and $y = f(x - a)$ represent translations of $y = f(x)$.

## Did you know?

### Just as you can transform shapes, you can also transform graphs

You can apply transformations such as translations and reflections to graphs just as you can to shapes.

The effects can be quite interesting, and can be used to help solve some difficult problems. Given a complex function it is often possible to use transformations to simplify it and then solve simple problems. These solutions can then be 'mapped back'.

This type of work is developed in courses which go beyond GCSE.

## Key terms

transformation
function
translation
one-way stretch

## You should already know:

✔ how to plot graphs

✔ the graphs of standard functions including trigonometric functions

✔ how to describe translations using vectors.

## Learn... 17.1 Transforming functions

You need to be able to use **transformations** on graphs.

If $y$ is a **function** of $x$, then it can be written as $y = f(x)$. A function of $x$ can be very simple, such as $y = x$, or as in the example, $y = x^2$. A function could be more complex such as $y = 3x^2 - 4x + 7$, and we can write $f(x) = 3x^2 - 4x + 7$

Here $y = f(x)$ is used to refer to any function of $x$.

### Translations of functions

The function $y = x^2$ has this table:

| $x$ | −3 | −2 | −1 | 0 | 1 | 2 | 3 |
|---|---|---|---|---|---|---|---|
| $y$ | 9 | 4 | 1 | 0 | 1 | 4 | 9 |

and the function $y = x^2 + 3$ has the table:

| $x$ | −3 | −2 | −1 | 0 | 1 | 2 | 3 |
|---|---|---|---|---|---|---|---|
| $y$ | 12 | 7 | 4 | 3 | 4 | 7 | 12 |

Plotting graphs for both functions on the same axes gives:

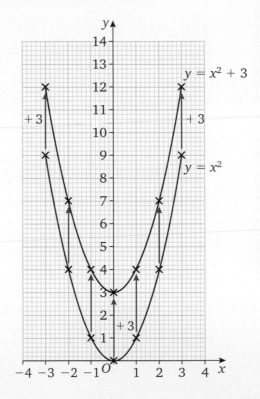

The graph of $y = x^2 + 3$, drawn in black, has exactly the same shape as the graph of $y = x^2$ but is 3 units above it. This is the effect of the '+ 3'.

In general, $y = x^2 + a$ will be the same shape as the graph of $y = x^2$, but will be $a$ units above it.

It is a **translation** with vector $\begin{pmatrix} 0 \\ a \end{pmatrix}$

This result applies to graphs of all functions, so the graph of $y = f(x) + a$ is a translation of the graph of $y = f(x)$ by a vector $\begin{pmatrix} 0 \\ a \end{pmatrix}$

This is true whether $a$ is positive or negative, for example:

- If $a$ is 4 then the translation vector is $\begin{pmatrix} 0 \\ 4 \end{pmatrix}$

- If $a$ is −2 then the translation vector is $\begin{pmatrix} 0 \\ -2 \end{pmatrix}$

It is important to note that $y - a = f(x)$ is the same as $y = f(x) + a$

Now consider $y = (x - 2)^2$

| $x$ | −1 | 0 | 1 | 2 | 3 | 4 | 5 |
|---|---|---|---|---|---|---|---|
| $y$ | 9 | 4 | 1 | 0 | 1 | 4 | 9 |

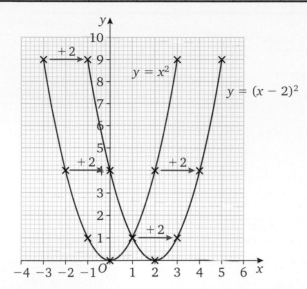

Every point on the graph of $y = x^2$ has 'moved' 2 units to the right.

The graph of $y = (x - 2)^2$ is a translation of the graph of $y = x^2$ by the vector $\begin{pmatrix} 2 \\ 0 \end{pmatrix}$

Similarly, the graph of $y = (x + 3)^2$ is a translation of the graph of $y = x^2$ by the vector $\begin{pmatrix} -3 \\ 0 \end{pmatrix}$

It may help to think of $y = (x + 3)^2$ as $y = (x - (-3))^2$ so $a$ is −3.

We conclude that $y = (x - a)^2$ is a translation of the graph of $y = x^2$ by the vector $\begin{pmatrix} a \\ 0 \end{pmatrix}$

In general, $y = f(x - a)$ is a translation of the graph of $y = f(x)$ by the vector $\begin{pmatrix} a \\ 0 \end{pmatrix}$

## Stretches

Now consider the function $y = 2x^2$

| $x$ | −3 | −2 | −1 | 0 | 1 | 2 | 3 |
|---|---|---|---|---|---|---|---|
| $y$ | 18 | 8 | 2 | 0 | 2 | 8 | 18 |

These points are plotted on the graph of $y = x^2$.

The graph shows that all the $y$-coordinates of $y = x^2$ have been multiplied by 2. This effect is called a stretch in the $y$-direction, with scale factor 2. Note that any points on the $x$-axis remain unchanged (because $0 \times 2 = 0$).

The graph of $y = 3x^2$ would be a stretch in the $y$-direction, with scale factor 3, of the graph of $y = x^2$

In general, the graph of $y = ax^2$ would be a stretch in the $y$-direction, with scale factor $a$, of the graph of $y = x^2$

As before, this result applies to graphs of all functions, so the graph of $y = af(x)$ is a **one-way stretch** in the $y$-direction, with scale factor $a$, of the graph of $y = f(x)$

If $a$ is negative, for example, −2, then all the $y$-coordinates are multiplied by this and the table of values becomes:

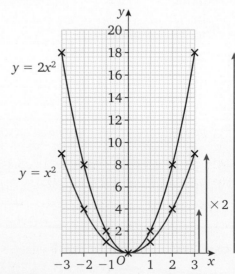

| $x$ | −3 | −2 | −1 | 0 | 1 | 2 | 3 |
|---|---|---|---|---|---|---|---|
| $y$ | −18 | −8 | −2 | 0 | −2 | −8 | −18 |

The result of this is a one-way stretch in the $y$-direction with scale factor 2 followed by a reflection in the $x$-axis. This can be expressed as a single transformation, a one-way stretch in the $y$-direction, scale factor −2.

It is important to note that $y = af(x)$ can be written as $\dfrac{y}{a} = f(x)$

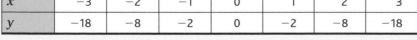

Now consider $y = \left(\dfrac{x}{2}\right)^2$

| $x$ | $-4$ | $-3$ | $-2$ | $-1$ | 0 | 1 | 2 | 3 | 4 |
|-----|------|------|------|------|---|---|---|---|---|
| $y$ | 4 | 2.25 | 1 | 0.25 | 0 | 0.25 | 1 | 2.25 | 4 |

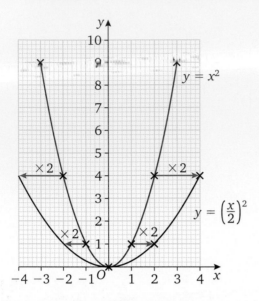

The graph shows that the $x$-coordinates of $y = \left(\dfrac{x}{2}\right)^2$ are exactly double the $x$-coordinates of $y = x^2$
This is a one-way stretch in the $x$-direction, scale factor 2.

Similarly, $y = (2x)^2$ is a one-way stretch in the $x$-direction, scale factor $\frac{1}{2}$, of the graph of $y = x^2$
It may help to think of $2x$ as being the same as $\dfrac{x}{\frac{1}{2}}$

We conclude that the graph of $y = \left(\dfrac{x}{a}\right)^2$ is a one-way stretch in the $x$-direction, scale factor $a$, of the graph of $y = x^2$

In general, the graph of $y = f\left(\dfrac{x}{a}\right)$ is a one-way stretch in the $x$-direction, scale factor $a$, of the graph of $y = f(x)$

## Summary

| Transformed function | Transformation |
|---|---|
| $y - a = f(x)$<br>$y = f(x) + a$ | translation by vector $\begin{pmatrix} 0 \\ a \end{pmatrix}$ |
| $y = f(x - a)$ | translation by vector $\begin{pmatrix} a \\ 0 \end{pmatrix}$ |
| $y = af(x)$<br>$\dfrac{y}{a} = f(x)$ | one-way stretch in $y$-direction, scale factor $a$ |
| $y = f\left(\dfrac{x}{a}\right)$ | one-way stretch in $x$-direction, scale factor $a$ |

*Example:*   Draw the graph of $y = \cos x$. Use your graph to plot the graphs of:

**a**   $y = \cos x - 3$

**b**   $y = 2\cos x$

**c**   $y = -\cos x$

In each case, state the transformation used.

**Solution:**     Plot the graph of $y = \cos x$

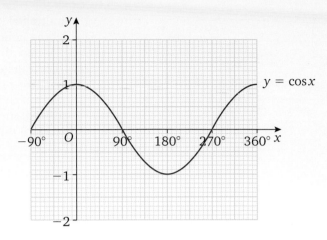

**a**

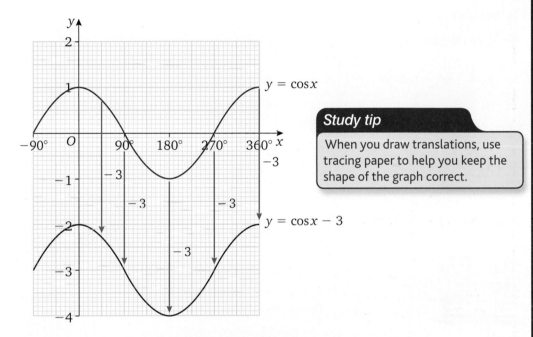

> **Study tip**
>
> When you draw translations, use tracing paper to help you keep the shape of the graph correct.

All the $y$-coordinates have 3 subtracted from them.

The transformation is: a translation with vector $\begin{pmatrix} 0 \\ -3 \end{pmatrix}$ or a translation three units in the negative $y$-direction.

**b**

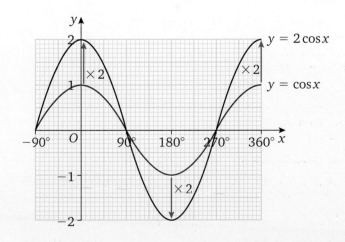

For the graph of $y = 2 \cos x$ all the $y$-coordinates will be multiplied by 2.

The transformation is: a stretch in the $y$-direction, factor 2.

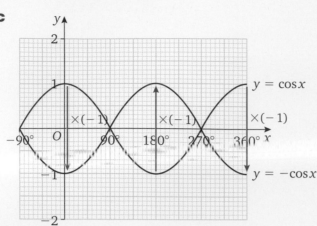

**c**

To get the graph of $y = -\cos x$ all the $y$-coordinates have been multiplied by $-1$.
All the points on the graph $y = \cos x$ that had positive $y$-coordinates now have a negative $y$-coordinate. The effect of this is to move all the points from one side of the $x$-axis to the other side.

The transformation is: a reflection in the $x$-axis.

## Practise... 17.1 Transforming functions ⓚ

D C B A A*

**1**

**a** Sketch and label each of these graphs.

**i** $y = x$      **iv** $y = x^3$

**ii** $y = x^2$      **v** $y = \sin x$

**iii** $y = \dfrac{1}{x}$      **vi** $y = \cos x$

**b** Translate each graph in part **a** using the vector $\begin{pmatrix} 0 \\ 4 \end{pmatrix}$

**c** Sketch the graphs in part **a** after a stretch in the $y$-direction scale factor 3.

**d** Label your sketches in parts **b** and **c** with their equations.

**2** For each set of graphs, do the following.

**a** Write down the equation of the red graph.

**b** By transforming the red graph, write the equation of each black graph.

**c** Write the transformation that produces each family of graphs.

**i**

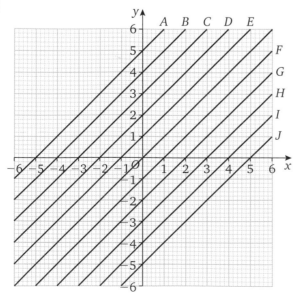

**ii**

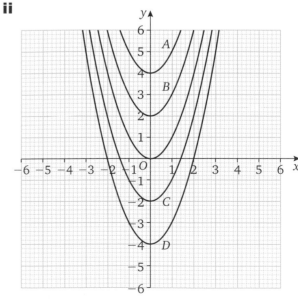

**3**  This diagram shows seven transformations of the graph of $y = \sin x$

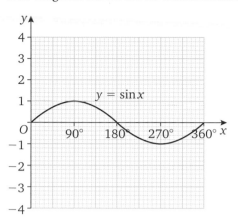

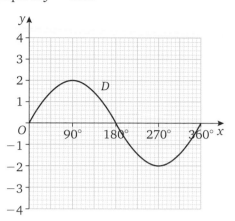

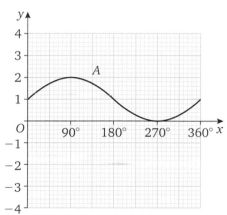

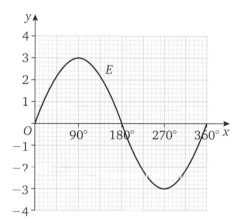

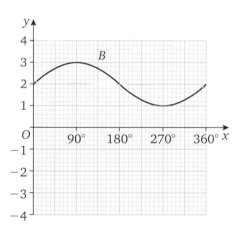

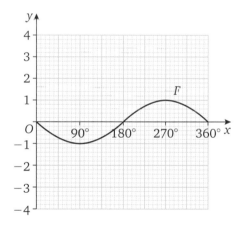

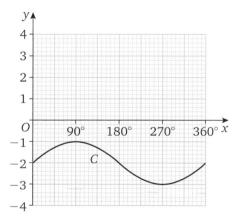

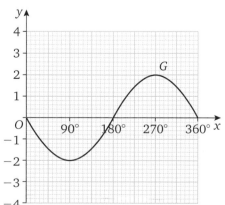

**a**  Match each graph with one of the following functions.

    **i**   $y = 2\sin x$      **iii**  $y = -\sin x$     **v**  $y = \sin x + 1$    **vii**  $y = \sin x - 2$

    **ii**  $y = 3\sin x$      **iv**  $y = -2\sin x$    **vi**  $y = \sin x + 2$

**b**  Describe the transformation that needs to be carried out to get the graph of each function from the graph of $y = \sin x$

**A\***

**4** This is the graph of $y = x^3 - 2x^2$

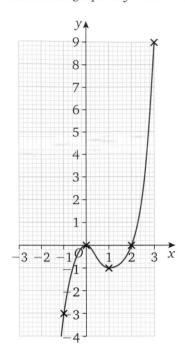

> **Hint**
>
> Think of the graph of $y = x^3 - 2x^2$ as the graph of $y = f(x)$

Sketch the graphs of:

**a** $y = x^3 - 2x^2 + 2$  **c** $y = 2x^3 - 4x^2$

**b** $y = x^3 - 2x^2 - 1$  **d** $y = 2x^2 - x^3$

**5** This is the graph of $y = \dfrac{1}{x}$

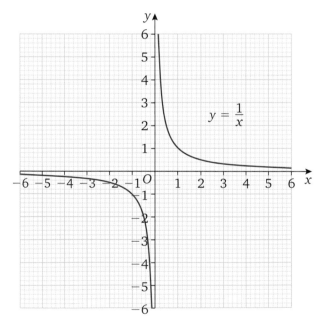

**a** Sketch each of these graphs.

**i** $y = \dfrac{1}{x} + 1$   **iii** $y = \dfrac{1}{x} - 1$   **v** $y = \dfrac{1}{2x}$

**ii** $y = \dfrac{1}{x} + 2$   **iv** $y = \dfrac{2}{x}$   **vi** $y = -\dfrac{1}{x}$

**b** Describe the transformation needed to get each graph you have drawn from the graph of $y = \dfrac{1}{x}$

**6**   For each of the graphs **a–c**, sketch the following transformations and describe the transformation in each case.

**A\***

   **i**    $y = -f(x)$        **ii**    $y = 2f(x)$        **iii**    $y = f(x - 1)$

   **a**    $y = f(x)$         **b**    $y = f(x)$          **c**    $y = f(x)$

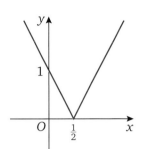 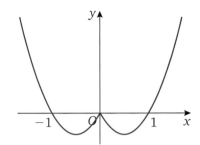 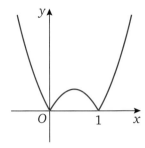

**7**   James, Ken, Hamish and Faisal have been given this graph by their teacher.

James says it is the graph of $y = 3\cos x$ because it starts at 3 on the $y$-axis.
Ken says it is the graph of $y = \cos x + 2$ because it goes up to 3 at its highest.
Hamish says it is the graph of $y = 2\cos x + 1$ because it is stretched and translated.
Faisal thinks that one of them is likely to be correct, but is not sure which one.

Who should Faisal choose? Explain your answer, and justify why he should not choose either of the others.

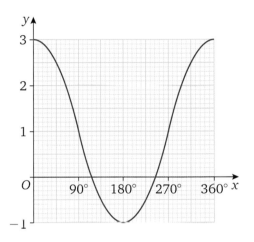

**8**   Lucy has been given the graph of $y = f(x)$ by her teacher.
He asks her to draw the graph of $y = af(x) + b$

   **a**    What transformations should she carry out and in which order should she do them?

   **b**    Check your answer on some examples using $f(x) = x^2$

**9**   What are the effects of changing the values of $a$, $b$ and $c$ in the function $y = a(x - b)^2 + c$?

Summarise your results in terms of simple transformations of the graph of $y = x^2$

# 17  Assess Ⓚ

**1**   **a**    Sketch the graph of $y = x^3$

   **b**    Sketch the graphs of:

      **i**    $y = x^3 + 2$         **iv**    $y = \frac{1}{2}x^3$

      **ii**    $y = x^3 - 2$         **v**    $y = -2x^3$

     **iii**    $y = 2x^3$

   **c**    Describe the transformation needed to obtain each graph you have drawn from the graph of $y = x^3$

**2**    Look at these graphs.

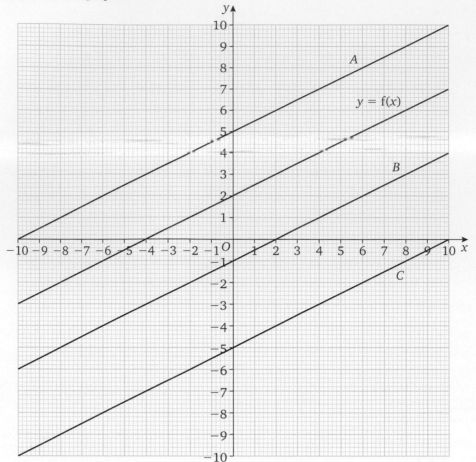

**a**    What is the equation of the line labelled $y = f(x)$?

**b**    For each of the graphs labelled $A$, $B$ and $C$, write their equations in the form $y = f(x) + a$

**c**    Work out the equations of lines $A$, $B$ and $C$ in the form $y = mx + c$ and show that you get the same answers as you did in part **b**.

**3**    Hamilton is given the graph of $y = f(x)$. He knows that the graph of $y = f(x) - 1$ is a translation of the graph of $y = f(x)$ by vector $\begin{pmatrix} 0 \\ -1 \end{pmatrix}$. He says that the graph of $y = f(x - 1)$ must be a translation by vector $\begin{pmatrix} -1 \\ 0 \end{pmatrix}$

Is Hamilton correct? Explain your answer.

# Practice questions  🄺

1    The graph of $y = 3 - x^2$ is sketched below.

Not drawn accurately

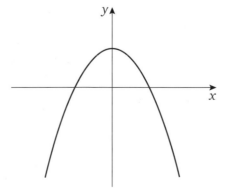

Copy the sketch and on the same axes, sketch the graph of $y = 7 - x^2$

*(1 mark)*

AQA 2009

# Glossary

**adjacent side** – in a right-angled triangle, the side adjacent to a known or required angle (but not the hypotenuse).

**alternate segment** – the angle between a tangent and a chord is equal to the angle in the alternate segment. For example, the red angles in the diagram are equal.

**angle of elevation** – the angle between a given line and the horizontal.

**angle subtended (subtended angle)** – the angle created by an object or line (e.g. the arc of a circle) at a given external point. The angle subtended by an arc (or chord) at the centre of a circle is twice the angle subtended at any point on the circumference.

**arc** – part of the circumference of a circle; a minor arc is less than half the circumference and a major arc is greater than half the circumference.

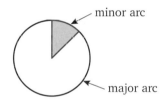

**back-to-back stem-and-leaf diagram** – a stem-and-leaf diagram where the stem is down the centre and the leaves from two distributions are either side for comparison.

**biased** – in the context of probability, not having the expected chance of happening.

**bisector** – a bisector is a line that cuts either an angle or a line into two equal parts.

**centre of enlargement** – the fixed point from which the enlargement is made.

**chord** – a straight line joining two points on the circumference of a circle.

**circular functions** – functions of the form $y = \sin x$ and $y = \cos x$ and $y = \tan x$

**coefficient** – the number (with its sign) in front of the letter representing the unknown, for example $4p$ (4 is the coefficient).

**column vector** – a way of writing a vector, for example $\binom{4}{3}$ which means a move of 4 units to the right and 3 units up.

**conditional probability** – the probability of an event (A), given that another (B) has already occurred.

**congruent** – exactly the same size and shape; one of the shapes might be rotated or flipped over.

**consecutive** – next to each other in a sequence. For example, the numbers 3.4 and 5 are consecutive.

**construction** – this is the process of drawing a diagram accurately with a 'straight edge' and compasses only.

**corresponding angles** – angles in the similar position between parallel lines and a transversal. For example, the angles marked $b$, which are on the same side of the transversal.

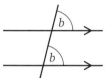

**cosine rule** – in a right-angled triangle, the length of the adjacent side divided by the length of the hypotenuse. Abbreviated to cos.

**cubic function** – an equation, expression or function in which the highest power of $x$ is 3. It may also include $x^2$ or $x$ terms and constants, for example $5x^3 + 2x^2 + 5x - 4 = 0$

**cumulative frequency diagram** – the name given to any diagram that shows the cumulative frequencies for a distribution.

**cyclic quadrilateral** – a quadrilateral with all four vertices on a circle.

**decimal places** – the number of digits after the decimal point. For example, the number 23.456 has three decimal places (4 tenths, 5 hundredths and 6 thousandths). Numbers can be rounded to different numbers of decimal places; 23.456 to 1 d.p. is 23.5

**denominator** – the bottom number of a fraction, indicating how many fractional parts the unit has been split into. In the fractions $\frac{4}{7}, \frac{23}{100}, \frac{6}{9}$ the denominators are 7 (indicating that the unit has been split into 7 parts, which are sevenths) 100 and 9

**dependent events** – events are dependent if the probability of the outcomes for the second event are changed by the outcome of the first event.

**depreciation** – a reduction in value (of used cars, for example).

**direct proportion** – if two variables are in direct proportion, one is equal to a constant multiple of the other. If one of the variables doubles then so does the other; if one of the variables halves then so does the other. In general, it means that $y = kx$ where $k$ is the constant of proportionality.

**discontinuous** – if a graph has breaks in it, it is discontinuous. For example, the graph of $y = \frac{1}{x}$ does not cross the point $x = 0$

**discount** – a reduction in the price. Sometimes this is for paying in cash or paying early.

**eliminate** – to remove one of the unknowns from a pair of simultaneous equations by adding or subtracting like terms. The unknown being eliminated must have a matching coefficient in both equations.

**enlargement** – an enlargement changes the size of an object according to a certain scale factor.

**equation** – a statement showing that two expressions are equal, for example, $2y - 17 = 15$

**equilateral** – having all sides of equal length.

**equivalent fractions** – two or more fractions that have the same value. Equivalent fractions can be made by multiplying or dividing the numerator and denominator of any fraction by the same number.

**event** – something that takes place that we want to find the probability of. For example, for finding the probability of 'getting an even number with one throw of a dice', the event is 'getting an even number with one throw of a dice'.

**expand** – to remove brackets to create an equivalent expression (expanding is the opposite of factorising).

**experimental probability** – the chance of a particular outcome based on results of experiments or previous data.

**exponential (function)** – a function where the base is a constant and the power is a vriable.

**exponential growth** – this occurs when the rate of growth is proportional to the quantity present. Repeated percentage increases leads to exponential growth.

**expression** – a mathematical statement written in symbols, for example, $3x + 1$ or $x^2 + 2x$

**factorise** – to include brackets by taking common factors (factorising is the opposite of expanding).

**fair** – without bias e.g. a fair coin has an equal chance of falling on heads or tails.

**formula** – a formula shows the relationship between two or more variables, for example, in a rectangle area = length × width, or $A = lw$

**frequency diagram** – any chart or diagram which compares the frequencies of objects.

**frequency polygon** – a frequency diagram for continuous data with a line joining the midpoints of the class intervals using the appropriate frequencies.

**frustum (of a cone)** – a cone with the top part cut off.

**function** – a function tells you what to do to the value of a variable to work out the value of a second variable. For example, if $y$ is a function of $x$, then the function will tell you what to do to the value of $x$ to work out the value of $y$. If $y$ is a function of $x$, then it can be written as $y = f(x)$

**histogram** – a diagram for continuous data with bars as rectangles whose areas represent the frequency.

**hypotenuse** – in a right-angled triangle, the longest side, opposite the right angle.

**identity** – two expressions linked by the $\equiv$ sign are true for all values of the variable, for example, $3x + 3 \equiv 3 (x + 1)$.

**image** – the shape following a transformation of the object, for example, reflection, rotation, translation or enlargement.

**independent events** – two events are independent if the outcome of the second is not affected by the outcome of the first.

**indirect proportion** – two variables, $x$ and $y$, are indirect proportion if $xy = k$ where $k$ is a constant. As one variable increases, the other decreases.

**inter-quartile range** – the upper quartile minus the lower quartile.

**line graph** – a diagram for continuous data, usually over a period of time.

**lower bound** – the lower limit on the possible size of a measurement and the lowest possible value it can take; for example, if a length is measured as 62 cm to the nearest centimetre the lower bound of the length is 61.5 cm.

**lower quartile** – the lower quartile ($Q_1$) is the value $\frac{1}{4}$ along a set of data.

**magnitude** – size.

**mixed number** – a fraction that has both a whole number and a fraction part, for example, $1\frac{4}{7}$, $3\frac{1}{2}$, $5\frac{3}{4}$

**mutually exclusive events** – events that are mutually exclusive cannot happen at the same time e.g. a 4 and an odd number.

**numerator** – the top number of a fraction, indicating how many parts there are in the fraction.

**object** – the shape before it undergoes a transformation, for example, translation, reflection, rotation or enlargement.

**one-way stretch** – a one-way stretch in the $x$-direction increases all the $x$-coordinates by a scale factor. Likewise, a one-way stretch in the $y$-direction increases all the $y$-coordinates by a scale factor.

**parabola** – the locus of a point that moves so that it is always the same distance from a fixed point and a given line.

**per annum** – means 'per year'.

**percentage** – the number of parts per hundred. For example, 15% means $\frac{15}{100}$

**perpendicular** – at right angles to; two lines at right angles to each other are perpendicular lines.

**quadrant** – one quarter of a circle.

**quadratic equation** – an equation in which the highest power of $x$ is 2. It may also include $x$ terms and constants, for example $5x^2 + 2x - 4 = 0$

**quadratic expression** – an expression containing terms where the highest power of the variable is 2.

**random** – outcomes are random if they have an equal or set probability but otherwise cannot be predicted.

**ratio** – a ratio is a means of comparing numbers or quantities. If two numbers or quantities are in the ratio $1 : 2$, the second is always twice as big as the first. If two quantities are in the ratio $2 : 5$, for every 2 parts of the first there are 5 parts of the second.

**reciprocal** – the reciprocal of a number is 1 divided by that number. Any number multiplied by its reciprocal equals 1. For example, the reciprocal of 6 is $\frac{1}{6}$ because $6 \times \frac{1}{6} = 1$ and $1 \div 6 = \frac{1}{6}$. The number 1 is its own reciprocal and the number zero has no reciprocal.

**relative frequency** – the fraction or proportion of the number of times out of the total that a particular outcome occurs.

**resultant vector** – the sum of two or more vectors.

**rounding** – a number can be expressed in an approximate form rather than exactly. For example, it may be written to the nearest integer or to the nearest thousand. This process is called rounding. The number 36 754 rounded to the nearest thousand is 37 000.

**scalar** – a quantity with size but not direction, for example, the number 2.

**scale factor** – the scale factor of an enlargement is the ratio of the corresponding sides on an object and its image.

**sector** – the area bounded by two radii and an arc in a circle.

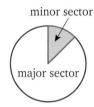

**segment** – the region bounded by an arc and a chord in a circle.

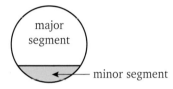

**significant figures** – the closer a digit is to the beginning of a number then the more important or significant it is. For example, in the number 23.657, 2 is the most significant figure. 23.657 = 20 correct to 1 s.f.

**similar** – shapes are similar (mathematically similar) if they have the same shape but different sizes. That is, one is an enlargement of the other.

**simultaneous equations** – a pair of equations containing two unknowns where both equations are true at the same time.

**sine rule** – in a right-angled triangle, the length of the opposite side divided by the length of the hypotenuse. Abbreviated to sin.

**stem-and-leaf diagrams** – frequency diagrams which use the actual values of the data split into a stem and leaves with a key.

**subject** – the subject of the formula $P = 2(l + w)$ is $P$ because the formula starts '$P = …$'.

**substitute** – in order to use a formula to work out the value of one of the variables you replace the letters by numbers. This is called substitution.

**substitution** – using an expression for one unknown in terms of another, obtained from one of a pair of simultaneous equations, to reduce the second equation to one with a single variable.

**supplementary angles** – two angles are supplementary if their sum is 180°.

**surd** – a number containing an irrational root, for example $2\sqrt{7}$.

**tangent rule** – in a right-angled triangle, the length of the opposite side divided by the length of the adjacent side. Abbreviated to tan.

**term** – a number, variable or the product of a number and a variable(s) such as 3, $x$ or $3x$.

**tetrahedron** – a solid made up of four triangular faces.

**theoretical probability** – the chance of a particular outcome based on equally likely outcomes.

**transformation** – reflections, rotations, translations and enlargements are examples of transformations as they transform the position, orientation or size of a shape.

**translation** – a transformation where every point moves the same distance in the same direction so that the object and the image are congruent.

**tree diagram** – a diagram used to calculate probabilities of combined events.

**trial** – a probability experiment consisting of a number of individual trials. For example, if an experiment is to 'throw a dice' and it is thrown 20 times, then that is 20 trials.

**trigonometry** – the study of the relationship between the length of sides and the size of angles in a triangle.

**two-way table** – a table showing information about two sets of data at the same time.

**unitary method** – a method of calculating quantities that are in proportion by first finding one unit.

**unitary ratio** – a ratio in the form $1 : n$ or $n : 1$; this form of ratio is helpful for comparison, as it shows clearly how much of one quantity there is for one unit of the other.

**upper bound** – the upper limit on the possible size of a measurement; for example, if a length is measured as 62 cm to the nearest centimetre, the upper bound of the length is 62.5 cm.

**upper quartile** – the upper quartile ($Q_3$) is the value $\frac{3}{4}$ along a set of ordered data.

**VAT (Value Added Tax)** – this tax is added on to the price of goods or services.

**variable** – a symbol such as $x$, $y$ or $z$ representing a quantity that can take different values.

**vector** – a quantity with magnitude (size) and direction. In this diagram, the arrow represents the direction and the length of the line represents the magnitude.

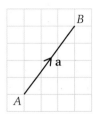

In print, this vector can be written as $\overrightarrow{AB}$ or **a**. In handwriting, this vector is usually written as $\overrightarrow{AB}$ or $\underline{a}$. The vector can also be described as a column vector:

where $\begin{pmatrix} x \\ y \end{pmatrix}$ ← $x$ is the horizontal displacement, ← $y$ is the vertical displacement

**vector sum** – the sum of two or more vectors.

**vertex, vertices** – the point where two or more edges meet.

# Index

Key terms are given in **bold** and can be found in the glossary.

accurate drawings 180–183
acute angles 110, 230
**adjacent side** calculations 109–110, 111
algebra 77–87, 110, 136–159, 171–172
**alternate segment** theorem 39, 41
amplitude 207
AND rule 69, 70
angle bisectors 183, 184–185, 194, 201–202
**angle of elevation** 116
**angle subtended** 33–34
angles
    calculating 109–116, 163–164, 229–233
    circle properties 33–37, 165–166, 250
    drawing triangles 180–181
    similar shapes 188
**arcs** 33, 180, 183, 201, 250–252
    *see also* **chords**
area(s) 249–258
    circles 103, 250–252
    ratios 100, 101
    scale factor 91
    surface areas 253–257
    triangles 235–236, 255
    units of 90

**back-to-back stem-and-leaf diagrams** 9
bearings 114
**biased** scores 65
BIDMAS 78
**bisectors** 38, 183–185, 194, 197, 201–202
bounds 14–15, 25, 56–58
box plots 19–24

'calculate' instruction 34
calculator use, tips 47, 49, 53, 110, 113, 121, 230
cancelling down fractions 73
capacity ratios 102
**centres of enlargement** 92–96
charts *see* diagrams; graphs
checking answers, tips 122, 145, 162, 164, 232
**chords** 33–34, 38–42
    *see also* **arcs**
circles
    angles in 33–37, 165–166, 250
    area of 103, 250–252
    locus of 201
    properties of 32–45
    quadrants 90
**circular functions** 207, 214–216
circumferences 33–34, 38
**coefficients** 139, 145, 147, 161
column layers 88
**column vectors** 240–241

common factors 141, 146
comparing data 20–21
'completing the square' method 145–146
**conditional probability** 72–74
cones 253–257
congruent shapes 89, 118, 193–197
**consecutive** numbers 156
consistent units 79
constant of proportionality (k) 130–131
**construction** 179–199, 201–204
Corinthian columns 88
**corresponding** sides 189, 193
**cosine/cosine rule** 109, 113, 214–216, 232–234
crop circles 32
**cubic** functions 207–211
cuboids 100–101, 116
**cumulative frequency diagrams** 14–20, 22–23
curves
    drawing 150–151
    for functions 264
    graph recognition 220
**cyclic quadrilaterals** 33, 36
cylinders 103

data
    comparing 20–21
    representing 7–31
**decimal place** rounding 51–52
decimals 46–61, 66
decreasing by percentages 121–125
degree mode, calculators 113
demand and supply 160
**denominator**, fractions 47, 53, 141
**dependent events** 72–74
**depreciation** 121
depth ratios 101
diagrams
    box-and-whisker 19–24
    constructions 197
    enlargements 92–100
    frequency 11–20, 22–28
    'not drawn accurately' 7, 34
    stem-and-leaf 8–11
    tree diagrams 69–74
    *see also* graphs
diameter, circles 38
'difference of two squares' expressions 138
**direct proportion** 130–133
**discontinuous** values 212
**discounts** 125
Doric columns 88
drawing shapes 92, 97, 116–118
    accurately 180–183
    quadratic graphs 150–151
    translations 263
    vectors 242–243

elevation angle 116
**elimination** method 161–163
emergency calls 228
**enlargements** 88–107, 129, 188–193
equal angles, circles 33
**equations** 81–82, 131, 264
  cubic functions 209, 211
  fraction solutions 144–145, 149
  graph recognition 219–220
  quadratic 136, 141–154, 171–176
  simultaneous 160–178
  vectors 244–245
**equidistant** points 201–202
**equilateral** triangles 183, 254
**equivalent fractions** 47
equivalent ratios 126
Euclid 179
events
  dependent 72–74
  independent 69–72
  mutually exclusive 63–65, 70
**expanding** 137
**experimental probability** 65
explaining answers, tips 203
**exponential**
  decay 123
  functions 207, 217–219
  **growth** 121–122, 124
**expressions** 53, 78, 81, 82, 137–140

**factorising** 137–143, 148
**fair** scores 65, 69
**formulae** 77–87
  areas 235, 253, 255
  changing subject of 81–85
  cosine rule 232–233
  proportions 131
  quadratic 147–149
  sine rule 229
  volumes 250, 253, 255
  writing 78–81
fractions 46–61
  cancelling down 73
  equation solutions 144–145, 149
  ratios and 126
  relative frequencies as 66
  simplifying 141
**frequency diagrams** 11–20, 22–28
**frequency polygons** 11–14, 24–25
frequency probability 65–69
**frustum** of cones 255
**functions** 207–227, 259–268

geometry 179–199, 244–246
graphs
  equation solutions 150–154, 167–170,
    172–176
  functions 208–211, 212–216, 217–219
  line graphs 11–14, 66–67
  of loci 219–223

paper size 211
proportions 130, 131, 132
recognition 219–223
transforming 259–268
*see also* diagrams
grid patterns 97, 98

harmonics 46
**histograms** 11, 24–28
**hypotenuse** of triangles 109–110

**identity** 81, 82, 155
**image** transformations 89
increasing by percentages 121–125
**independent events** 69–72
**indirect proportion** 130–133
integers, rounding 51–52, 57
**inter-quartile range** 14–15
interest rates 217, 219
inverse proportion graphs 131
inverse sine function 230
Ionic columns 88
isosceles triangles 39, 41, 118, 163–164,
    244

$k$ (constant of proportionality) 130–131
Katoomba railway 108

length ratios 101
lightning 62, 80
line bisectors 183–186, 201
**line graphs** 11–14, 66–67
line–plane angle 116
line of symmetry 118, 151
linear equations 167–170, 171–176
**locus/loci** 200–206, 219–223
loss percentage 124, 125
**lower bound** 25, 56–57
**lower quartiles** 14–15, 19–21

**magnitude**, vectors 240
**maximum** value, bounds 57
median 9, 14–15, 19–21, 27
**minimum** value, bounds 57
misleading diagrams 7
**mixed number** fractions 49
mobile phone masts 200, 228
multiplier method 121, 126–127
multiplying out 137, 139, 155, 161
multiplying vectors 241
music 46
**mutually exclusive events** 63–65, 70

negative scale factors 97–99
negative values
  algebraic proof 156
  functions 211, 261, 264
  quadratic equations 142, 146–148
  vectors 245
**numerator**, fractions 47, 53, 141

**objects**
  centre of 94
  transformations 89
obtuse angles 230
**one-way stretches** 261
opposite angles, circles 33
**opposite side** calculations 109–110, 114
OR rule 63, 70
ordering fractions 53

**parabolas** 150–151, 220
parallel vectors 240–241
patterns for enlargements 97, 98
**per annum** interest rates 217, 219
**percentages** 120–135
perfect squares 145
perimeter ratios 99, 101
**perpendiculars** 38, 183–186, 197, 201
plane–line angle 116
population growth 121–122, 124
powers, functions 211, 218
prisms 253
probability 62–76
profit percentage 124, 125
proof questions 147, 155–157, 194, 197
proportions 126–133
pyramids 249, 253–257
Pythagoras' theorem 39, 116–117

**quadrants** 90, 149
**quadratic equations** 136, 141–154, 171–176
**quadratic expressions** 137–140
quadratic formula 147–149
quadratics 136–159
quadrilaterals 33, 36, 188
quartiles 14–15, 19–21

radius, circles 38–39, 201
railway lines 108
**random** events 63
**ratios** 89, 99–102, 109, 120–135
**reciprocals** 54–55, 212–214
rectangles 81, 92–93, 100–101
**recurring decimals** 53
reflections 89
**relative frequency** 65–69
representing data 7–31
**resultant vectors** 244
right angles
  circles 33
  triangles 109–113, 116–118
rotations 89, 97
**rounding** 51–55, 57, 233

sailing boats 243
**scalar** numbers 241
**scale factors** 89–93, 94, 96–105, 189
**sectors** 250–252
**segments** 39, 41, 250
semicircle properties 33

shapes
  congruent shapes 89, 118, 193–197
  functions 212, 215, 264
  similar shapes 89, 99–105, 188–193
  transforming 259, 263
  *see also* drawing shapes
sides
  calculating 109–113, 114, 229
  congruent shapes 193
  drawing triangles 180–181
  similar shapes 189
**significant figures** 52
**similar** shapes 89, 99–105, 188–193
simplest form answers 64, 73, 126
simplifying fractions 141
**simultaneous equations** 160–178
**sine/sine rule** 109, 113, 214–216, 229–231
sound waves 207
speed equation 145
spheres 253–257
squared numbers 138, 145–146, 147, 232
squared paper use 242
**stem-and-leaf diagrams** 8–11
straight line equations 173–175
stretches, functions 261–262
**subject** change, formulae 81–85
**substitution** method 78–81, 161, 163–167,
    171–172, 211
subtended angles 33–34
**supplementary angles** 33
supply and demand 160
**surd** form answers 145, 148
surface areas 253–257
symbols 120, 155
symmetry 118, 151, 215

tables of values 150–151, 172–174, 208, 211–212
**tangents** 38–42, 109, 113–114
**terminating decimals** 53
**terms**, expressions 82
**tetrahedrons** 254
**theoretical probability** 65
three-dimensional trigonometry 116–118
tracing paper use 263
**transformations** 89, 259–268
  *see also* **enlargements**
**translations** 89, 260–261, 263
**tree diagrams** 69–74
**trials** 65
triangles
  accurate drawings 180–183
  areas 235–236, 255
  congruent shapes 193–197
  enlargements 93, 99–100
  equilateral 183, 254
  isosceles 39, 41, 118, 163–164, 244
  right-angled 109–113, 116–118
  similar shapes 188–192
  sine rule 229–230
trigonometric functions 207, 214–216

trigonometry 108–119, 228–238
two-way tables 74

unitary method 126–127, 250
unitary ratios 126
units
    enlargements 90
    formulae 79
    percentages 124
upper bound 14–15, 25, 56–57
upper quartiles 14–15, 19–21

Value Added Tax (VAT) 122
variables 130, 161

VAT (Value Added Tax) 122
vector sum 243
vectors 239–248
vertex/vertices 92–94, 253
volume(s) 90–91, 101–103, 249–258

wind 239, 243
'working' stages, exams 78, 107, 189
writing
    formulae 78–81
    percentages 124–126

$x$-values 168, 170, 208–210, 213–214, 218